La BIBLE Commentary

Deuteronomy thru Ruth

Volume 2

Contributing Editors:

DAVID HATCHER
J. HAMPTON KEATHLEY, TH.M
DR. STEPHEN LESTON
DR. ROBERT RAYBURN
DR. DEREK W. H. THOMAS

Consulting Editor:

DR. TREMPER LONGMAN

BARBOUR
PUBLISHING

ISBN 978-1-62029-772-8

Produced with the assistance of Christopher. D. Hudson & Associates. Contributing writers include: Elizabeth Arlene, Anita Palmer, Heather Rippetoe, Carol Smith, and Jane Vogel

Published by Barbour Publishing, Inc., P.O. Box 719, Uhrichsville, Ohio 44683, www.barbourbooks.com

The maps that appear in this volume are taken from *Bible Atlas and Companion* published by Barbour Publishing. (ISBN: 978-1-59789-779-2)

Our mission is to publish and distribute inspirational products offering exceptional value and biblical encouragement to the masses.

Member of the
Evangelical Christian
Publishers Association

TABLE OF CONTENTS

DEUTERONOMY

INTRODUCTION TO DEUTERONOMY

Deuteronomy might be called the Romans of the Old Testament. It is chock-full of the great themes of scripture. It is a wonderfully down-to-earth and practical book that provides counsel about both the large and small issues and questions of life. It addresses itself both to private matters such as the inner conflicts of the believing soul, the way of faith under trial, marriage and family, and to such public and corporate issues such as worship and the proper stewardship of the environment.

AUTHOR

Moses is clearly identified as the author of Deuteronomy in verse 1. Moses' authorship is claimed throughout Deuteronomy (1:5, 9; 5:1; 27:8; 29:2; 31:1, 30) as well as in other Old Testament books (1 Kings 2:3; 8:53; 2 Kings 14:6; 18:6, 12). Jesus also identified Moses as the author of Deuteronomy (Matthew 19:7–8; Mark 10:3–5; John 5:46–47), as did Peter (Acts 3:22), Stephen (Acts 7:37–38), and Paul (Romans 10:19; 1 Corinthians 9:9).

The final chapter, recording Moses' death and burial (34:1–12), was most likely added by another writer after Moses' death.

PURPOSE

The title *Deuteronomy* means "second law." In this book, Moses reiterates and expands on the laws God has already given Israel and calls them to renew their covenant with God by pledging their obedience.

OCCASION

The book of Deuteronomy records Moses' last words to the people of Israel as they are poised to enter the promised land after forty years of wandering in the wilderness. Moses reminds the people of all that the Lord has done for them to this point and calls them to a life of faithful obedience in the land they are about to receive.

STRUCTURE

At the time that Deuteronomy was written (around 1400 BC), "suzerainty treaties"—treaties of sovereignty of a stronger king over a weaker one—were common. Deuteronomy appears to be an almost perfect example of the ancient Middle Eastern treaty, a literary form that would have been easily appreciated and understood in Moses' day:

- Opening preamble (paralleled in 1:1–5)
- Historical introduction (1:6–4:49)
- The particular stipulations of the treaty (chapters 5–26)
- What blessings and curses would result from keeping or breaking the treaty (chapters 27–28; 32–33)
- Some form of oath taking (chapters 29–30)
- Provisions for the perpetuation of the covenant after the death of the particular kings who signed it (chapter 31)

DEUTERONOMY 1:1–46

FAITH BEFORE WORKS

Setting Up the Section

When Deuteronomy commences, Israel as a nation is poised on the eastern bank of the Jordan River opposite Jericho. Two months later, she will cross the river, on dry land, into the promised land for the first time. It is at this juncture in her history that God initiates a renewal of the covenant He had established with the Israelites when they were camped at Sinai (Exodus 19–24). Chapter 1 records the preamble to this renewal and the beginning of a lengthy review of God's dealings with Israel. The historical prologue, which begins here in chapter 1, serves to provide a rationale for obedience to the commandments which occupy the largest part of the book.

1:1–5

PREAMBLE

Deuteronomy appears to be an almost perfect example of the ancient Middle Eastern treaty form. It begins, as did the treaties of that time, with a preamble (1:1–5), giving the geographical and historical setting.

Critical Observation

Archaeological discoveries of international treaties have shed new light on the literary structure of the book of Deuteronomy. Ancient Middle Eastern treaties had a standard form:

- Opening preamble (paralleled in 1:1–5)

- Historical introduction (1:6–4:49)

- Particular stipulations of the treaty (chapters 5–26)

- What blessings and curses would result from keeping or breaking the treaty (chapters 27–28; 32–33)

- Some form of oath (chapters 29–30)

- Provisions for the perpetuation of the covenant after the death of the particular kings who signed it (chapter 31)

GOD'S FAITHFULNESS COMES FIRST

Moses begins by reminding Israel that their favored status as God's children and their wonderful prospects as a people have nothing to do with them or anything they have done. They can take no credit for the land and prosperity that is soon to be theirs—or for the spiritual life and bounty of which the promised land is a sign and seal. The promise being fulfilled was made generations before to their forefather, Abraham. God is faithful to His promises.

The Lord had promised Abraham that his descendants would be as numerous as the stars in the sky (Genesis 15:5; 22:17; 26:4). Moses observes that this promise has come true (Deuteronomy 1:10) and with it the conclusion that leading the people is more work than one man can do (1:9–12). Moses reminds the people that they approved the appointment of leaders and agreed to be subject to their authority (1:13–18). Chapters 16–18 will further refine the system of leadership in Israel.

THE NECESSITY OF FAITH

The account of Israel's cowardly refusal to enter the land that God had promised is an instructive beginning to the book of Deuteronomy, because it shows that God's fundamental requirement is not obedience to the law, but faith.

The event that Moses recounts had happened thirty-eight years earlier at Kadesh Barnea (1:19). As Moses recollects in verse 21, the Lord has already given them the land, as it were, and all they have to do is walk in and take possession. But they are unnerved by the spies' reports of fortified cities and warlike people (1:22–28). The Lord has already proved His might and His faithfulness to His people by bringing them out of Egypt and providing their food and water in the wilderness (1:29–33). Now they stand poised to enter the promised land, but they do not do so. Verse 32 indicates it's a faith issue: "You did not believe the LORD your God" (ESV).

Demystifying Deuteronomy

Most ancient Middle Eastern treaties were "suzerainty treaties," or treaties of sovereignty of a stronger king over a weaker one. The Lord had given Moses this covenantal revelation in the form drawn from the custom of ancient Middle Eastern diplomacy. It provides a wonderful example of God's condescension, of His employing a literary form that would have been easily appreciated and understood in Moses' day. He wanted to be understood and wanted His covenant to be kept.

When the people realize that as a result of their lack of faith they will never be permitted to enter Canaan (1:34–40), they see the error of their ways and march across the border (1:41–43). The Lord does not go with them, and they are soundly thrashed by Canaanite armies and chased back into the wilderness (1:44). They gather in the camp and weep before the Lord, but He will not relent (1:45–46).

It is clear enough that what lies behind the Lord's unwillingness to listen to Israel's cries is His knowledge that their hearts are far from Him. They are bitterly sorry for the consequences of their stupidity, but they still have neither true faith in the Lord nor true reverence for Him. Numbers 14:24, the original account of this episode, reveals that the Lord does not punish Caleb the same way, because Caleb has a different spirit. It is not the disobedience itself that is so important; God is always forgiving the disobedience of His people. The problem is the people do not obey God, because they neither trust His Word nor love Him for His goodness to them.

Take It Home

First things first: faith then obedience. First the glad acceptance of God's gracious salvation; then a life lived in demonstration of undying gratitude to God. Deuteronomy spends most of its time teaching us how to live so as to demonstrate our love and gratitude to God—how God would have us think and speak and act. But it begins by reminding us that the only obedience that pleases God is that which flows from the love and gratitude of a person who knows full well that he or she has been saved by the grace and mercy and goodness and power of God alone. To a very great degree, what kind of Christian you are will be determined by just how fully you appreciate the grace of God.

DEUTERONOMY 2:1–37
FROM WANDERING TO CONQUEST

Setting Up the Section

Moses, at the end of the forty years of desert wanderings, is recalling for the people their history. Chapter 1 ends with the Lord's decree that the generation who left Egypt will not enter the promised land of Canaan. Chapter 2 begins the saga of Israel's forty-year sojourn in the wilderness.

📄 2:1–23

MERCY OVER ALL HIS WORKS

Poised on the brink of the promised land, the Israelites now have to turn around and retrace their steps toward the Red Sea (2:1). Hidden in this narrative of Israel's travels through the wilderness from Kadesh Barnea to the Arnon Gorge is a lovely and profoundly important truth: The Lord shows kindness to the large part of humanity that lies beyond the boundaries of the church and His kingdom.

Verses 1–8 show the Lord's concern for the people living in Seir. The Lord gives careful instructions to Israel that she is not to engage them in battle, for God has no intention of letting Israel take the land from them (2:5). What is more, all the food and water they consume while passing through is to be paid for in cash, which they could easily afford because God has provided; they lack nothing (2:6).

Similar instructions about how to treat the Moabites (Deuteronomy 2:9, 17–19) bracket the three short verses relating the passage of thirty-eight years and the death of an entire generation of fighting men (2:14–16). Historical asides about the previous inhabitants of the land (2:10–12, 20–23) remind the readers that in these cases, as in the case of Israel's conquest of Canaan, it is the Lord who drives out the nations (2:21–22) and who gives ownership of the land (2:7, 9, 12, 19).

Critical Observation

The mercy of God toward all people, not just believers, often goes by the name of "common grace," to distinguish it from particular and saving grace.

📖 2:24–37

HARD SAYINGS

Verse 24 signals a change in the way God commands Israel to deal with other nations. They *will* engage in battle, but according to God's plan (2:24–25). The Lord is telling them what will occur. Peace can still be genuinely offered (2:26–29).

Deuteronomy 2:30–37 not only recounts the first victory recorded in the book, but also introduces some hard sayings. Verse 30 states that God hardens Sihon's heart so that he will not allow Israel to pass through his territory peacefully, because God had determined to give Sihon and his kingdom into Israel's hand. This is the only explanation given of this statement.

Critical Observation

The word translated *destroyed* in verse 34 is the Hebrew term which means "to dedicate or devote something to God." Sometimes it has a positive sense—such as when objects are devoted for use in the temple and its worship—but more often it refers to the compulsory devotion of something which impedes or hinders God's work. In that case, the object is devoted to utter destruction. That is the idea here.

It is clear that it is the Lord who wins the battle for Israel (2:31–33, 36). Verses 34–37 are the account of the utter annihilation which Israel bestowed upon Sihon's kingdom. No one is left; not men, not women, not even children. That God would use these means is a tough truth to understand.

Demystifying Deuteronomy

Why would a holy God condone such annihilation? Such destruction is a judgment on the wickedness of the people destroyed (see 9:4). Keep in mind that God had already given the nations ample time to repent. In fact, He had delayed Israel's conquest for some four hundred years for this reason (Genesis 15:16). In the end, however, Israel was not spiritually strong enough to withstand the influence of pagan nations, and judgment fell (see Deuteronomy 20:17–18).

Take It Home

The Lord tests our faith intellectually by forcing us to reckon with realities we find difficult to accept. When faced with such hard sayings, we either subject His Word to our own thinking and pass judgment on God and His ways, or we acknowledge that, though we cannot comprehend it, if God has said it, it must be true and right.

The hard sayings here in Deuteronomy 2 are good examples. Will we believe that God is infinitely pure, unstained by sin in any way? Or will we reason that God's sovereign disposal of even the hearts and minds of humanity, as here He hardens Sihon's heart, must impeach the divine purity and make God a partner in sin?

Will we take God at His word? That is the test such a hard saying puts to our faith. We must live each day in the certainty that everything we read in scripture is absolutely true and to be practiced and trusted in, even though much of it is beyond our full comprehension.

DEUTERONOMY 3:1–29

MOSES' LAST BATTLE

Holy War	3:1–11
Division of the Land	3:12–23
Unanswered Prayer	3:24–29

Setting Up the Section

Chapter 3 continues the historical prologue that precedes the covenant laws and decrees that make up the bulk of Deuteronomy. The Israelites' desert wanderings have come to an end, and they are engaged in the business of conquering and claiming the land.

📄 3:1–11

HOLY WAR

It is essential for a true estimation and appreciation of this history to realize that the destruction of Bashan (3:1–11) is, in fact, God's judgment and God's doing. Israel is His instrument. This point is made in verse 2, where it is clear that, in the campaign against Og, Moses and Israel are acting on orders given them by God. It isn't Moses' idea to destroy the women and children; it is a direct order from the Lord Himself.

Demystifying Deuteronomy

The conquest of Bashan took the Israelites off their route somewhat, as they went north of the point where they would cross the Jordan into Canaan. From a military point of view, the conquest of Bashan was necessary to protect Israel's right flank as she crossed the river for her main assault on the cities of Canaan. History records that several other armies conquering Palestine from the same direction proceeded on the same military principle.

In respect to both the specific instructions Moses is given and to the general instructions God gave Israel for waging her wars, Israel does precisely as she is told by the Lord God when she exterminates the population of Bashan. Therefore, whatever we may at first think about what Israel does here, we are forced to reckon with the fact that it is done under God's instruction.

The word rendered "destroyed" in verse 6 is in fact a technical term and means, more precisely, "devoted"—separated for a holy use. It is true that these people were devoted to destruction, but they were destroyed precisely to further the interests of the kingdom of God. They are destroyed because they stand in the way of God's good purpose. That is the sense of the word *destroyed*, which is also used in much more positive ways to refer to things which are consecrated to the service of God.

Critical Observation

Leaving no survivors was not always the outcome of an Israelite conquest. Outside of Canaan (the land the Israelites were in inhabiting), the women and children were spared. The men (who would serve as warriors against the Israelites) were killed. Inside Canaan, all were destroyed; but keep in mind that even in those situations, should the people surrender, they were spared (see 20:10–15).

Bashan had always been an idolatrous and crudely sinful people. Centuries before this incident, they had been notoriously evil in their ways. But God had been patient with them. He had endured their unbelief and the ugly corruption of their life for hundreds of years. Indeed, He consigned His own chosen people, Israel, to live in bondage in Egypt for four hundred years, in large part because He was unwilling to move against these Amorite peoples until the cup of their iniquity was full to the brim, as He tells Abraham (see Genesis 15:16) some six hundred years before Moses moved against Og, king of Bashan.

Christians who know that God's judgment is always just and righteous will know that the wickedness of this people must have been very great to be judged so severely. The warfare described here is a preview of hell where all God's enemies—men, women, and children—will suffer.

Demystifying Deuteronomy

The culture of Bashan appealed to the bestial in human nature in a very direct way. Not only were their gods particularly violent and vicious, but the people's worship of these gods was idolatrous and utterly debauched. Cult prostitution and fertility rites were a major feature of what they called "worship." Whether child sacrifice was also a feature at this time has not been certainly established, but it was in later years. One of the goddesses of the Canaanite pantheon, Anat, is represented laughing with joy over the dismemberment of young and old alike, gleefully collecting the heads and the hands.

In the laws governing Israel's warfare, given in Deuteronomy 20, the Lord says plainly why He wants certain peoples devoted in this way, especially the peoples who would be Israel's neighbors, if left to live in the land Israel is to occupy and possess (see 20:18). It is to keep Israel from catching the moral and spiritual diseases of these people. God knew that a pure, devout, and faithful people of God could not long exist if thoroughly mixed with a radioactively wicked, corrupt, and sensually powerful culture.

As it happens, Israel does not destroy all of these peoples, and their influence does terribly corrupt the people of God, to the spiritual death of vast multitudes of them.

📖 3:12–23

DIVISION OF THE LAND

The accounts of Israel's history that precede the law-giving conclude with a summary of the allotment of land Israel had conquered up to this point (3:12–17). All the land that had been taken was east of the Jordan River; Israel had not yet crossed into Canaan proper. Only the tribes of Reuben, Gad, and the half tribe of Manasseh receive land east of the Jordan—perhaps because they had a lot of livestock (3:19) and needed a large range for them.

Verses 18–23 detail the trans-Jordan tribes' responsibilities to the rest of Israel. They are to accompany the other tribes across the Jordan and fight alongside them. Only after all the tribes have received their territories may any man settle down in his new home.

q 3:24–29

UNANSWERED PRAYER

We have in verses 12–29 one of the most striking and important examples of God saying "no" to the prayer of one of His children. Moses' prayer recorded here (3:24–25), asking God to relent and allow him to set foot in the promised land, is apparently not his first. During the months, perhaps years, that had passed from striking the rock (see Numbers 20:1–13) to this point, with Israel poised on the west side of the Jordan, ready at last to enter Canaan, Moses had apparently often pled with the Lord. That is the suggestion of Deuteronomy 3:26, where we read that the Lord says, "That is enough. Do not speak to me anymore about this matter" (NIV).

In this particular case, the Lord seems to have decided it was necessary to say no to Moses so that the people of Israel, already suffering from a seriously inadequate view of their own sinfulness, would not be further confirmed in their tendency to take sin lightly. Moses reminds the Israelites that it is because of them that he was provoked to commit the sin for which now he is paying so steep a price (3:26). In Moses' punishment, the Lord is sending a message to Israel concerning the seriousness with which He takes their disobedience.

Further, the Lord forbids Moses to cross the Jordan in part because He wants Joshua properly prepared for the task that will fall to him when Israel enters the promised land (3:28). Once Moses understands that he is not to cross the river, he can devote all his energy to preparing Joshua to take his place.

DEUTERONOMY 4:1–49

LAWS AND ORDERS

Setting Up the Section

The first three chapters of Deuteronomy recall God's faithfulness and power. Now Moses begins to lay out the commandments that God calls Israel to obey in response to what He has already done.

q 4:1–14

THE GRACE OF LAW

Before setting out any specific laws, Moses speaks more generally about the importance of obedience (4:1–8). The obedience which Israel is here summoned to give to God is not for the purpose of making them God's children; it is not for earning salvation. This obedience they owe to God *because* God has saved them and because they are already His children. Throughout the chapter, beginning with verse 2, the law is referred to as "the commands of *the LORD your God.*" The Israelites are already God's people.

While obedience does not earn salvation, it does convey certain benefits. Obedience removes the threat of punishment (4:3–4). Living by the commandments of God will make this people wise and understanding, so wise as to be the envy of their neighbors (4:5–8). The law is God's good gift and blessing to His people, demonstrating His nearness and involvement in their lives (4:7).

Just as the Lord is the God of Israel's forefathers (4:1), He is the God of the generations yet to come as well. This generation is to teach God's law to their children (4:9).

There is a significant difference in obeying commandments to earn God's approval and acceptance and obeying commandments because one has already been graciously given God's approval and acceptance. The latter is the case here, very clearly. Israel does not receive the law of God at Mount Sinai (4:10–13) until after she is delivered from her bondage in Egypt. Salvation comes first, then obedience; grace first, then the believer's grateful response to God's goodness.

God's law is not some set of unreasonable and onerous requirements which God imposes simply to test His people's loyalty or fortitude. God's law is His wisdom, His instructions for how human life should be lived if it is to be lived right. It is God's fatherly counsel to His children so that they might live happily, fruitfully, and safely in the land He is giving them (4:14).

📖 **4:15–31**

KEEP YOURSELVES FROM IDOLS

There is no particular reason why Israel should be so captivated by idols, but Moses here clearly regards this as the standing danger of her religious life. God has never appeared to His people in a form that they could pattern an idol after. They had never seen God—a point Moses reminds them of (4:15). They are not to make or worship an image of any shape—not images of humans, birds, animals, or fish (4:16–18). Nor are they to worship any object of God's making, such as the sun, moon, and stars (4:19). As Moses points out, having delivered them from bondage in Egypt as He did, God has every right to demand that He be worshiped by His people in the way that He deems right and proper (4:20, 23–24).

Demystifying Deuteronomy

The peoples of the ancient Middle Eastern world made and worshiped idols of every kind. Gods and goddesses were represented as animals—fish, bulls, calves, and the like—or as human beings in figurine form, or as poles and pillars. What is more, as indicated in Deuteronomy 4:19, they not only worshiped gods through images which represented them, but they also actually considered heavenly bodies as gods themselves. Idolatry was a universal institution and a part of the fabric of life for all of these people, save one: Israel herself.

Despite God's clear command, Israel drifts toward idol worship over and over again. Indeed, while Moses is still at the top of Mount Sinai, receiving the law from the hand of God, Israel is at the foot of the mountain cavorting before a golden calf, with bitter consequences, as Moses reminds them (4:21–22).

Critical Observation

Old Testament history is the long story of Israel's partial success and then complete failure to live up to the true understanding of God she had been given. She was always being lured into idol worship. First, it would be the worship of the Lord her God but with the use of idols. After all, all the other nations worshiped their gods by means of idols. But it would eventually cease altogether to be the worship of the Lord and become instead the worship of the idols and the gods they represented: Baal, Ashtoreth, Molech, and the like. One of the great themes of the Old Testament prophets is their condemnation of Israel and Judah for taking over the worship of idols from neighboring nations. But it took the destruction of the nation of Israel and the long bitter years of captivity in Babylon before that kind of idolatry was finally exterminated in Israel.

Moses warns Israel not to forget what kind of God the living and true God is: invisible, immortal, transcendent in glory, infinite in power and might (4:24–25). All idolatry thus becomes both dangerous and utterly foolish. It will bring God's punishments instead of His blessings—for Israel it means that they will lose the promised land (4:26–27)—and it will turn the idolaters into fools, spending their lives chasing after the ridiculous. That is the dripping irony of verse 28. Idolatry practiced long enough will finally bring a person to a state of complete blindness about life. It will bring people who know better to worship objects they themselves have made; it will make people who have long since learned that money cannot buy happiness to seek after more of it still more avidly; it will make people who have sought the meaning of life in pleasure or power or fame completely incapable of serving another master. It is a form of madness. And it is what happens when God finally, as an act of judgment, hands idolaters over to their idolatry.

Take It Home

Idolatry is by no means a problem for Old Testament Israel only. It is a constant danger to God's people still today. By our very nature, we all worship something. It is in our nature to give our allegiance to something or someone. God made us this way so that we might worship and serve Him. Sin has corrupted this tendency, but it did not remove or destroy it. If a man or woman will not worship the living God, then he or she will worship someone or something else.

The Bible takes full account of the fact that one can be an idolater in many other ways than by bowing down to figurines representative of an imaginary god. An idol is anything which claims from us the loyalty and the service we owe to God alone. Today, as in former times, many people worship many idols at the same time: pleasure, power, money, fame, political ideas, and so on. The church is likewise crammed full of idolaters. Every time we give loyalty to something else over God, we are idolaters.

Yet this warning is not without hope. Those who look for the true God will find Him (4:29). Those who repent will learn the mercy of the faithful, covenant God (4:30–31).

4:32–40

OUR HISTORY

We have in verses 32–40 the climactic conclusion of the historical prologue and some of the most beautiful prose in the book of Deuteronomy. The elevated style is the result of the subject matter: the glorious works of Almighty God.

The answer to the rhetorical questions in verses 32–34 is clearly, "No." Christians today, however, can answer, "Yes," and speak of the historical events of Christ's incarnation and resurrection of which these Old Testament events are foretastes.

The monotheism alluded to in verse 35 is an essential implication of Israel's history. They never thought to ask, as people have often since, whether God exists. They had seen Him at work.

The discipline of verse 36 is that of a father disciplining his child. (This is made explicit in 8:5.) God has established a parent-child relationship between Himself and His people.

Moses here speaks to the people as if they were personally present at the Exodus and Mount Sinai, even though many of them clearly had not been. The oldest among those to whom Moses is speaking had been children during those days of the deliverance from Egypt and the two years at Sinai, but many more would have been born in the years since Israel left Sinai and began her wanderings in the wilderness.

Moses has a very practical purpose in speaking this way to his contemporaries. Reminding them of their history, he expects them (and us) to live according to it. He wants them to consider the past, take it seriously, and draw from it courage to face the challenges of life in the promised land. He desires his listeners to fear God and develop a solemn determination to keep His commandments, to be ever thankful and hopeful, and possess a sense of great obligation to pass this history on to future generations (4:40).

4:41–49

SOME UNFINISHED BUSINESS

At the conclusion of this historical prologue, Moses tends to some logistical details for the tribes receiving territories east of the Jordan. He establishes cities of refuge, one for each tribe (4:41–43).

Verses 44–49 once again describe the geographical locations of the territories Israel has taken possession of, anchoring this account firmly in historical time and place.

DEUTERONOMY 5:1–33

LOVE, FEAR, AND OBEDIENCE

Setting Up the Section

The book of Deuteronomy follows the pattern of ancient Middle Eastern treaties. The preamble in chapter 1:1–5 gives the historical and geographical setting. The historical prologue in chapters 1:6–4:49 comprises a lengthy review of God's dealings with Israel and serves to provide a rationale for obedience. In chapter 5, we begin the particular stipulations of the covenant: the commandments which occupy the largest part of the book.

📄 **5:1–22**

THE TEN COMMANDMENTS

Moses' words recorded in Deuteronomy 5:1–5, like those in chapter 4, address the people as if the Ten Commandments have been given directly to them, rather than to the generation before (The Lord made a covenant with *us* at Horeb [5:2]; He spoke to *you* from the mountain [5:4]; *you* were afraid of the fire on the mountain [5:5]). In the statement recorded in verse 3, Moses seems to draw special attention to this foreshortening of history by saying that God made His covenant at Sinai not with the people who were present there at the time, but with those who would come after them.

The Ten Commandments recorded in verses 6–21 are already familiar to the Israelites. Moses repeats them as a summary of the covenant the people had to affirm for themselves. As Moses conveys in verses 1–5, the people could not simply inherit the covenant of their forefathers; they had to own it for themselves.

Critical Observation

The Ten Commandments are not simply ten of the many laws that God gave His people; they are not even the ten most important of those laws. The Ten Commandments are a summary of the *entire* law of God. All the rest of the commandments in God's Word are applications or elaborations of these fundamental duties. Their character as a general summary is further indicated by the fact that both in the Old and the New Testaments these ten can be further summarized by only two commandments: to love God with all your heart and soul and to love your neighbor as yourself (see, for example, Deuteronomy 6:5; Luke 10:27).

📖 **5:23–33**

HOW BLESSED ARE THEY WHO FEAR THE LORD

After repeating the Ten Commandments that God had delivered to the people through him (5:22), Moses recalls the scene at the foot of Mount Sinai after the law had been given. The glory of God's presence continued to surround the mountain through the majesty of fire, thunder, and darkness, and the people cowered in fear (5:23–24). They felt they could not stand any further exposure to the glory of God or it would literally kill them (5:25–26), so they pleaded with Moses to approach the Lord and to speak on their behalf (5:27).

Some of this fear is clearly the result of their faithlessness. They did not have a true and living trust in God; they feared God for His justice and His wrath and His power. But that is not the whole explanation. God does not dispute the request the people make of Moses. Indeed, He commends it, as it reads in verse 28. And then He goes on to say that His people will always fear Him as they feared at Sinai. It is only through this fear that they will be blessed and things will go well with them and their children forever (5:29).

Critical Observation

What does it mean to fear the Lord? True fear of God is a positive, not negative, thing; it is an expression of high regard for God, not of alienation or repulsion. It is taking God as seriously as His majesty requires, not hating to be near or with Him.

Holy fear does not drive out all other emotions before it or displace all other emotional states. The fear of the Lord coexists with joy.

The fear of God spoken of here could be defined as an apprehension of the true majesty and glory of God. It is the awe one should have in the presence of God's greatness and wonder; it is high reverence, which is appropriate to creatures before their Creator, finite persons before the infinite and Almighty God.

It is easy for Israel to have such reverence and fear; they have, with their own eyes, seen terrific, breathtaking, heart-shuddering manifestations of the divine majesty. They know the vastness that separates them from God and how it feels to be so small before something so infinitely great.

If God's people truly fear Him as they should, that fear will bring them blessing and prosperity (5:30–33). Nothing leads to obedience more certainly than a true reverence for God, than some sense of His majesty, His immensity. Before such a God, a God who sits enthroned in the heavens, any and all disobedience seems absurd, irrational, and unquestionably wicked. Sin is not likely to find much welcome in a soul often overwhelmed with God's sublime splendor.

Take It Home

God gave Israel the law after He had already delivered them from their slavery in Egypt. They did not need to earn their deliverance by obeying the law. Rather, the law served another purpose: to show God's people how they ought to live out love and gratitude to their Redeemer.

In the same way, Christians keep the commandments of God not in order to be saved—that would be legalism and not the gospel of grace—but because they have been saved by grace and wish to live a life that glorifies God. The law of God shows us the way. Obedience is a response of love to a God who has not only delivered us from the wrath to come by the death of His Son, but has given us such wise and sound counsel that our lives might be rich and full and good. God has given His laws to us and laid us under obligation to keep them because we are His children—He loves us and wants the very best for us.

DEUTERONOMY 6:1–25

GOD-FEARING CHILDREN

Talk the Talk 6:1–9
Walk the Walk 6:10–25

Setting Up the Section

Deuteronomy 5 looked to the previous generation and emphasized how essential it was for the current generation to inhabit as their own the covenant made with their parents and grandparents. Deuteronomy 6 takes a forward view to the next generation. In it we read of God's exhortations for parents to nurture their children in the faith of the covenant God.

📄 6:1–9

TALK THE TALK

After exhorting the people to fear the Lord as had the generation at Sinai (4:29), Moses extends that charge—and the promised blessings—to their children and the children after them (6:1–3).

Two essentials form the core of what each generation must know: the truth about who God is (6:4) and how the people are to relate to Him (6:5). This covenant succession from parents to children is too important to be left to chance. Parents must be intentional and passionate about passing on the faith. The picture is not of disinterested parents who set their children to memorizing the catechism or who suppose their obligation is satisfied by taking the children to church. The picture is of parents who are eager and determined to see their children enter into an ever deeper understanding of God's Word and gratitude for God's great works. Here are parents who, with remarkable diligence and great affection, teach the truth of God to their children until they are sure their children understand it and apply it to the practical issues of life, until it is written indelibly in their hearts (6:6–7).

Critical Observation

Most of the significant characters of biblical history were sons and daughters of the covenant and were raised in the faith. Godly successions of faith and love litter the pages of scripture: Seth, Enoch, Noah; Abraham, Isaac, Jacob, Joseph; Boaz, Jesse, David, Solomon; Lois, Eunice, Timothy; and so on. The godly Hebrew kings, the heroes of faith listed in Hebrews 11, and John the Baptist all were children once in homes where fathers and mothers faithfully kept the command to nurture their children in the faith.

Verses 7–10 say it plainly. The Word of God is never to be far from the lips and should often be popping into the conversation that fathers and mothers have with their children. What are the commandments that parents are to impress upon the hearts of their children? They are the commandments, we read in verse 5, which are summed up in this: that they are to love God with absolutely everything they have.

Demystifying Deuteronomy

Many observant Jews take literally the injunctions in Deuteronomy 6:8–9. They bind small, scripture-filled leather cases, called *tefillin*, on their arms and foreheads, and post small cases containing the words of Deuteronomy 6:4–9, called *mezuzahs*, on their doorframes.

📖 6:10–25

WALK THE WALK

Children cannot follow where their parents do not lead. So parents are called upon to maintain their own close walk with God. In prosperity, they must not let materialism crowd out God (6:10–12). In a secular culture, they must not follow the crowd (6:13–15). In times of deprivation, they must not succumb to ingratitude (6:16). At all times, they are to do what is right and trust the Lord with the consequences (6:17–19).

And how will parents know if the grace of God is impacting their children's lives? Their children will begin turning to them to ask the great questions of life (6:20), giving them the opportunity yet again to recount the mighty works of God by which He saved His people (6:21–23) and to teach them nothing is more important than keeping every one of God's commands, in the fear of God, holding nothing back.

Take It Home

Are your children learning from your words, example, and expectations that you care for nothing more than this: that their lives be joyfully spent serving the Lord Christ? Do they know that your primary and ultimate goal for them is to do all they can for the sake of their Redeemer and yours?

DEUTERONOMY 7:1–26

GIFTS AND REWARDS

Setting Up the Section

Some refer to the book of Deuteronomy as the Romans of the Old Testament. Well, then, we should not be at all surprised to find in it such a strong statement of the doctrine of divine election, the very doctrine to which Paul devotes such considerable and famous attention in his letter to the Romans.

📄 **7:1–11**

GOD'S ELECTING GRACE

Verse 1 of chapter 7 establishes once again that it is God who drives out the nations so that Israel may possess the land. Here we find a strong statement of the principle of sovereign and electing grace. Out of all the peoples of the world, God chose Israel to be His own people. He chose her, not because she deserved His favor—she most certainly did not—but entirely and mysteriously because He loved her. As the apostle Paul would later put it: "It does not, therefore, depend on man's desire or effort, but on God's mercy" (Romans 9:16 NIV).

Critical Observation

The doctrine of election is that God has been pleased from all eternity to choose certain men and women out of fallen humanity whom, and for His love's sake, He has determined to save by Jesus Christ. This is a controversial doctrine; those who disagree with it contend that

1) election makes God unjust, choosing to save some and not others;

2) this doctrine of divine election robs humans of their free will and thus destroys human responsibility.

Election is given a double aspect here in Deuteronomy 7. If it is true that God has chosen Israel, it is also true that He has not chosen the other nations (7:1-5). God makes this distinction between sinful and unworthy people, to call some to Him and to leave others unsummoned (7:7-10). The election of Israel as a people was the first step in that process by which God set apart to Himself those who would be saved. It is His gracious choice in each case, not human action or merit, that is the final explanation for anyone's salvation.

As verse 11 makes clear, Moses' point is not merely that God has chosen His people, but that they should be deeply grateful for the salvation they do not deserve but have been given as a gift, and that in their gratitude they ought to seek the Lord's pleasure by keeping His commands.

📄 7:12-26

THE GOSPEL OF PROSPERITY

Verses 12-15 contain the remarkable promise of blessing that the Lord makes to His people if they walk faithfully and obediently before Him. If they are faithful to His covenant, He will make their lives rich and happy in every way. They will enjoy good health. Their farms will prosper and they will become very successful, while all their enemies will suffer ruin. It is a dramatic passage in its extravagance and in the absence of all qualification or limitation.

In the most literal sense, these words—this promise of blessing for covenant faithfulness—are true. The fact of the matter is that, as a general rule, those who live godly lives by a living faith in the Lord, and by careful and scrupulous obedience to His commands, do prosper in the kinds of ways that are mentioned here in Deuteronomy 7. This is the constant theme of the book of Proverbs. A person who lives faithfully and responsibly before the Lord will say and do those things which make for a fruitful life. It is a simple fact often and everywhere to be observed. The English Puritans, for example, became a prosperous people as a direct consequence of their faithfulness to the way of life and ethics taught in scripture, which they embraced because they loved and trusted the Lord.

A faithful member of God's covenant community—who has, by the grace of God, come to trust the Lord and commit himself to the Word of God—will be an honest and hard-working man, a kind and generous man, and a man who sees life as rich with opportunity and possibility because it is under the rule of his Father in heaven. Such a man does well in this world and finds great reward in it.

Demystifying Deuteronomy

While chapter 7 was being written, Israel was poised on the brink of entering the promised land. But Canaan was not only a fertile and beautiful land which God had given His people; it also represented their spiritual inheritance, the blessings of the eternal promised land. A great point of this is made in the New Testament letter to the Hebrews, especially in chapter 11. There we read that Canaan was never as significant as a piece of real estate as it was as a figure, an enacted prophecy of the heavenly country which God's people, by faith, were headed. The promise of great blessing for covenantal faithfulness is also true in the sense that it will eventually be perfectly fulfilled, in even the most literal way, in the life of God's faithful people in the world to come.

This promise of great blessing for covenantal faithfulness is also true in the sense that the physical blessings mentioned here, as often in scripture, represent spiritual blessings and the general blessedness of God's people who live under His favor. When the Lord promised physical blessings, He meant much more than that, and any spiritual man or woman would want and seek more than that.

Critical Observation

The great problem posed by such promises as this one in Deuteronomy 7:12–16 is, of course, that the Bible itself bears abundant witness to the fact that godly and righteous people do not always enjoy such a wealth of worldly riches and reward; often they experience the reverse. Sometimes it is for a time that a godly man undergoes great tribulation and must walk heavily in this world, such as Job. But often the faithful of the Lord have lived their whole lives in comparative poverty, suffering trials of various kinds. What is more, contrary to the expectation of Deuteronomy 7:17–26, the scripture itself more than once raises the point that the wicked seem to enjoy a greater prosperity than the righteous.

Scripture points the way to a proper understanding. Very often the blessings of salvation, the far greater blessings of peace with God, the forgiveness of sins, eternal life, and the joy of salvation and communion with the Lord are represented under the figure of physical prosperity. When we read in verse 13, for example, of wine and oil being the blessing of the Lord, we are reminded how many times in the scripture wine and oil are symbols of happiness and joy and fulfillment in life (see Job 29:4–6).

In verses 16–26 we read the flip side of the promises in verses 12–15: Not only will God's faithful people prosper, but the wicked nations around them will suffer defeat at their hands. This defeat is also a part of Israel's faithfulness: God's people are to destroy the idols in Canaan so that they will not be tempted into idolatry (7:25). Those who are not faithful in rejecting these rival "gods" will not receive the promises of the faithful, but rather destruction (7:26).

Take It Home

The extravagant promise that was made to Israel in Deuteronomy 7 is also made to God's people today. We are to understand it as a general promise of prosperity for those who trust and obey the Lord, a promise of still far greater blessings of the soul and heart which are represented by these physical blessings spoken of, and a promise of literal and complete fulfillment and prosperity of life in the world to come, the true and eternal promised land.

Are the choices you make day by day based on your conviction that what God will give you for faithfulness to Him will always vastly surpass what you could get for yourself if you sought your own pleasure, success, or prosperity? Is it obvious to those who watch you that what is supremely important to you is to love and serve the Lord? Do you invest your money, your time, and your effort according to this promise in Deuteronomy 7 and many others like it in scripture? Or do you seek first the other things and give only partial and divided attention to the kingdom of God?

DEUTERONOMY 8:1–20

FORGET NOT ALL HIS BENEFITS

Setting Up the Section

You would think that Israel's escape from Egypt and desert wanderings would have been so indelibly printed on every Israelite heart that forgetting it would be nearly impossible. But Moses knew human nature too well to think that. He knew that when they entered the lush and fruitful land that God was giving them, and settled down into their new homes and began enjoying their wealth and prosperity, it would be entirely natural for them to forget all about the desert and all that God had done for them, even forget that the new land and prosperity was His gift to them. Moses knew full well what the human heart is capable of, and how it can so quickly begin to take credit itself for the Lord's achievements.

📖 8:1–5

REMEMBER WHAT GOD HAS DONE

In this chapter of Deuteronomy, Moses warns the people of God of the ease with which they can forget the Lord and His great kindnesses to them. He urges them to be careful not to do so, but to remember the Lord and all that He has done (8:1).

This generation has much to remember. They have just finished long years in the wilderness, which were necessary, after all, only because their parents had rebelled against the Lord and faithlessly refused to trust His promise to bring them into Canaan in triumph, even though He had brought them so miraculously and triumphantly out of bondage in Egypt (8:2). They should also remember how often they had tested the Lord and complained against Him and how, nevertheless, He patiently and generously met their needs with manna, clothing, and with fatherly discipline (8:3–5).

📄 8:6–14

GIVE GOD CREDIT

The appropriate response to what God has done, Moses points out, is to obey Him, walk with Him, and give reverence to Him (8:6–8). And God's blessings are not simply part of Israel's history; at that moment God was in the process of bringing Israel into a good land of their own (8:7–9). The blessings of prosperity, it seems, come with their own temptations: to become proud and forget God (8:10–14).

Critical Observation

This pattern of remembering God's work and responding in gratitude parallels in miniature the entire book of Deuteronomy, in which Moses first recounts God's history of faithfulness to Israel and then calls Israel to obedience.

📄 8:15–18

KEEP REMEMBERING

To emphasize his point, Moses again reiterates what God has done and that which Israel is to remember. How true had all of God's promises proven themselves to be; how safely Israel had lived according to the Word of God. It was not by their own skill or effort or endurance that they had managed those long years in the desert, but by the goodness and provision of God. All of this was fresh in their minds as they sat poised on the eastern bank of the Jordan, ready to cross and possess the promised land.

Demystifying Deuteronomy

While the land of Canaan may not seem like a fertile land by North American standards, it was more fertile and verdant in antiquity especially before the land was raped by the Ottomans. Also keep in mind that the Israelites were seeing the land compared to desert, where Israel had wandered for forty years, and to Egypt, which depended on irrigation. It was indeed a good land (8:7–8).

Moses warns the people that they must resist this natural tendency to forget the Lord and His works. Instead, they must set themselves to remembering them, every day and in every way calling to mind the Lord and all His benefits. Moses doesn't think that Israel will actually forget the Exodus and the wilderness in the sense that the people will no longer know that these things happened. But what Moses means is that they must remember them in a spiritual way, being forever impressed on their hearts so that the Exodus and the wilderness continue generations afterward to awaken faith, hope, and love in the hearts of God's people.

📖 8:19–20

FOLLOW GOD'S WAYS

If you are going to live a faithful life, Moses tells the Israelites, then make a determined and heartfelt effort to keep God's commandments, for love's sake (8:19–20).

The kind of remembering Moses is speaking of here is that which stirs the heart, breaks pride and willfulness, and awakens faith, hope, and love.

Take It Home

What we read here in Deuteronomy 8 we will often read in the Bible. Remembering has a great deal to do with living the Christian life—remembering what God has done for us in the distant past and remembering our own lives and our own experience of the Lord. And the Christian man or woman, boy or girl, who keeps the Lord and His works in remembrance is the person who will most joyfully and zealously live the Christian life.

How will you keep the memory of the Lord, His word, and His works in front of you? With a verse stuck to the door of your refrigerator? Through keeping a journal? In weekly worship with other believers?

DEUTERONOMY 9:1–29

UNRIGHTEOUSNESS

Setting Up the Section

Interestingly, all of the examples Moses uses to demonstrate how unworthy Israel is of the gift she is about to receive are from the life of the previous generation, not this generation about to cross into the promised land. Those who aroused the Lord's anger at Mount Sinai, who cavorted before the golden calf, and then who later rebelled at Kadesh Barnea—they all lie dead and buried back in the wilderness. They had forfeited the promised land by their faithlessness. But, with that sense of family solidarity which is so common to the Bible, the present generation is addressed as if they, too, had been at Horeb, they, too, had worshiped the golden calf, they, too, had participated in the cowardly refusal to enter the promised land at Kadesh Barnea.

📄 **9:1–6**

NOT FOR YOUR RIGHTEOUSNESS

Moses again assures the people that they will be successful in conquering the land—successful even against the fearsome Anakites (9:1–2). And he reminds them yet again that their success will not be a result of their own strength but of the Lord's power and faithfulness (9:3).

Critical Observation

It is significant that Moses assures the people they will conquer the Anakites. These are the very people that terrified the Israelites so much that they refused to enter the land forty years earlier (see Numbers 13:26–33). The Anakites were very tall and very strong, and some thought they were descended from a race of giants.

This ought to be a cause of humility for the Israelites, but Moses recognizes that Israel may turn it into a source of pride (9:4). So Moses clearly states, not once, but twice, that God's driving out of the nations is not because of Israel's righteousness, but because of the nations' unrighteousness and because of God's faithfulness to His covenant promises (9:5–6). The fact is, they, too, are guilty of the sins of their parents. Their parents were unworthy of the promised land, but the current generation is as well. They, too, are stubborn people, always saying and doing things that offended the Lord. And here the Lord is reminding them, in the most emphatic way, that the land He is about to give them they do not deserve.

Demystifying Deuteronomy

Israel is described as a "stiff-necked" people (9:6, 13 NIV). The description is a farming expression for an animal that would not be led by a rope around its neck. It portrays Israel as stubborn and resistant to God's leading.

📖 **9:7–29**

THE GOLDEN CALF

In chapter 8, we read the charge to remember what God has done. Now the charge is to remember what Israel had done (8:7). It is not a list to be proud of. At the very moment that God is carving His covenant with Israel into stone (9:8–11), Israel is making a golden statue and calling it the God who had led them out of Egypt (9:12–22).

Demystifying Deuteronomy

The full account of the golden calf is in Exodus 32. The calf could have been modeled after the Egyptian god Apis, which the Israelites knew from Egypt, or after the Canaanite god Baal, both of which took the shape of a calf or bull.

Next, Moses lists three other places where the people had angered the Lord: Taberah, Massah, and Kibroth Hattaavah. In each of these places, the people doubted God's provision and complained about what He did provide. At Taberah, the people's complaints angered the Lord so much that He sent fire to burn the outskirts of the camp (Numbers 11:1–3). Massah is the place where the people claimed that Moses (and, by implication, God) had led them into the desert to die of thirst (Exodus 17). Kibroth Hattaavah was the place where the people complained that they were sick of manna and whined that the food had been better in Egypt (Numbers 11:4–35).

Finally, Moses reminds the people of the sin that led to forty years of desert wandering: the refusal to enter the promised land because their fear of the Canaanites was greater than their trust in the Lord (Deuteronomy 9:23–24). They escaped destruction, Moses explains, only because God was faithful to His promises to Abraham, Isaac, and Jacob (9:25–29). Again, the message is that the gift of the promised land is because God is faithful, not because Israel is deserving.

Take It Home

In Deuteronomy 9, the spirit of God is speaking as surely to us as He was speaking at that moment to the people of Israel. We, too, are an unrighteous people who have been given a great gift—a still more wonderful promised land—which we do not deserve. We, too, are always forgetting and slighting that tremendously important fact.

DEUTERONOMY 10:1–22

A FAITHLESS PEOPLE; A FAITHFUL GOD

Two More Tablets	10:1–11
With All the Heart	10:12–22

Setting Up the Section

The Bible was written in largest part not to the world but to the people of God. Most of its contents, both in the Old Testament and the New Testament, are directly addressed to the church and the people of God. And for that reason one of its greatest themes is the possibility and the temptation, and the frequent reality and danger, of formalism in the Christian faith—of a faith which is not a matter of the heart.

The tragic story of the Old Testament is of a people who were religious in an outward way but whose hearts were far from God. Moses has repeated some of that history to the people; now he calls them specifically to give their whole hearts to God.

📖 10:1–11

TWO MORE TABLETS

Verses 1–5 continue the account of what happened immediately after Israel's blatant unfaithfulness when they made the golden calf (chapter 9). Israel had broken covenant with God when they made that calf, and any other treaty-maker would have considered that covenant over. But God does not turn away; instead, He rewrites the very same words of covenant treaty that He had written on the stone tablets that Moses had broken. God gives the people another chance—exactly the same opportunity He had given them before they turned to idolatry, just as if they had never betrayed Him.

Verses 6–9 are a parenthetical summary not only of the people's travels but of the development of the priesthood. Aaron, the original priest, dies (10:6), and the Lord sets apart the tribe of Levi to serve as priests (10:8).

Demystifying Deuteronomy

Deuteronomy 10:9 states that the Levites would inherit no land. Their needs were provided for in the stipulations about offerings: Part of the meat and grain offered to God was to feed the priests (see Leviticus 6:18; 7:28–36).

Verses 10–11 provide a flashback to the time at Horeb and return the focus back to entering the promised land.

📖 **10:12–22**

WITH ALL THE HEART

Moses reiterates the earlier theme of the importance of the heart in a true and right relationship with God. He tells Israel that they must serve the Lord with all their heart and soul (10:12). Verse 13 elaborates on that: Serving God involves observing God's commands and decrees.

Verses 14–15 reiterate once again both God's supremacy—everything belongs to Him—and His gracious choice to love Israel above all other nations. Verse 16 returns to the issue of the heart. The first part of circumcising hearts is to practice dependence upon the Lord for sanctification, for, as Deuteronomy 30:6 will show, it is really the Lord who does the circumcising. For this work of making hearts right before God, they are utterly dependent upon the Lord. He calls His people to do something, but He must bless what they do, and He alone can make it effective.

Critical Observation

Circumcision was the original sign of God's covenant with Abraham and Abraham's descendants (Genesis 17). It was an outward, physical sign, but the command in Deuteronomy to circumcise one's heart indicates that circumcision was always intended to reflect an internal reality, not merely external obedience.

Moses seems to be saying that it is the heart that matters and there will never be true loyalty to God and faithfulness to His covenant unless it comes from the heart.

Critical Observation

What Moses says here in Deuteronomy 10, about the circumcision of the heart, Paul will later say in Romans 2:28–29: "For you are not a true Jew just because you were born of Jewish parents or because you have gone through the ceremony of circumcision. No, a true Jew is one whose heart is right with God" (NLT).

Take It Home

Christianity is uniquely, among the religions of the world, a matter of the heart. It condemns in no uncertain terms religious activity and performance which is not as much a matter of the heart as it is of outward behavior. From the beginning to the end of the Bible, we are reminded that the living God sees the heart, inspects the heart, and judges according to what is in the heart. The life of true faith is not the doing of certain religious acts, but rather, in one's heart, the fear of God, love for God, desire for God, joy in God, and gratitude to God.

DEUTERONOMY 11:1–32

LOVE AND OBEDIENCE

Setting Up the Section

It is imperative that the Israelites understand that the key to staying in the land is to obey God. All obedience to God starts with love. A person who does not love God cannot obey God. For this reason, Moses reiterates the call to love.

📄 **11:1–7**

THE CALL TO LOVE GOD

Everything that happened in the history of Israel had been for the purpose of motivating the people to love God with their whole hearts. For this reason, as they are called to love God (11:1), they are to remember all that He has done for them (11:2). He rescued them (11:3–4), provided for them (11:5), and disciplined them (11:6–7) so that they would grow in their obedience to Him. The call to love is grounded in the love that God had given to them.

Critical Observation

This chapter is laid out in a logical sequence. It begins with the call to love God, then moves to the call to obey God, and ends with the consequences for both obedience and for disobedience. This order is theologically important. To work it backward would look like this:

- If you obey, you are blessed; if you disobey, you are cursed.

- Therefore, you must obey.

- The only way to obey is to love God, for all obedience is motivated by love.

📄 **11:8–25**

THE CALL TO OBEY GOD

The strength of the Israelites to take possession of the land and to secure for themselves a place to live in peace, safety, and security is directly related to their obedience. Their abilities to conquer stronger enemies and to live long in the land (4:40; 5:16; 6:2; 25:15; 32:47) are ultimately matters of obedience, not military skill or sound military leadership (11:8–9). This is the uniqueness of this nation. Their focus is not to be on becoming better soldiers or leaders; their focus is to be on loving God and following all He says.

Mentioning the contrasts between the promised land and Egypt (11:10–12) was no doubt prompted by those who wanted to return there, as Dathan and Abiram had (11:6). The land of Canaan had far more potential than Egypt ever had. What God provided clearly exceeded what Egypt offered. The people in Egypt had to depend on irrigation; God's people would have rain from heaven (11:11). Unlike human irrigation, rain is in the complete control of God. Thus, God is again showing the people that He will care for them and give them what they need to survive (11:12).

Because of the importance of obedience and the seduction of false religion, Moses again warns Israel against worshiping other gods (11:16). Many of the gods worshiped in Canaan were fertility gods (gods of grain, oil, rain, etc.). If the people transfer their trust for the prosperity of their land to one or more of these false gods, the Lord will withdraw His gifts of rain and produce (11:17).

These commandments about staying away from false gods are so important that the people are to have them always in their hearts and minds (11:18). God's laws are to be always in front of them and their children (11:19–21).

In return for their obedience, the Lord will grant Israel supernatural success against all her enemies—no matter how large and strong they are (11:22–24). He will put terror and fear in their enemies so that they are not able to fight successfully against Israel (11:25). God will deliver this nation and provide for her in extraordinary ways.

Demystifying Deuteronomy

Moses was very clear that love and obedience are intrinsically connected (6:5–6; 7:9; 10:12–13; 11:13, 22; 19:9; 30:6, 8, 16, 20). In Hebrew, the command to love the Lord carries with it something more than just a feeling; it carries the idea that a person will follow God in a very personal and intimate relationship and then express that desire to follow in obedience to His revealed will. Thus, it means more than just a close relationship; it is a relationship that causes one to be united with God in intent and purpose.

📄 11:26–32

THE CONSEQUENCES FOR OBEDIENCE AND DISOBEDIENCE

The Lord clearly set before the people the simple reality for obedience: If you obey, you will be blessed; if you disobey, you will be cursed (11:26–28). Longevity, prosperity, and security are not based on following pagan practice, but on loving God and following Him all the days of their lives. A formal proclamation of blessings and curses will reemphasize this truth once the people enter the land. (The blessings and curses proclaimed from Mount Ebel are recorded in 27:9–26.)

Take It Home

Many people take these words to ancient Israel to mean that obedience is the key to all business success today. In other words, *if I want to get rich, I must follow these commands.* This is an inappropriate application. The proper application is that God blesses obedience and punishes disobedience. The fact is that Israel could not obey God. Early on they began serving other gods. Therefore, what we must look at is *how do we obey God?* The answer is found in trusting the person and work of Jesus Christ. When the love of Christ takes residence in one's life, then he or she will have the right motivation to obey God, and God will bless the person for His glory (Galatians 4–5).

DEUTERONOMY 12:1–32

FORM AND FREEDOM IN WORSHIP

Setting Up the Section

This chapter opens the next major section of Deuteronomy. The first four chapters are a historical introduction, or prologue, an account of the previous relationship between the Lord and His people Israel. Chapters 5–11 set out the general commandments or stipulations of the covenant with repeated exhortations to Israel to keep the covenant which God had made with her. Chapter 12 begins the third and longest section of the book, stretching from 12:1 to 26:15. These chapters contain the specific stipulations, or legislation, covering matters as diverse as worship and the management of criminal cases in court.

📖 12:1–4

DESTRUCTION OF IDOLS

Chapter 12 begins and ends with brief sections of warning, serving as bookends to the larger sections of positive instructions in between. These laws are designed for the life of Israel once she is resident in the promised land (12:1). Pluralism and religious tolerance is not to be a part of Israel's experience. The people are not only to avoid pagan forms of worship; they are to destroy both the places of worship and the instruments used in that worship (12:2–3). This introductory section concludes with the summary prohibition, "You must not worship the Lord your God in their way" (12:4 NIV).

Demystifying Deuteronomy

The sacred stones referred to in 12:3 are stone monuments used in Canaanite worship, probably engraved to represent Canaanite gods. Asherah poles were wooden poles set up to honor Asherah, the Canaanite goddess of love and war.

📖 12:5–28

ONE PLACE OF WORSHIP

Verses 5–28 contain regulations governing the right worship of God. Verse 5 refers to the yet unidentified place where the sacrifices are to be offered to the Lord. Eventually, of course, this would be Jerusalem with its temple.

The Lord here tells His people that in true worship there is no conflict between form and freedom. That is, though they must worship God in a certain way, according to rules He has laid down, the worship does not need to be without vitality and sincerity and pleasure.

Worship itself in this chapter is identified with the sincere and joyful engagement of the heart. The worship of Israelite people at the sanctuary is described as an act of joy. In verse 7, the people who brought their sacrifices—and note that, characteristically, they worshiped not as individuals but as families—are to come and rejoice. Again in verse 12, when they come to offer sacrifices and pay their tithes, they were in those acts of worship to rejoice before God. Once again, in verse 18, as they eat their sacrifices and special offerings at the tabernacle and temple, they are to rejoice before the Lord with their families, servants, and the Levites who are there to assist their worship.

The worship God desires from His people is not to be a mere performance, a going through of motions, a series of acts done in a spirit of mere duty or obligation. The God who looks upon the heart and weighs the heart has from the earliest times demanded that the honor and worship which His people pay Him be as much a matter of their heart as of their performance of certain rituals and duties. He has done great things for them and is giving them the land as inheritance (12:9–10). What they celebrate when they come to worship Him is nothing less than the forgiveness of their sins and God's gift to them of Himself and of everlasting life. Surely any true worship, any true thanksgiving, would be offered with joy.

Notice another concern in this chapter about the right worship of God: that worship must be offered according to the directions and the specifications of God's law. The Holy Spirit, through Moses, insists that worship be joyful, but He is still more insistent that Israel's worship of God be offered according to the many laws and regulations which have been laid down. They may not worship in various places as the pagans do, but only where God says (12:5). They must worship the Lord in the specific ways they have been taught, with certain kinds of offerings and gifts to be given in a certain way (12:6, 9). More regulations follow regarding these sacrificial meals and the proper way they are to be taken (12:15–28).

Verse 8 summarizes all of this material in a nutshell: "Your pattern of worship will change. Today all of you are doing as you please" (NLT).

AVOIDING SNARES

The second bookend to this passage again warns against the problem and the temptation Israel would face upon entering the promised land (12:29). True worship of the true God might not appear nearly as exciting or as entertaining as the worship of the Canaanites (12:31). That kind of worship is easy to find—they were fully engaged in sexual and violent acts (12:31).

Critical Observation

Unfortunately, not all of God's people listened to these warnings. No sooner had Israel settled in the promised land than there were people attracted and lured into Canaanite worship. It was this problem, this running after Canaanite worship, which finally ruined the faith of Israel in the Old Testament. In chasing after the worldly way, they finally stopped worshiping God altogether and began to worship only themselves and false gods—though still claiming to be true Israelites.

These warnings are all brought to a conclusion in verse 32, where the Lord says again that Israel is to worship Him only as He has taught them.

Take It Home

God wants our worship of Him to be full of true joy in our hearts, but He wants it to be offered according to His Word and law. He clearly does not see the two things to be in contradiction at all: True worship is to be at the same time both joyful and lawful.

True worship requires preparation and determination. And one must practice true joy in the Lord so that nothing is done as a mere duty, but all is happily a work of love and thanksgiving to God. It is work, hard work, but those who have learned to worship God this way will attest to its ultimate satisfaction. It is work so rewarding as not to be thought work at all.

DEUTERONOMY 13:1–18

CONTEND OR DIE

Setting Up the Section

Deuteronomy 13 continues the warnings about worshiping other gods. Here, however, the source of temptation is not the Canaanites, as in chapter 12, but rather people among the Israelites themselves.

📖 13:1–5

AMONG RELIGIOUS LEADERS

Deuteronomy 13 contains the same warning repeated three different times, but each time with reference to a different group of people within the covenant community who may tempt the people to infidelity to God and His Word.

Critical Observation

The New Testament is just as severe as the Old in its condemnation of false teaching and in the steps it requires to be taken to protect the church from it. Execution has been changed to excommunication, but the issue is the same: The heresies that people foster in the church destroy the soul and bring the wrath of God. No one is to toy with eternal damnation.

In verses 1–5, the Israelites are warned that their own prophets may undermine the truth and that Israel must stand ready to oppose even those with authority and reputation if they contradict the Word of God. The remarkable warning in verse 2, that false teachers may be able to work miraculous signs, reminds us that Moses is writing in an age of miracles—even Egyptian magicians had performed at least one miracle. It is a further demonstration of the general fact that falsehood will always have its powerful inducements and arguments—if not miracles, then through the appearance of compassion or broadmindedness or the approbation of the world.

We read that these false teachers will entice God's people to follow other gods. But this is the biblical judgment as to the true meaning of their message. Very few false teachers come out and say, "Let's abandon God's truth and follow this new way." They almost always say that they are really the defenders and promoters of God's truth, as Aaron does when he calls the revelry around the golden calf a festival to the Lord (Exodus 32:5).

WITHIN THE FAMILY

Verses 6–11 warn the people even against members of their own families, whose wanderings from the truth they would be most likely to excuse and whose punishment they would be most reticent to impose. It would not be a difficult thing to name any number of sons (or husbands, or wives, or brothers) of godly people whose teaching led God's people astray through the generations.

The Lord requires the most severe punishment for those who are found guilty of infidelity to the Word of God: execution (13:5, 9–11, 15). The reason is just this: This falsehood will kill the souls of many others who turn away from the Lord (13:10). As Moses says in verse 11, only punishments as severe as this will serve to prevent others from embracing the same deadly errors and evils.

Demystifying Deuteronomy

It is characteristic of the Lord's teaching in the Bible to devote Himself to one aspect or part of a subject in one place and to leave other aspects of the same theme for consideration in another place and time. Here in Deuteronomy 13, the Lord is instructing His people that they are to contend for the truth and that any disloyalty to the Word of God, any effort to weaken the church's commitment to God's revealed will in the Bible, is to be vigorously and thoroughly exposed and punished.

IN THE TOWNS

Finally, in verses 12–18, Moses warns that in the towns especially there may be a general revolt that takes place against the Word and law of God as fashions and tastes change from time to time. One commentator speaks of "urban revolutionaries," but he is probably referring to people with modern ideas who appear in every generation, arguing that in one way or another the Word of God is out-of-date and needs revision.

If the Israelites catch even a whiff of the scent of such infidelity, they are to take immediate action to find out whether the rumors and reports have substance (13:12–14). They are not to wait to see if heresy comes to full flower; they are to make every effort to locate it and nip it in the bud.

Take It Home

We live in a relativistic age in which the greatest sin is to judge and condemn the convictions of others. In an age like ours, which in some important ways is very similar to that of Canaan in the time of Moses, there will be constant pressure on the truth. And Moses' point is that pressure will be everywhere: in the teaching ministry of the church itself, in our own Christian families, and in new consensuses forming in the Christian population. If we are not constantly on guard, we will be overwhelmed by falsehoods insinuating themselves into the body of the church.

And so that we are not and cannot be seen to be hypocrites, let us first promise the Lord again that before we defend that truth and contend for it in every part, we will first obey it and believe it ourselves. The best defenders of God's truth are always those who truly believe that "Man does not live on bread alone, but on every word that proceeds from the mouth of the LORD" (Deuteronomy 8:3 NIV; Matthew 4.4 NIV).

DEUTERONOMY 14:1–29

A HOLY, GIVING PEOPLE

The Holiness of the Laity   14:1–21
To Tithe or Not to Tithe   14:22–29

Setting Up the Section

Deuteronomy, in its recapitulation of the commandments about clean and unclean animals, gives but a brief account of the laws of cleanliness. This paragraph in Deuteronomy 14 should be understood as representing the much longer legislation touching ceremonial cleanliness in Leviticus 11–15.

14:1–21

THE HOLINESS OF THE LAITY

There is much that remains obscure in these particular laws distinguishing between clean and unclean animals, recorded here in 14:1–21. In fact, the identity of some of the animals named in the verses is not certain. But, more important, the principle of why one animal is clean and another unclean is also by no means certain.

Demystifying Deuteronomy

Leviticus 11–15 records not only the laws distinguishing between clean and unclean animals, but about uncleanness contracted by a woman through childbirth, uncleanness from skin diseases, uncleanness in one's home from the appearance of mildew, and uncleanness contracted by men and women from discharges from the sexual organs. In each case, the law describes how Israelites became unclean, what the consequences of that uncleanness are, and how they are to remove the uncleanness.

There are at least five major theories to explain this distinction between clean and unclean animals.

First, there are those who maintain that the division is entirely arbitrary. God divided the animals this way and gave these laws as a test of obedience. But this distinction between clean and unclean animals is of very great antiquity. It already existed in the days of Noah, as we learn from Genesis 7:2. This suggests that there was some basis for this distinction and that this basis was known to various peoples of the ancient world.

Second, others argue that the division between clean and unclean animals is due to the use of the same animals in pagan worship, but this explanation hardly accounts for all the facts. Pagan religions also made extensive use of the bull, sheep, and goat, even in sacrificial ritual, and these are all considered to be clean animals.

Third, one of the most popular explanations for this distinction between clean and unclean animals is that it is rooted in hygienic considerations. Many of the unclean animals were, in fact, carriers of diseases, and would have been known to be so in the ancient world. But this explanation likewise leaves much unexplained. Why, for example, is the camel unclean? And if hygiene is the right approach, why does Jesus do away with the distinction?

Others argue a fourth theory, namely that animals are categorized as clean or unclean according to a symbolic significance: the clean animals representing traits Israel is to emulate. For example, chewing the cud reminds one of contemplative meditation upon God's law. Sheep remind one of the shepherd. Pigs, on the other hand, suggest nothing positive. This explanation, however, leaves much more unexplained than it can account for.

Finally, there is a new interpretation gaining ground among biblical scholars. One might describe it as the "sociological explanation." It argues that in any culture there is an instinctive recognition of certain things as the standard or ideal against which other things are judged. Birds with wings and two bent legs that eat seeds are proper, or normal, birds. Killer birds and straight-legged birds do not conform to the ideal, and are thus improper and unclean. Fish with scales and fins conform to the ideal concept of fish. Others that do not are unclean. Because the cow, sheep, and goat are the standard fare in the ancient Near East, and hence normal, those animals that do not conform to their pattern of cud-chewing and cloven hoof are abnormal and unclean.

It does not appear, then, that any perfectly satisfactory explanation has been yet advanced to explain why certain animals are clean and certain unclean. Perhaps the true explanation lies in a combination of several of these theories. But it is not necessary for us to know everything about the origin of such laws in order to receive instruction from Deuteronomy 14.

Moses himself indicates the general significance of this legislation about clean and unclean animals with the statement he makes in verses 1–2 and again in verse 21: "You are a people holy to the LORD your God." God's people are to live as a mirror in which God's own holiness is reflected in the world. All of God's people—not just priests—are to be holy.

These laws bring the demands of divine holiness into every aspect of a faithful Israelite's life. At every turn, he or she is faced with the demand that God's people be holy because God is holy and in their midst. God's holiness is to prevail also at their tables and at the taking of meals; they are the people of God, and in their eating and drinking, as in every other part of their lives, they are to be holy as their God is holy. The family could not sit down to a meal without the requirements of their heavenly Father's holiness impinging upon them. In this way, Israel is constantly impressed with the need to be fit for God's service, fit to approach Him, to worship Him, and fit to reflect something of His glory in the world.

Take It Home

While the purpose of the distinction between clean and unclean animals functioned primarily to distinguish between Israelite (Jew) and Gentile, there is significance behind the regulation that still has meaning for us today. We, too, are required to be holy, because our heavenly Father is holy. And though the demands of God's holiness upon us are not illustrated and taught and recollected in the same way they were in the days of Moses, the demands themselves are just as comprehensive, searching, and universal as they were in that ancient time when, no matter where an Israelite turned, he bumped into reminders of the fact that he had to behave as a child of the holy God.

📄 14:22–29

TO TITHE OR NOT TO TITHE

The Israelites are required by the law of God to tithe (14:22). As verse 23 makes clear, they are to tithe not only from their harvested crops, but also from their livestock. One-tenth had to be given as an actual gift to the Lord (Leviticus 27:13).

In this passage, Moses spells out three purposes of tithing. First, it provides for worship for the entire household (14:13–16). The sanctuary meal would have been one of the great occasions of the year for an Israelite family (14:23, 26), and their tithe is put against the cost of the meal. Moses spells out the lesson of the tithe in verse 23. God's people are to tithe in order to learn to revere Him.

A second purpose of tithing is to provide for others (14:27–29). The Levites are able to devote themselves to the priesthood because the people's tithes provided for them (14:27, 29); they did not have to work in the fields or tend flocks in order to make a living. Also, tithing provided a communal storehouse from which to feed the needy—the outsiders, the fatherless, and the widows (14:29).

And finally, regular tithing is God's appointed way to drive home to His people that their prosperity does not depend, as appearances might suggest, on the bounty of the land or their own skill as farmers and herdsmen, but upon the blessing and the provision of their heavenly Father (14:29). The people, with their produce and income, give back a portion to the One who has given it all to them in the first place; year after year they must reckon with the fact that everything they have is a gift from God.

DEUTERONOMY 15:1–23

HOLY EXTRAVAGANCE

Canceling Debts	15:1–11
Freeing Servants	15:12–18
Firstborn Animals	15:19–23

Setting Up the Section

Deuteronomy 15 flows thematically from the previous chapter. Deuteronomy 14 concludes with a concern for the poor and the tithe as a means of providing for the poor. Deuteronomy 15 continues the concern for the disadvantaged—in this case, those in debt and those who have to sell themselves as servants.

📄 **15:1–11**

CANCELING DEBTS

God weaves mercy into the fabric of Israel's life by commanding that debts be canceled every seven years (15:1–2). Opinions vary as to whether the entire debt was to be permanently terminated, or whether payments were only suspended for the seventh year. It's likely the latter is more probable, and this provision has to do with the fact that according to the Law of Moses, in that same seventh year the land was to lie fallow. Many poor people, without the income of the land, would be unable to make payments on their debt and would, therefore, experience even greater hardship, such as being forced into servanthood, which is discussed in verses 12–18.

Critical Observation

Debts were to be canceled every seventh year. The number seven was significant among many ancient Near Eastern peoples—possibly having to do with the cycles of the moon. But for the Israelites, the number seven stood for something that was complete—reflecting the seven days of creation.

If the Israelites follow this law, there will be no poverty in Israel (15:4–8).

Verses 7–11, however, acknowledge that this condition will not be faithfully met. Therefore, the people need instruction about being generous to the poor. The requirement of charity extends past the letter of the law to the attitude of the heart (15:9–10).

📖 15:12–18

FREEING SERVANTS

The servanthood referred to in verses 12–18 could as easily be called slavery. Unlike slavery as we think of it today, this form of slavery provided a solution to the person who could no longer support himself. He could sell himself with the assurance that his servitude was only temporary (15:12) and that he would not go away empty-handed when his time of service ends (15:13–14). Lest the wealthy think this freeing of servants is too much to ask, God reminds them that they were slaves in Egypt and were given their freedom by God (15:15). God's lavish love for them has become the pattern of their lives; loving God and wanting to honor Him, they seek to imitate Him in the extravagance of love.

Demystifying Deuteronomy

One of the unique and remarkable features of the Mosaic Law is its genuine concern for the individual member of society, and especially the poorer and weaker members. Elsewhere in the ancient Near East, men were treated according to their social and economic status. In the Code of Hammurabi, for example, the slave and the underprivileged counted less before the law. But in Israel, the needy were the special concern of the Lord, and the covenant community was expected to ensure their welfare.

The Israelites' laws were wonderfully different from those of the people around them, because they were the people of God. God required things of them that a worldly calculation would never think of or approve. But then, by faith, Israel could enter a world and see a truth that was hidden from unbelievers.

A servant can choose to forgo emancipation and remain in service to his master (15:16). David later describes the custom of piercing a servant's earlobe to show his willingness to serve God (Psalm 40:6), and the writer of Hebrews quotes David when describing Jesus' willingness to become a servant (Hebrews 10:5–10).

This section concludes with a practical word: "Do not consider it a hardship to set your servant free, because his service to you these six years has been worth twice as much as that of a hired hand" (Deuteronomy 15:18 NIV).

FIRSTBORN ANIMALS

Verses 19–23 briefly touch on setting aside the firstborn animals for the Lord. Like the tithed animals (14:22–29), these animals belong to the Lord and may be eaten only by those who offer them. This section, along with the section on tithing in chapter 14, frames the instructions on debts and servants, putting concern for the impoverished in the context of what is owed to God.

Take It Home

The simple question posed to us by these commandments in Deuteronomy 15 is this: What in your life is the equivalent to this extravagance and immoderation? In what way have you cancelled debts, freed slaves, and given up the firstborn of your flocks and herds? What do you do for no other reason than God's grace to you demands a lavish response from you? As is mentioned three times in this chapter (verses 6, 10, 18), God reserves His blessing for those who serve Him in this abandoned way.

DEUTERONOMY 16:1–17

THE GOD OF HOLIDAYS

Passover	16:1–8
Feast of Weeks	16:9–12
Feast of Tabernacles	16:13–17

Setting Up the Section

The chapter gives only a summary statement on the three great yearly feasts of the Israelite calendar. More complete legislation is found in Exodus 12; 23:14–17; Leviticus 23; and Numbers 28:16–31.

PASSOVER

The month of Abib (16:1) is later called *Nisan*. On today's Jewish calendar, it marks the beginning of the religious year. The festival of Passover (16:2–4) celebrates the Angel of Death passing over the homes of believing Israelites in Egypt (Exodus 12:14–20).

While only the adult males are required to attend the Passover ritual at the central tabernacle, and later the temple in Jerusalem (Deuteronomy 16:5, 16), every Israelite family participates in their homes, starting in the evening (16:6) as on the first Passover. The tents to which the men are to return (16:7) are their temporary lodgings at the sanctuary where they stay for the six days of the festival (16:8).

Critical Observation

The Hebrew word for "feast" used in these verses is *Hag*, which reminds us of the Muslim annual pilgrimage to Mecca, the Haj. The idea of pilgrimage belongs to the Hebrew word as well.

📖 **16:9–12**

FEAST OF WEEKS

The Feast of Weeks is so called because it begins seven weeks after the offering of a sheaf of new grain (16:9). The date is given more precisely in Leviticus 23:15–16 as fifty days after the beginning of Passover, which is the reason the festival is also called Pentecost (*pente* means "fifty"). In Exodus and Numbers, it is also called Harvest and Firstfruits, because the freewill offering (16:10) comes from the first produce of the harvest.

The celebration includes a trip to Jerusalem and the temple, wonderful food, grand ceremonies, and no normal labor, allowing free time for sightseeing and recreation—and all of it is made more special because of the sacred and holy connotations in the festival itself (16:11–12).

Demystifying Deuteronomy

The three feasts described here (Passover, the Feast of Weeks, and the Feast of Tabernacles) are still celebrated by observant Jews today. Passover begins on the fifteenth day of the month of Nisan on the Israelite calendar—sometime in March or April of the Gregorian calendar. The Feast of Weeks begins on the sixth of Sivan (in May or June), and the Feast of Tabernacles on the fifteenth of Tishri (late September through October).

📖 **16:13–17**

FEAST OF TABERNACLES

The Feast of Tabernacles (16:13–15), or Booths, is celebrated at the autumn harvest of produce (grapes, olives, dates, figs). In Exodus it is also called the Feast of Ingathering. Part of the festival is camping out for the week, living in booths as a reminder of their camping in the wilderness following the exodus from Egypt. Every Israelite man is required to celebrate these three feasts every year (16:16). Giving to God (via the tabernacle or temple offerings) is an essential part of all three festivals (16:17).

Take It Home

Isn't it remarkable that God should require of His people that they take so many holidays? That He should want to be remembered by His people over a meal? That He should seek to build their faith in such a happy and festive way? This is a point hardly confined to the Old Testament pilgrimage feasts; it's a theme woven through all the Bible. We are to be a festive people.

Deuteronomy 16 is a call to all of us to live festive lives, in our families and in our church fellowship. It is our inheritance as the people of God, part of our calling, ministry, witness, and most importantly, it is to God's honor.

DEUTERONOMY 16:18–17:13

UNDER AUTHORITY

Judges   16:18–20
Responsibility of Every Believer   16:21–17:7
Law Courts   17:8–13

Setting Up the Section

In this section, God is saying that His people must be under His authority and live their lives under that authority. These verses are about judges, trials, and punishment, but that is all to demonstrate that God requires His will be done in the community of His people. All of this instruction is to that end and purpose.

📄 16:18–20

JUDGES

Each town has its own legal system, though there is also a central, or national, system. The officials referred to in verse 18 likely hold a role similar to that of police officers. Judges and officials must rule according to the will of God. They are to enact justice—which is to enforce the laws and commandments of God and those only (16:19). If by the faithful exercise of their office the judges ensure that God's people are living according to God's Word, the people of God will live and prosper in the land (16:20). Contrarily, if they do not, as we read often in Deuteronomy, they will lose both God's blessing and the land.

Demystifying Deuteronomy

The judges referred to in 16:18 are the leaders whose appointment was described in Deuteronomy 1:9–18.

🗎 16:21–17:7

RESPONSIBILITY OF EVERY BELIEVER

The judges and officials, along with other government officials of Israel, are appointed by the Lord precisely to ensure that His people remain faithful and obedient to Him. The people have already been commanded to tear down the Asherah poles at Canaanite centers of worship when they enter the land (chapter 12), and now they are told not to set up any of their own, nor to offer defective sacrifices (16:21–17:1).

Deuteronomy 17:2–7 is closely related to 4:15–24 and 13:1–8 in its discussion of God-pleasing worship. Disloyalty to God is equivalent to treason and undermines the security of the people. When God's people refuse to live in submission to God's authority, terrible consequences ensue (16:5–6). By casting the first stone, the witnesses are laid under the onus of murder if they testify falsely (17:7).

🗎 17:8–13

LAW COURTS

It isn't at all hard to imagine what the difficulties in judgment (17:8) might be, for they were the same as we face today. Difficulties arise when courts are faced with a set of complex circumstances that the law doesn't precisely address. Such cases are to be submitted to priests for judgment (17:9–11). The priest's comprehensive knowledge of the scripture helps ensure that the judgment rendered is in keeping with God's Word. No doubt, after a time, a body of precedents will be compiled to aid judges in adjudicating cases, just as in modern times.

Critical Observation

In Deuteronomy 17:10–11, the command to obey the priests and judges is, "Do not turn aside from what they tell you, to the right or to the left." This is exactly the same kind of language used for obedience to the law of God: "So be careful to do what the LORD your God has commanded you; do not turn aside to the right or to the left" (Deuteronomy 5:32 NIV); "Do not turn aside from any of the commands I give you today, to the right or to the left, following other gods and serving them" (Deuteronomy 28:14 NIV). The use of this language reinforces the message that obedience to God's appointed leaders is obedience to God Himself.

In verse 12, the point is made again that priests and judges are ministers of the Lord. A minister is one who does not act for himself or in his own name but carries the authority of another and speaks and acts in His name and with His authority.

The whole reason for priests and judges is to ensure that God Himself is obeyed. When sin is tolerated and wickedness goes unpunished, the commitment of the whole community to the law of God and the life of obedience is undermined. This is the point of verse 13. Faithful discipline, correction, and, if necessary, even the most extreme punishments, are carried out so that the obedience and faithfulness of others will be preserved and fostered. If unfaithfulness is tolerated, it will soon become the normal way of life. This is why God is so severe in His demand for the punishment and the correction of such conduct among His people.

Take It Home

God calls His people to obey Him by obeying His officers, those entrusted to rule on His behalf and in His name. In the Christian church today, you will quickly run into individuals who make a great show of their submission to the Lord and their zeal to keep His commandments but who won't heed or obey any particular church government or any particular group of elders. These people are defying the Word of God in this unwillingness to submit to those who have been given authority within their church. And their claim to be submissive to God Himself is, in this way, demonstrated to be pretence and hypocrisy.

DEUTERONOMY 17:14–18:22

THE THREE OFFICES

The King	17:14–20
The Priests	18:1–8
The Prophet	18:9–22

Setting Up the Section

Deuteronomy 17:14–18:22 is a highly interesting passage of scripture for the way in which it places together the three great offices of the Old Testament religious structure. God communicates His presence directly to the hearts of His people by His Spirit, and He also uses people as instruments of His presence. He speaks to His people through prophets, He grants forgiveness of sins and maintains fellowship with them through priests, and He rules over them through kings.

📖 17:14–20

THE KING

The instructions here assume that in the future Israel will want a king (17:14). In these guidelines, God is not *recommending* that Israel have a king, but rather *allowing* her to have one. The instructions that follow (17:15–20) will provide for a godly king and a godly reign. This passage makes clear that, like the judges and courts, the king is God's officer, intended to rule on God's behalf. Unfortunately, the many wives and much gold that Moses warns against (17:17) do indeed lead future kings astray.

Demystifying Deuteronomy

Deuteronomy 17:14 says that the Israelites will want to appoint a king over the land. First Samuel 8 records that, although God warned the Israelites about the hardships of serving a king, they insisted, just as God had predicted: "We want a king over us. Then we will be like all the other nations. . ." (1 Samuel 8:19–20 NIV).

📖 18:1–8

THE PRIESTS

Every man in the tribe of Levi is part of the priesthood (18:1). Rather than working the land, they are to offer sacrifices on behalf of the people. Since their work does not produce a livelihood, the Levites are to be supported by the rest of the people (18:2–8). Like the judges, courts, and king, priests exercise their office for the Lord's sake and in His name (18:7, 15).

📖 18:9–22

THE PROPHET

Between sections devoted to Israel's priesthood and prophecy, several verses forbid them to recognize or make any use of the priestly and prophetic practices of Canaan (18:9). God forbids sacrifices offered to false gods, and here He specifically forbids human sacrifice as well (18:10). Divination, interpreting omens, and consulting the dead (18:10) are ways of trying to predict the future or discover things through human intervention, rather than God's divine intervention through His prophet. Israel is to separate herself from these practices (18:12–14).

Critical Observation

Peter (in Acts 3:22–23) quotes Deuteronomy 18:15 about the prophet to come. He says Jesus is a prophet like Moses but greater than Moses.

Moses promises that God will raise up a prophet like him (18:15). A prophet's job is to deliver God's messages to God's people. Moses reminds Israel that he fulfilled this prophetic role at Horeb (18:16–20). Prophecy that is proven wrong or that conflicts with God's Word is evidence of a false prophet (18:21–22).

Critical Observation

This is not information of mere historical importance. The offices of prophet, priest, and king—and the officers who filled them in the ancient epoch—were enacted and living prophecies of Jesus Christ. These offices are one of the most important ways God chose to reveal in advance what the Messiah would be, what He would do, and how He would save His people from their sins.

All of this about the Savior being a prophet, priest, and king is taken up in detail in the New Testament and applied to Jesus Christ (Matthew 27:11; Luke 4:17–19; Hebrews 5:5–6). All the other prophets in the Bible were a part of the prophetic work of Jesus Christ, but He Himself is its culmination and completion. He is the Word of God. All that we need to know, He has taught us by His Word and Spirit.

In our guilt, we are estranged from God and subject to His wrath. And so Christ, the High Priest, came and offered a sacrifice to satisfy divine justice and make us friends with God again. And, when the work was done, He ascended to heaven and there continues to be our High Priest by interceding for us.

Take It Home

In the old days in Israel, if people got wind that there was a prophet in the area, they dropped what they were doing and ran to hear him speak so that they might know what God was saying to them. People went to the priest to unburden themselves of their sins and their problems and to request prayer. The people also gathered before their king to declare their allegiance to him and to promise him their obedience. We ought to do no less today, for One who is far greater in every way, and far better able to help us, is now our Prophet, Priest, and King.

DEUTERONOMY 19:1–21
LEST INNOCENT BLOOD BE SHED

Setting Up the Section

The apparent subject of the chapter is the laws governing murder and its punishment. But, really, the subject of the chapter is the purpose of all of these laws, which is stated in Deuteronomy 19:10—that innocent blood not be shed in the land. This is the purpose of all that we read in this chapter.

📖 19:1–14

CITIES OF REFUGE

In addition to the three cities already set aside east of the Jordan mentioned in Deuteronomy 4:41–43, the people are to establish three cities on the west of the Jordan. This is an expansion of the law of Exodus 21:12–14, according to which the altar is a sanctuary, or asylum, for someone who has accidentally killed another. There he cannot be molested by anyone bent on vengeance. But when Israel enters the land, the altar is too far away, and a person fleeing to it might not reach it before being overtaken by the avenger of blood. Hence three centrally located cities (Deuteronomy 19:1–7).

Demystifying Deuteronomy

The term "cities of refuge," which many translations use as a paragraph heading, does not appear in this chapter, but it is used in Numbers 35:6, 11 for these same cities.

The avenger of blood (19:6) is not merely a hotheaded relative bent on revenge but the kinsman who by culture and law is responsible to see that justice is carried out.

The cities of refuge are not only for the purpose of asylum; they are also places of punishment, for while manslaughter may not be murder, in many cases it is still wrong. In Numbers 35:25–28, where the more comprehensive explanation of these cities is found, the law states that in some cases, once a person is found to be guilty of manslaughter, he is to be returned to the city of refuge and remain there until the death of the high priest. If he leaves that city, the avenger of blood is free to take his life. In effect, the city of refuge then becomes a prison, though certainly not like modern prisons.

The purpose of these cities of refuge is that no innocent blood is shed. Executing an innocent man is equivalent to murder, making the community as a whole guilty of bloodshed (19:10). Another way that innocent blood might be shed is to let a murderer go unpunished (19:11–12). If executing an innocent man is a crime to be avoided at all costs, so is the failure to punish a murderer by execution. Failure in that case also renders the community guilty of bloodshed (19:13).

A boundary stone marks the edge of a person's property (19:14). To move it is essentially to rob a person of that portion of land.

📖 19:15–21

WITNESSES

All of this information about cities of refuge and trials to discriminate between what is truly murder and what is something less is to ensure that no one be executed for anything other than a capital crime.

Trials are to be conducted in every case. One witness, even an eyewitness, is not sufficient to prove the guilt of an accused murderer. There must be two or three, which is a cryptic way of saying that the evidence must be incontestable (19:15). The scripture clearly entertains the possibility that guilty men might go free for want of adequate evidence.

Witnesses are sworn to the truth upon the most serious penalty should they be found to have perjured themselves (19:16–17). If a witness's lie results in the condemning of an innocent man to death, the witness is executed (19:18–19).

The point made in verse 20 is the principle of deterrence. Swift, sure, and just punishment is to deter others from the commission of the same crime. Failure to provide such punishment, by implication, will lead others to a greater willingness to commit such crimes.

Critical Observation

The law of retaliation in verse 21 is also found in Exodus 21:23–25 and Leviticus 24:17–20.

The principle of justice by equity is stated in Deuteronomy 19:21—punishments are to be, as far as possible, the exact equivalent of the crime. An eye for an eye, a hand for a hand, and a life for a life means that justice requires a murderer forfeit his own life. Anything less or more is not retribution in proportion to the crime. Other ancient Near Eastern law codes (famously, the Code of Hammurabi) sometimes insisted on excessive punishments, so the guidelines here function to guard from that excess.

Take It Home

The perspective of scripture is twofold. First, being made in the image of God, the life of a human is sacred, and this in itself makes it a crime of unimaginable proportion for one person to murder another. Because we are made in the image of God, it is a form of deicide (of God-killing) as well as homicide to lift up our hand against our neighbor.

Second, justice is a matter of equity and, in the case of a criminal, his receiving what is due. Humans instinctively, if not always consistently, recognize the wrong of a small crime being punished with a great penalty—a man being sent to Devil's Island for stealing a loaf of bread for his hungry family—or contrarily, of a great crime being punished with a small penalty. This is the principle expressed in the statue of justice as a woman with eyes blindfolded holding balances or scales in her hand. Crime lies on one side of the balance, punishment on the other, and the scales are to be even at the end of the matter. Justice requires an impartial reckoning of a punishment which fits the crime.

DEUTERONOMY 20:1–20

THE COMMANDS OF GOD ARE NOT A BURDEN

Exemptions from Military Service	20:1–9
Offering Peace	20:10–20

Setting Up the Section

Chapter 20 begins a section of the book of Deuteronomy devoted to particular laws addressing many different issues. In certain cases, they reiterate points that have already been made in previous chapters. This chapter, for example, recapitulates some of what was already stated in chapter 7: laws governing the conduct of war.

📖 **20:1–9**

EXEMPTIONS FROM MILITARY SERVICE

Israel's strength lay not in the size or equipment of her army, but in her God, and this is a matter not only of faith, but of her own experience. Egypt has a far greater army than the ill-equipped and untrained Israelite people, but it is the vaunted army of Egypt that is destroyed in the Red Sea (20:1). Before the battle, the priest is to remind the soldiers of the fact that God is worth many armies (20:2–4).

The officers mentioned in verse 5 probably refer to officials of the tribes of Israel, not to army officers, as is confirmed in verse 9. These men, knowing their tribe, would know which ones qualify to be exempted from service (20:5–8). God thinks it important to ensure that no man dying in battle should be deprived of the pleasure of seeing his new vineyard begin to bear fruit, and that no young man miss the joy of marrying his bride. God doesn't require the same thing of the fainthearted that He does of the brave.

Demystifying Deuteronomy

The point briefly made in verse 6 is made with more detail in Leviticus 19:23–25, with reference to fruit-bearing plants in general—trees as well as vines. For the first three years, no fruit was to be taken. The fourth year, the fruit was to be dedicated to the Lord, and from the fifth year on, the fruit was to be harvested and sold or eaten. Those who were engaged in this lengthy process—one which was very important for the long-term production of the land—were exempted from army service. God is always after His people's welfare. He didn't want farms and orchards and vineyards ruined because the men who had to cultivate and care for them were absent at the critical period.

It is clear that Israel, at least at this early stage, does not maintain a standing army or has very little of one. For each war, the army has to be recruited separately (20:9).

Take It Home

Chief among the lessons taught by the laws on exemption from military service is this: As the apostle John would later say, God's commandments are not burdensome. These verses are simply teaching in another way that the law of God is one of God's great gifts to His people, and it is intended to lead them into a life that is rich, secure, satisfying, and fruitful.

All of us chafe under the commandments of God. We have a rebellious streak, and, much like little children, we resent being told what to do. God's commands are kindly given and well-meant, and the one who lives by them is going to find a great reward. In Deuteronomy 20:1–9, we are being taught to love and cherish the laws and commandments of God as not only right, but good and health-giving.

20:10–20

OFFERING PEACE

It is often overlooked that outside of the promised land, God commands that the Israelites offer peace before attacking cities (20:10). Only if the rulers of the city reject the offer of peace are the Israelites to attack (20:11–13). Even then, the women and children are to be spared (20:14–15). Deuteronomy 15 outlines rights of the captives and provisions for incorporating them into the Israelite community.

The rules are different for the neighboring cities, however (20:16). The laws laid out in Deuteronomy 7:1–6 are summarized here (20:17), along with the reason for them: to keep Israel from being led astray (20:18).

Ancient military powers often destroyed everything they found on the land they conquered. But God's covenant with Noah extends to the earth as well; the trees are not to be destroyed (20:19–20). This provision allows the land to remain productive.

DEUTERONOMY 21:1–23

LAWS FOR DIFFICULT SITUATIONS

Setting Up the Section

This chapter gives laws that govern three sets of issues. The first is what to do on the discovery of a murdered body when there is no way to ascertain who committed the crime. The second set of laws governs family life, and the third set of laws governs how to handle the remains of a person who has been executed for a crime.

📖 21:1–9

UNSOLVED MURDER

The point of mentioning a field in the land from God (21:1) is that a person murdered in the promised land is killed on sacred soil. For this reason, the sin is elevated—it isn't just a sin against this person who dies and his family, but also a sin against God because it desecrates His land. The process is set up to preserve the honor of God and make right what has been desecrated. In this, the holiness of God is seen as something to take very seriously.

Having determined the nearest town by measurement (21:2), the elders and judges of the district (see 16:18) will instruct the elders of that town the prescribed duties for making things right.

The fact that the animal and field have never been worked (21:3–4) suggests that they are undefiled, never having been ritually contaminated by humans. Something clean has to be offered for the unclean act of a murder. The heifer is to be killed in a very specific manner—it must have its neck broken (21:4).

Critical Observation

By breaking the heifer's neck, there would be no blood shed, for this offering was different from a traditional sin offering, which requires the shedding of blood (Leviticus 17:11). Blood sacrifices always had to be offered on altars at recognized centers (see Deuteronomy 12), therefore shedding this blood at a random town would not be acceptable.

The priests, chosen by the Lord not only to offer sacrifices and pronounce blessings but also to function in judicial capacities (see 17:9; 19:17), assume a role in the proceedings (21:5). Since the murderer is unknown, it is the guilt or innocence of the community at large that is at stake. The entire point of this ritual is to make the community clean.

The town elders, on behalf of all the people, are to symbolize the innocence of the community by washing their hands over the carcass of the heifer, state their collective innocence of the deed, plead with the Lord to accept their act of exculpation, and absolve them of any blame for the death of the victim (21:6–9).

📄 **21:10–21**

WIVES AND CHILDREN

A bride taken as a captive is to shave her head, trim her nails, discard her native clothing, and fulfill a month of mourning for her parents before becoming a wife of an Israelite (21:10–13). All these procedures represent cutting off all ties to the former life. It is important that the bride enter into her new life fully and unreservedly.

Demystifying Deuteronomy

The cities attacked in this scenario would be distant cities (20:10–15)—which probably means they were not Canaanite cities (for it was against the law to marry Canaanites—see Exodus 34:16; Deuteronomy 7:3).

The reality is, because of the sinful nature of humanity, not all relationships will be successful. The husband could therefore end the marriage by simply releasing his wife to go wherever she wishes. He is forbidden to sell her as property or regard her as a slave.

Critical Observation

It is important to note that Deuteronomy 21:14 is not endorsing divorce. Jesus says (in Mark 10:5) that these laws are in place to protect the women, not to endorse a behavior. The laws were in place so that a woman would be treated in a respectable manner even if her husband chose to send her away.

A husband's attitude toward his wife is not to affect his legal responsibilities to her and her children. If he has two wives and the one he does not love gives him the firstborn male, he cannot favor the firstborn son of the wife that he does love (21:15–16). The matter of law that is pertinent here is the proper bestowal of inheritance rights. On the basis of what appears to be a long-standing custom, the eldest son is to receive a double portion of his father's estate (21:17). This is a stipulation first recorded here in biblical law.

The motive for this is clearly articulated: The firstborn is the first sign of his father's strength (21:17). What this means is that a man first gives indication of his virility and capacity to sire succeeding generations when his first son is born (see Genesis 49:3; Psalm 105:36). It is only fitting that the son who gives the father such recognition be recognized himself for what he symbolizes. Therefore, the rights of the firstborn are not based upon feelings or relationships but on what the firstborn son represents.

At the basic level of civil society is the family. A child who cannot obey his parents shows that he or she does not possess the fundamental skill to function properly in a society. In this case, the parents have a responsibility to the society at large to deal with this issue.

Specifically, the charge is that a child who is stubborn-minded (21:18) against his father and mother is disobeying the fifth commandment (to honor your father and your mother, Deuteronomy 5:16). This rebellious son is to be brought to the gate (21:19), that is, the broad plaza just outside the gate where matters of public interest are conducted. The court before which the case is presented consists of elders (21:20), not those of a district or the whole nation but the rulers of the local village. It is they who hear the evidence and rule on the case.

Once the case is heard and the elders judge the child to be guilty as charged, the townsmen execute the felon by stoning. Only by this drastic means can the evil be purged (21:21) from the community. Since this child proves to be nothing more than a plague on the society, he has to be removed. This is the last step in dealing with a child's rebellion—not the first step. It is done only after evidence of uncontrollable and dangerous rebellion that would cause the whole of society to be hindered.

📄 21:22–23

CAPITAL PUNISHMENT

The cause of death might not be by hanging, for in this text the act of hanging follows the person's having been put to death (21:22). The purpose of such a postmortem hanging is to provide a sober warning to the community of the serious consequences of the crime committed.

The corpse is to be brought down and buried before sunset because the curse applied to the criminal would otherwise accrue to the community and the land as a whole (21:23).

Take It Home

Why an individual who was put on display on a tree was considered especially cursed is not clear. What is clear is that God wanted the people to recognize that someone hanging from wood was under God's curse. This is a foreshadowing of the cross. The apostle Paul quotes Deuteronomy 21:23 when talking about Jesus: "Christ redeemed us from the curse of the law by becoming a curse for us—for it is written, 'Cursed is everyone who is hanged on a tree'" (Galatians 3:13 ESV). When Jesus was hanging on the cross, cursed, He took on our guilt and the punishment that we deserved. Imagine the love that inspired Jesus to willingly take God's curse upon Himself!

DEUTERONOMY 22:1–30
LAWS ABOUT LOVE AND SEX

One's Brother's Keeper   22:1–8
Marriage Violations   22:9–30

Setting Up the Section

The laws here deal with the sixth and seventh of the Ten Commandments and the themes that lie beneath them—the sanctity of life and marriage.

📖 **22:1–8**

ONE'S BROTHER'S KEEPER

The brother referred to in verse 1 is not related by blood but by membership in the same spiritual community. There is to be no "finders, keepers" among brothers; possession is not nine-tenths of the law. Any straying animal or lost possession is to be returned (22:1–3), and each person is to be responsible for caring for his neighbor's animals if the owner is away (22:4).

Take It Home

Our natural tendency is to reduce the obligation we owe to others to doing them no harm. In these laws in Deuteronomy 22:1–4, we indeed are forbidden to harm our neighbors; but far more than that, we are required actually to do them good. We are not simply to leave them in the condition we find them in, but we are to improve their lot and help them. They are to be the better for our encounter with them.

There is nothing in it for the one who keeps these laws. At least, there is no gain in any outward or material sense. If you find a lost animal you are to catch it, take it home, care for it—perhaps at some considerable expense to yourself—and then when you locate the owner or he finds you, you are to return the animal to him at no charge! Your neighbor's need has become your obligation.

Not many of us have cows, but we all have lost things we need others to help us find. All of us in one way or another need a bit more of what others have in abundance. How different might the community of believers be, and how much more powerful might our witness to the world be, if only we would make one large step forward in loving one another and caring for one another heartily and positively as God commands us here in Deuteronomy to do.

The command about clothing (22:5) is not a statement about fashion so much as it is about real confusion of genders, specifically transvestism. Some suggest this command is related to pagan practices in the nations around Israel at that time.

The instruction to leave a mother bird on the nest (22:6) is a law of conservation. The potential for future supply is not to be destroyed for the sake of immediate gain. Only if the Israelites take care of the resources around them will it be well with them (24:7).

Roofs were flat and used for sleeping in the summer, for certain chores, and for entertaining, so it is not inconceivable that someone could fall off an unfenced roof (22:8). Protecting people from this danger is the homeowner's responsibility.

📄 22:9–30

MARRIAGE VIOLATIONS

Although many Bible translations put verses 9–12 with the commands in verses 1–6, simply classifying them as "various laws," their relationship to the laws about marriage are closer than it might appear at first reading. Maintaining a separation between different kinds of seeds (22:9), animals (22:10), and fabrics (22:11) reflects the separation Israel is to maintain between herself and the nations around her. Failure to stay separate eventually leads to God's charge of spiritual adultery (see, for example, Jeremiah 3).

Critical Observation

The distinctions in verses 10–11 are more than random examples. The ox (22:10) was a symbol of the Israelites, while the Canaanites were represented by the donkey. Israelite priests wore clothes of wool (22:11); Canaanite priests wore clothes of linen. The imagery here, like the prohibition elsewhere against intermarrying with the Canaanites, illustrates Israel's call to maintain purity and an identity distinct from the pagan nations around her.

If a man slanderously accuses his wife of not being a virgin when they married (21:13–14), her parents can bring proof of her virginity (blood on the bedclothes—verse 17) to the city elders (21:15–17), who will require the husband to pay a fine to the girl's father and deny the right to divorce (21:18–19).

Should the charge be true, however, the woman will be stoned (21:20–21). Note that the men of the village, not just the husband, carry out the execution, indicating, as does the comment about purging Israel, that the sin affects the entire community. The same holds true for those caught in adultery (21:22).

The laws about sex between single, unmarried people take into account a number of factors. First, the offense is more serious if the woman is engaged to another man (21:23, 25, 28). If the liaison took place in the city, both the offending man and the woman are considered equally deserving of execution (21:24), on the assumption that the sex was consensual (if the woman had cried for help in a city, someone would have heard and rescued her). She could not get away with falsely accusing her lover of rape. In the country, however, the woman is given the benefit of the doubt; she may have resisted without anyone being close enough to hear her. In this case, only the rapist receives the death penalty (21:25–27).

Demystifying Deuteronomy

Engagement in ancient Israel was more like marriage than engagements in Western cultures today. The engaged woman described in Deuteronomy 21:23–27 is also referred to as her fiancé's wife (21:24). Unfaithfulness to her betrothed received the same penalty as adultery—death. Likewise, a man who had intercourse with a woman engaged to another man—whether consensually or by rape—was also accounted an adulterer.

A man who raped a woman who was not engaged (21:28) did not receive the death penalty, but he was responsible both to marry the woman and to pay a bride-price to her father (Exodus 22:16–17; Deuteronomy 21:29).

Although in some cases a man's father's wife might not have been the man's mother (if his father had been widowed and remarried, for instance, or in the case of polygamy), marrying her was forbidden; it would dishonor the father (Deuteronomy 21:39).

DEUTERONOMY 23:1–25

VARIOUS LAWS

Setting Up the Section

Chapter 23 continues the laying out of laws relating to a variety of situations.

📖 23:1–8

EXCLUSION FROM THE ASSEMBLY OF THE LORD

These laws were established for those who were being excluded from the corporate worship services of God. The assembly of the Lord (23:1–3) refers to the gathering of the people for corporate worship.

First, no castrated man is allowed (23:1).

Verse 2 can be translated to exclude either those born of a forbidden marriage or those of illegitimate birth. In either case, it refers to a child of an incestuous relationship, a child born out of pagan worship, or a child born outside of marriage. Such a child comes from that which is an affront to God's laws and is thus not allowed at the ceremonies.

The Ammonites and Moabites (23:3) are not allowed to join the worship of Israel because they refused to provide a break and water to the Israelites as they were moving toward the promised land (23:4). In addition, Balak the Moabite king hired Balaam to curse Israel (Numbers 22:2–6; Deuteronomy 23:4–5). Because of their rejection of the children of God, the Israelites are not to seek any reconciliation with these people (23:6). The Moabites and the Ammonites descended from the incestuous relationship between Lot and his daughters (Genesis 19:29–38) and so would have been excluded as those of illegitimate birth as well.

Critical Observation

A later exception to this prohibition against relationships with Moabites is the case of Ruth, a Moabite woman who married into an Israelite family. After being widowed, she returned to the land of Israel with her also widowed mother-in-law, Naomi. Ruth embraced Naomi's people and Naomi's God. Her story can be read in the Old Testament book of Ruth (Ruth 1).

Edomites, however, are considered the Israelites' brothers (Deuteronomy 23:7–8) because they descended from Esau, the brother of Israel's patriarch, Jacob.

Critical Observation

The key to understanding the laws about exclusion from the assembly is that they dealt with the ceremonial aspects of worship. These were not laws excluding people from believing in God, loving God, or having eternal life. These laws were in place to govern the ceremonial worship for the nation of Israel. Since that worship dealt with Israel's sin and redemption, it had to be done in a way that was according to the holiness of God.

📖 23:9–14

UNCLEANNESS IN THE MILITARY CAMP

God wants the army to remember that He is the One who fought for them, and He is in their presence (23:14). With this in mind, they must not be trite about the way they handle their human waste (24:12–13). If a man has nocturnal emissions, out of respect for God, he is required to stay outside the camp until he has bathed himself (23:10–11). This way the camp of the Lord remains clean—for both health reasons and also so that the people will remember that God must always be treated with respect and dignity (23:14).

SLAVERY

The slaves referred to in verse 15 are not Israelites. In most Middle Eastern treaties there is a provision that slaves seeking refuge are to be returned to their owners. But Israel is not to have allegiances to other nations. Slaves from other countries who come to seek sanctuary (refuge) in Israel are to be accepted (23:16). This law no doubt reminds Israel that their treaty is with God, and they do not need any political alliance with another nation.

PROSTITUTION

Another way that Israel is to be different is in the way that they reject the practice of temple prostitution (23:17). This practice was common in the Near East. God rejects this type of religious practice because it degrades sex and it degrades holy worship.

Demystifying Deuteronomy

Unfortunately, Israel failed to observe the command against temple prostitution (1 Kings 14:24; 15:12; 22:46; 2 Kings 23:7; Hosea 4:14). This unfaithfulness was one of the reasons that God later let Israel be conquered and taken into exile.

In addition to temple prostitution, the nation is not to practice prostitution at all. The money that is gained from this is degraded money, and therefore a vow is not to be paid with money obtained in this manner (23:18).

LOANS AND INTEREST

The context of this law is of a brother who has become poor or is in severe need (see Exodus 22:25; Leviticus 25:35–37); he is not borrowing money to engage in a capitalistic endeavor. The point is that to charge a poor brother interest will only worsen his condition. Mercy, kindness, and grace are all virtues that must mark this nation (Deuteronomy 23:19).

An Israelite is permitted to charge a foreigner interest (23:20). This is because he is not a member of the covenant community. Most likely the loan is for business purposes, and it isn't unreasonable to charge interest in this case.

VOWS

In this law (23:21), God wants the Israelites to make sure that when they speak, they speak with honesty and integrity. The vow is a commitment that is not forced upon anyone—it is made out of the volition of the person (23:22–23). Yet, once it is made, it is to be kept without question.

23:24–25

EATING IN A NEIGHBOR'S FIELDS

A traveler is given the right to revive himself from a vineyard or grain field but is not given the right to take grapes with him or to harvest in the field (23:24–25). Since the Lord has been gracious in providing for the farmer, the farmer in turn should be gracious to a stranger traveling through his land. Yet the person in need must not take advantage of the one giving; he must show proper respect for the one from whom he is taking food.

DEUTERONOMY 24:1–22

VARIOUS LAWS CONTINUED

Laws about Marriage	24:1–5
Laws Mostly about the Needy	24:6–22

Setting Up the Section

Deuteronomy 24 continues the rather lengthy section devoted to various laws touching many different aspects of life. There is no clearly discernible principle of organization in these chapters. The laws are not even grouped together according to theme, as is clear from the English versions that use paragraph titles such as "Various Laws" and "Miscellaneous Laws."

24:1–5

LAWS ABOUT MARRIAGE

The Old Testament always regards divorce as a tragedy (see Malachi 2:16). The commands in Deuteronomy 24:1–4, then, are given to regulate an already existing practice rather than introducing a new idea. The idea of indecency (24:1) cannot refer to adultery, for which the penalty is death (22:22). It cannot refer to the wife's premarital intercourse with another man, for which the penalty is also death (22:20–21). The precise meaning of the phrase is unknown. If a man finds something indecent, the certificate of divorce he writes is apparently given to the woman for her protection under the law. This certificate keeps her from being completely rejected by society. She is allowed to be free and cared for by another man or her father (24:2).

If after being divorced, a woman remarries and her second husband divorces her or dies, her first husband is not permitted to remarry her since she has been defiled. The word translated *defiled* is often used to describe a man who has committed adultery (Leviticus 18:20). So the use of this word to describe a woman who has been divorced and remarried to the same man suggests that divorce is viewed in a negative light, even though Moses permits it. A remarriage to her former husband is equal to adultery and, therefore, detestable to the Lord (Deuteronomy 24:3–4). The purpose of this law seems to be to prevent trivial divorce and to present divorce in its proper light.

Critical Observation

Jesus' interpretation of Deuteronomy 24:1–4 indicates that divorce (like polygamy) goes against the divine ideal for marriage (see Matthew 19:3–9).

Marriage is held in high honor. Thus the nation is to allow a man to get settled into his new relationship after marriage. It is considered cruel to send a recently married man to war (20:7; 24:5). If he is killed in combat, he will probably have no children to preserve his name in Israel. A newly married man is also to be free of other responsibilities in order to have time to adjust and bring happiness to his wife.

Demystifying Deuteronomy

Deuteronomy 25:5–10 shows how important it was for a man to leave a child to preserve his name.

📖 24:6–22

LAWS MOSTLY ABOUT THE NEEDY

Millstones (24:6) were used daily in homes to grind grain in preparing meals. To take both or one of these as collateral for a debt would deprive a man of his daily bread and therefore contradict the spirit of generosity. Thus, when a loan is made, collateral should never be something that will hurt someone.

The crime of kidnapping (24:7) was common in the ancient Middle East. The law codes of Mesopotamia and the Hittite Empire both mention this issue. In fact, it is still an issue today in this area. Since the kidnapper is depriving his victim of his freedom, the kidnapper is to be punished by death—as though he has taken the victim's life.

Leprous diseases (24:8) refer to a broad range of skin diseases, not exclusively leprosy. Instead of repeating the legislation concerning these diseases, Moses refers the people to his original instruction in Leviticus 13–14. Motivation to obey this ceremonial legislation is furnished by Miriam (24:9), who opposed Moses and is struck with leprosy (see Numbers 12).

A borrower typically gives something to the lender as collateral (Deuteronomy 24:6, 10). For a lender to go inside the borrower's house suggests that the borrower is not trustworthy—as if the lender needs to keep an eye on him to ensure that he will hand over the collateral. By keeping the lender outside the house (24:11), both the borrower's dignity and his possessions are safeguarded—the lender does not have the option to take anything he might want as a pledge.

If the borrower is so poor that all he can offer as a pledge is his cloak (which serves as a blanket at night), then the lender is to return it before nightfall (24:12–13). By acting in this manner, the lender shows love, kindness, and mercy, which must govern all civil relationships in Israel.

This kindness is to be extended to resident aliens as well as to fellow Israelites (24:14). If a man is so poor that he is making ends meet day-to-day, he has the right to receive his wages every day (24:15). This is not merely a suggestion about how an employer should act; it is a requirement. Not to do so is a sin.

The edict that fathers should not be executed for their children's crimes (24:16) must be held in tension with other teaching and laws. This refers primarily to legal responsibility, but even then, there are exceptions (such as Achan's family in Joshua 7).

Verse 17 instructs God's people to pay special attention to protecting the powerless in society: foreigners without a say in the governance in the community, those without fathers to speak and act on their behalf, and widows, who have no voice in society. Lest they forget, Moses reminds the people that they were all once powerless slaves in Egypt (24:18). Just as the Lord looked out for them, they are to look out for others.

Another way of looking out for the needy is by making it possible for them to provide for themselves honestly. Women, in particular, have few vocational options other than prostitution. The practice of leaving part of every harvest—whether it be in the field (24:19), the orchard (24:20), or the vineyard (24:21)—allows those who do not own land to work honestly for their food.

Demystifying Deuteronomy

The practice of leaving part of the harvest for the needy is key to the story of Ruth. God rewarded Boaz, who was so generous that he left extra sheaves, by putting him in the family line of both King David and Jesus Christ.

As in verse 18, Moses again reminds the people that they are not so different from those who are in need of their help (24:22).

Take It Home

The deliverance from Egypt, mentioned in verses 18 and 22, is the great Old Testament picture of our redemption in Jesus Christ. As the Israelites were to respond to God's mercy to them by being merciful to others, so we are to be merciful, kind, and generous to others, because Christ is immeasurably kind and merciful and generous to us. Because He became poor for us, then impoverishing ourselves for others not only makes eminent sense, but it is what we most desperately want to do.

These laws, then, dig down into our motives and absolutely require us genuinely to love others and to love mercy. Without God's grace and mercy animating our hearts, these laws will never be kept. On the other hand, as the Bible says, if God's grace is alive in our hearts, if we love Christ because He first loved us, it is inevitable that the love of others will follow in turn.

DEUTERONOMY 25:1–19

LIVING BEFORE THE HOLY GOD

Setting Up the Section

All of the details of the laws in Deuteronomy 25 point to two important things: God is holy and He is everywhere. Thus these laws highlight the incredible detail with which God's holiness should be taken and how much every person should recognize God's presence every day and everywhere.

📄 **25:1–3**

DISPUTES

Vigilante justice has no place in Israel. They are to allow a judge to handle disputes (25:1) and determine the appropriate punishment (25:2). The guilty party is not to be flogged more than forty times, so as to provide a consequence without permanently hurting the person (25:3).

📄 **25:4**

WORKING OXEN

The command not to muzzle an ox while it is treading grain (25:4) stresses kindness and fairness to the animals that help the people survive. Mercy and kindness should extend to animals.

Critical Observation

Deuteronomy 25:4 is quoted in two New Testament books: 1 Corinthians 9:9 and 1 Timothy 5:18, where the use of the passage makes the point that if God cares about a working ox, how much more must He care about human laborers, especially those laboring for His kingdom.

📄 **25:5–10**

LEVIRATE MARRIAGE

The marriage described in Deuteronomy 25:5–10 is also called *levirate*, from the Latin word that means "brother-in-law." This marriage happens when the deceased relative has died without a male heir. The point of the levirate marriage is to provide a male heir who, in turn, can care for the parents in their old age and keep the property in the family.

God is so concerned about people not losing their family line that the first son born from the levirate marriage is given the deceased brother's name (25:6). This shows that God cares about family legacy.

Take It Home

For God's New Testament people, biological bloodlines are no longer what determine family; the true Israelites, or children of Abraham, are those who believe in Jesus Christ (Galatians 3:7). In what ways do God's people today demonstrate the value of adding new believers to the family of God? What will be your personal legacy?

If a widow's brother-in-law refuses to fulfill his duty, she is to tell the elders of his town about it (25:7). She could then remove one of his sandals and spit in his face (25:9). This would mark him, for the entire town to see, as a man who does not care for others (25:10).

Demystifying Deuteronomy

The levirate law and a variation of the ritual with the sandal are played out in the life story of Ruth (Ruth 4:1–8).

📄 **25:11–12**

HOW NOT TO STOP A FIGHT

This law is the only time when physical mutilation serves as punishment (25:11–12). This command intends to protect both womanly modesty and the capacity of a man to produce heirs. This also shows God's seriousness in regard to the next generation, which is probably why this law follows the one on levirate marriages.

📄 **25:13–16**

HONEST BUSINESS DEALINGS

Israel is to be content with what God has provided for them. For this reason, they are to be totally honest in their business dealings (25:13–14). This form of business dealing is a way of proclaiming one's faith in the Lord's ability to support him and give him long life (25:15–16).

THE DESTRUCTION OF THE AMALEKITES

The Israelites are to wipe out the Amalekites when they enter the land. The reason is clear: Since the Amalekites have shown no mercy to Israel (25:17–18), they are to receive none. Israel is to blot out the memory of Amalek from under heaven (25:19).

Demystifying Deuteronomy

The Amalekites were a nomadic desert tribe ranging from Sinai northward to upper Arabia. Their genealogy is traced to Amalek, son of Eliphaz, and grandson of Esau (Genesis 36:12). God wanted the Israelites to punish these people for what they had done in showing no mercy to the Israelites (Exodus 17:8–16; Numbers 14:39–45).

DEUTERONOMY 26:1–19

PRESENTATIONS

Firstfruits	26:1–11
The Presentation of the Tithe	26:12–15
The Declaration of Intent	26:16–19

Setting Up the Section

The book of Deuteronomy is a reiteration of the law for the children of those who were brought out of Egypt and allowed to enter into the promised land. Since all that is said here is a reiteration of the law for those entering the land, it is stated in its simplest form. Chapter 26 describes some of the rituals that are to be followed as soon as they enter the land.

FIRSTFRUITS

When Israel takes possession of the promised land, they are to celebrate the first ritual of taking the firstfruits (the initial produce of the harvest; see Leviticus 23:9–14) to the priest at the central sanctuary (26:1–2). The declaration "I have entered the land" (26:3 NASB) is a testimony to the Lord's faithfulness in bringing the nation into the land He had promised. In this way, at the very beginning of their new life, each one has the opportunity to come before God and acknowledge His great deliverance while presenting the basket of firstfruits (26:4).

The second part of the ritual is declaration of the Lord's faithfulness. This confession highlights both God's faithfulness and the miraculous nature with which Israel received the promised land. This confession is quite a confession. It includes Israel's heritage—her father Jacob, a wandering Aramean (26:5); Israel's growth (26:5); Israel's bondage in Egypt (26:6–7); deliverance from Egypt (26:8); and God's provision in the promised land (26:9). At this point the basket is again presented (26:10) and celebration ensues (26:11).

Critical Observation

Tithing and giving firstfruits were not unfamiliar requirements for the Israelites. Legislation regarding firstfruits and the tithe had already been given in Deuteronomy (14:28–29; 18:3–5). What is unique in this passage, however, is the declaration ritual for each offering (26:3, 5, 13). It seems that these declarations were meant to be practiced only once: for the firstfruits after Israel's first harvest and for the tithe after being in the land three years. They were given in order to celebrate Israel's transition from a nomadic existence to a settled community through the power of the Lord.

📖 **26:12–15**

THE PRESENTATION OF THE TITHE

After the third year in the land, the people are to pay a tithe to the Lord. This tithe is to be given to those in need (Levite, strangers, orphans, widows) so that there will be food for them to eat in their towns (26:12). It is a sacred offering, intended to show the same mercy and kindness that they themselves had received (26:13). Because of its sacredness, the offering could be given only by someone who is ritually clean, as described in the declaration accompanying this offering (26:14).

The prayer for blessing in verse 15 emphasizes Israel's dependence on the Lord and on His grace. He is so transcendent that He dwells in heaven, but at the same time He is so near to His people that He hears their prayers on earth. God is good and provides for His people.

Take It Home

The provision of the Lord is the subject of celebration in the ceremonies associated with both firstfruits and tithes. Since God provided for His people, they should in turn provide for others. The same is true for God's people today. All that God does for us is intended to shape our ethics. In this way, we will reflect the image of God that we were created to bear (Genesis 1:26).

THE DECLARATION OF INTENT

This section is very important because it ends with a call for commitment. Everything that will happen in Israel depends upon adherence to the law of God. This nation is to be different. Their ethics, morality, practices, business, and their entire infrastructure are to derive their ethical moorings from God. As a result, the nation must be committed to God.

Demystifying Deuteronomy

Deuteronomy 26:16–19 is the conclusion to the entire section that began in chapter 5:1, where Moses begins to reiterate the law (see the "Critical Observation" at Deuteronomy 1:1–5).

Two things are mentioned here: the responsibility of Israel and the responsibility of God.

Israel is to devote herself to obey carefully and unreservedly the Lord's decrees and laws (26:16). Israel is formally accepting the terms laid out in the law of God that have just been restated for her (26:17). In other words, the people are saying that they want to be bound by this structure and framework. By this, they are accepting the responsibility to love and serve God by obeying all of His statutes.

With the same type of terminology, the Lord formally acknowledges His obligation to Israel: to be her God and to make her His most valued nation on earth (26:18). God is committed to this nation, and He will provide all that they need to grow and prosper. The reiteration of Israel's responsibility (26:18) reminds Israel that her special status of honor depends on her obedience to Him. To be the Lord's treasured possession means that He will exalt Israel high above all the nations (26:19).

DEUTERONOMY 27:1-26

BLESSINGS AND CURSES, PART 1

Setting Up the Section

Deuteronomy 27 begins a new section in the ancient Near Eastern treaty form that structures the book (see the "Critical Observation" note at 1:1–5). Following the opening preamble (1:1–5), historical introduction (1:6–4:49), and the particular stipulations of the treaty (chapters 5–26), chapter 27 opens the section of blessings and curses that will result from keeping or breaking the treaty.

📖 27:1-10

THE LAW DISPLAYED AND AN ALTAR BUILT

Moses and all the leaders of Israel command the people again to obey all the commands of God (27:1). They must remember that the entire key to their success depends upon their obedience to God.

They are to write all the words of the law on large stone tablets coated with plaster.

The meaning of the phrase "all the words of this law" (27:3, 8) probably refers to the entire book of Deuteronomy rather than just parts of it.

Demystifying Deuteronomy

The writing of laws on large stones coated with plaster was a common practice in Egypt. It was a way of preserving the words of important documents for generations.

The stones are to be set up on Mount Ebal (27:4–6), at the base of which lies the city of Shechem. The altar will commemorate God's faithfulness in giving them the land. There are two possible reasons for not using any iron tools (27:5). Because the nation probably did not have any access to iron, they had to get it from the surrounding nations. This would put them into contact with the nations and might cause them to stumble. A second reason could be that the altar should not have any human additions that would cause humans to get the glory.

Critical Observation

Shechem was the place that the Lord first appeared to Abraham. It was also the place where Abraham built his first altar to the Lord (Genesis 12:6–7). The choice of this location emphasizes God's faithfulness to the original promises to Abraham and highlights that the time for God to make good on this promise is near.

The covenant is to be renewed not only by writing the law but also with sacrificial offerings (27:7). The burnt offerings express the people's total dependence on the Lord. The fellowship offerings express their thankfulness to Him and their joy in His provision.

The final reminder to write the law very clearly (27:8) emphasizes the supreme importance of the role of God's law in the promised land. It is important that God's law be central to all that happens. This section, then, ends with a second call to obey God (27:9–10).

27:11–26

THE ANNOUNCEMENT OF THE CURSES

After the altar is set up on Mount Ebal, six tribes are to assemble on Mount Gerizim to bless the people (27:12), and six are to assemble on Mount Ebal to pronounce curses (27:13). The six tribes on Mount Gerizim are from Jacob's wives, Rachel and Leah. Four of the six tribes on Mount Ebal are descended from Jacob's concubines, Bilhah and Zilpah. The other two are Reuben, Jacob's firstborn who forfeited his birthright through incest (Genesis 35:22; 49:3–4), and Zebulun, Leah's youngest son.

A curse is a condemnation by God. In other words, it is a divinely made consequence in which a person who has violated the law of God must face the discipline that God ordains for the violation of that law. Deuteronomy 27:15–26 records twelve curses. Many of them pertain to actions done by individuals in secret. Eight of the twelve are violations of the Ten Commandments.

Deuteronomy 27:15 addresses idolatry. God hates idolatry, both public and private. If a person tries to keep his or her idolatry secret, the Lord will see it and the idolater will be cursed.

Critical Observation

All the people, by responding with *Amen* to each curse, are acknowledging that they understand and agree to the proclamation.

Verse 16 has to do with parents. Anyone showing dishonor to parents is cursed. This again shows that God is a God who believes that authority should be respected. God takes the family lineage seriously.

Verse 17 deals with honesty. Anyone who steals from his or her neighbor by moving the landmark is cursed. Some might try this by moving the boundary markers in the middle of the night.

Verse 18 concerns abuse. A blind man cannot care for himself. If someone comes along pretending to care for a blind man but really seeks to take advantage of him, this person is cursed. This curse probably applies to all who mistreat the weak and oppressed members of the community (Leviticus 19:14).

Verse 19 declares a curse for oppression. It would also have been easy for an Israelite to take advantage of these generally poor classes of people. But God will defend them. Strength and power are to help, not hurt, the weak.

Verses 20–23 have to do with immorality. These four curses are directed to one who engages in one of four forbidden sexual relationships. The marriage bed is to be held in high honor, and sexual relations are not to be perverted by taking them out of a proper marriage context. Some of these perversions show that when sexual relations are taken outside of God's context, they turn into horrible and degrading practices.

The tenth and eleventh curses deal with an attempt to violate the sixth commandment, which prohibits murder (27:24–25). Human life is to be preserved. Taking someone's life is an action that is cursed by God.

Verse 26 spells out a final curse against disobedience to any of God's laws. God desires a wholehearted obedience to the law in every area of life. God wants the people to understand that all disobedience to His law will be punished.

Take It Home

There are Christians, alas, who come to think of the Christian life as some heavy task that must be done in order not to get hammered with some heaven-sent punishment. What a weary way to live! But that entirely misses the point. To think this way is to behave as children who pout and sulk because their parents refuse to let them grab the pan on the stove while the soup is boiling in it. They cannot see the love in the warning!

God's punishment for disobedience reveals His love, care, and interest in our welfare.

DEUTERONOMY 28:1–68

BLESSINGS AND CURSES, PART 2

The Blessings   28:1–14

The Curses   28:15–68

Setting Up the Section

In this chapter, Moses sets before Israel the blessings and curses of the covenant they are renewing. The curses section (28:15–68) is about four times longer than the blessings section (28:1–14). This underscores the importance of obedience. God is making the point that if you fail to obey, there is no such thing as success; every area of life will be impacted in a great way. This commitment is intended to make a strong point—they should obey God.

📄 28:1–14

THE BLESSINGS

God's gift of the promised land is an act of grace and mercy. But Israel's continued success in the land is conditioned on the people's obedience. This covenant was made with a people who had already been redeemed by God's gracious deliverance from Egypt (as will be spelled out again in 29:1–8). Their deliverance was not conditioned by their obedience; only their blessing in the land was conditioned in this way (28:1–2). This covenant enables Israel to enjoy unhindered fellowship with God in the fullness of His blessing. One of those blessings is the exalting of Israel above all other nations (28:1). God will make this nation great. God outlines some very specific blessings for their obedience.

If Israel obeys the Lord, then every aspect of life will be blessed greatly by God. Both the merchant and the farmer will be blessed (28:3). Israel can expect fertility in both humanity and animals (28:4). There will always be food in her homes for daily meals (28:5), the land will never experience a famine, and in all their daily work, Israelites will enjoy God's blessings (28:6). In their obedience they will find happiness and fulfillment.

Critical Observation

Verses 3–6 were probably read aloud in covenant-renewal ceremonies in order to state the blessings of covenant obedience. What follows in verses 7–14 is probably Moses' elaboration of those blessings.

Three areas of blessing are singled out.

The first one deals with Israel's relationship to the nations around them. Israel will have supernatural military success and financial prosperity that will cause them to be above other nations (28:7). The fruit of this is that they will never borrow from other nations, and they will always lead and never follow (28:12–13).

The second deals with agricultural endeavors. Israel will experience abundant prosperity in her farming and family life (28:8, 11).

Take It Home

It can sometimes trouble believers that God promises such earthly blessings to those who prove faithful to His covenant. Large families, large harvests, good health, political and military security, and the like, are the blessings promised here. Should He not instead have promised such things as peace and purity of heart, the nearness of God, and eternal joy in the world to come?

Of course, those things are promised to those who trust and obey the Lord; and in the context of the Bible, we ought to take these promises of earthly prosperity as containing in themselves and pointing to the more spiritual blessings which God pours out on those who love Him. God does, of course, reward His faithful children with many earthly benefits. But the Bible also teaches clearly enough that a faithful Christian can suffer ill-health or financial reverses that are in no way the curse or punishment of God.

All through the Bible, the physical and the earthly is taken to stand for the spiritual and the heavenly—in large part because we respond better to what we can see, touch, and taste. The faithful in Old Testament days understood well enough that the promised land, Canaan, stood for the blessings of eternal life and the heavenly country. When God spoke to His people of their earthly life in the promised land, He was saying much more to them about spiritual good and heaven.

The Lord Jesus spoke the same way. He promised that those who sacrifice houses and fields for His sake would receive in this life one hundred times as many houses and fields. But He was not speaking literally of houses and fields. The apostles, for example, who had made such sacrifices of property and earthly possessions, did not finish their lives as wealthy landowners. The outward blessing—which God does give as a general rule—is still more important as a sign of the unseen and everlasting blessings God gives to those He loves.

The third deals with Israel's reputation. By being God's obedient and holy people, the Israelites will enjoy such a close relationship with God that they will be a testimony to all the peoples on earth who witness it (28:9–10).

All three of these blessings will come to Israel if they obey God (28:14). What if they do not obey God?

THE CURSES

Just as obedience will bring blessings, so disobedience will bring curses. No middle ground exists (28:15).

The four curses in verses 16–19 are the exact opposite of the four blessings cited in verses 3–6. The point here is that all the great blessings will be undone with disobedience to God. Disobedience is ultimately rejection of God and His ways. If you reject God, there are grave consequences.

In addition to reversing the blessings mentioned above, there will also be eleven more major judgments that will come upon Israel for disobeying: destruction (28:20), disease (28:21–22), drought (28:23–24), defeat in battle (28:25–26), diseases of Egypt (28:27–29), oppression and robbery (28:30–35), exile (28:36–37), crop failure and economic destruction (28:38–48), siege by the enemy (28:49–57), and disease that brings death and exile (28:58–68).

Demystifying Deuteronomy

Keep in mind that these curses were written specifically to Israel in Canaan. We cannot expect these literal curses to come our way if we disobey. Nevertheless, we must take obedience to God seriously. We must know that blessings do follow obedience, and consequences follow disobedience.

Each of these judgments essentially has one goal: to turn Israel from disobedience. God's heart is to turn the nation back to Him through these punishments. The point here is that the process that leads to this level of pain and destruction is disobedience. Israel must know that she has to obey God. If they fail in this area, then all the blessings will be taken away, and pain and destruction will follow. They should take this seriously.

DEUTERONOMY 29:1–29

AN APPEAL TO OBEY

Setting Up the Section

Chapter 29 opens with the conclusion of the reiteration of the covenant. At this point, Moses begins to unfold a summary of the covenant to highlight what the Israelites should keep foremost in their minds.

📖 29:1–8

REVIEW OF THE LORD'S FAITHFULNESS AND ISRAEL'S DISOBEDIENCE

This review (29:2–8) is unique for one reason—it makes the point that Israel has not really understood the significance of what God has done for them. They do not understand the real significance of the deliverance from Egypt or the hand of God in their life. Because their minds do not fully grasp what God is ultimately doing, it is easy for them to rebel against God (29:4). To miss the heart of God is to miss the motivation to obey.

Critical Observation

The two places mentioned in verse 1 are significant. Horeb is the same location as Mount Sinai, where God gave the Ten Commandments at the beginning of the Israelite journey. Here, in Moab, the people are at the end of the journey, almost to their destination.

📖 29:9–15

THE COVENANT

In verse 9, Moses brings the nation back to the most fundamental of all issues, one that is a running theme in Deuteronomy—obedience. The people must obey God in order to prosper. The word *today* occurs several times (29:10, 15), as well as *this day* (29:12–13 NIV). Moses is focusing on the present. He wants the people at that moment in time to realize they need to commit themselves to God, and God is going to commit Himself to them. This moment is all a part of God's plan to make good on His promise to Abraham.

Yet, there is more than just the moment focused on in this text. The scope of this covenant renewal also includes future generations ("those who are not here today"; 29:15 NIV). Therefore, the obedience of that present generation has a great effect on those not yet born. They are to pass on to the next generation the importance of obedience to God. With this great call to multigenerational obedience, Moses will again focus on the curses that befall disobedience.

Take It Home

This multigenerational principle is true for us today. We, too, must make sure that we pass on to the next generation their role and focus on obedience to God.

📄 **29:16–29**

THE CURSES FOR DISOBEDIENCE

Moses reminds the Israelites that they are not naive concerning idolatry. They witnessed it in Egypt and had fallen into idolatry on the way to Canaan (Exodus 32; Numbers 25). These people understood how one act of idolatry was a bitter poison. For this reason, they are told to be diligent against this sin when they enter the land of Canaan. Once they enter this land, they will face new temptations to idolatry over and over again.

Demystifying Deuteronomy

The word *poison* in verse 18 refers to wormwood, a plant known for its bitter pulp. Wormwood is often associated with poison in scripture (Jeremiah 9:15; 23:15; Amos 5:7; 6:12).

These words are reminders that if the people are not vigilant, then an idolatrous foothold can take place through a single person who might think he or she is safe from judgment because the Lord has said Israel is His people. In other words, a deceiver might come in and think that Israel is off limits from the judgment of God. If they allow this person to come in, this foothold could flower into a downfall of faith that will certainly bring God's judgment. If this happens, everyone in Israel will suffer in the judgment that God will bring to the nation, and anyone who brings such sin into Israel can never escape the consequences of that sin (29:19–21).

Not only will judgment fall on the one who introduced idolatry, but also on the whole nation, because they let themselves be swept away by the false worship. The judgments will be so severe that it is compared to the judgment that fell on Sodom and Gomorrah, and Admah and Zeboiim (Genesis 14:2). The land will be covered with salt and sulfur and thus destroyed and unable to support life.

The devastation will be so intense that the nations will ask why Israel's God allowed it to happen. The judgment will be so severe that it will seem almost unlikely that God would bring such a harsh punishment upon His own people. The point is that God hates all rebellion, no matter who does it. Therefore, God will make good on His word—if the people use the land for idolatry, then the people will be taken from the land (Deuteronomy 29:22–28).

In verse 29, the secrets probably refer to future details that God has not revealed to the nation. There are many things that God has not yet revealed to Israel—things according to His will that no one knows. God is bigger and working with a view of history that no one can see or understand. Yet what He has revealed (future judgment for disobedience, future blessing for obedience, His requirements for holiness, etc.) is enough to encourage the Israelites to follow all the words of the law. Even though they do not know it all—they know enough to obey.

Take It Home

As with the Israelites, people today also want to know more than God reveals, and because they do not have exhaustive knowledge, they fight God. Yet, what God has revealed is enough to be accountable for. This is what Israel needed to remember and what the modern church should never forget.

DEUTERONOMY 30:1–20

BLESSINGS FOR OBEDIENCE

Setting Up the Section

In chapter 29, the language seems to assume the reality that the people of Israel will fall into exile because of their tendency toward idolatry. Chapter 30, then, is the good news—they will eventually be brought out of exile. God will not abandon His people, even in the midst of the worst punishment—that of losing the land they believe God had promised them.

📖 30:1–10

RESTORATION

While chapter 30 sheds some light on the end of the journey the Israelites have set out upon, their repentance from idolatry will be insufficient to reverse all the effects. For this reason, God Himself will intervene and with tender compassion gather the nation and bring her back to her land. This restoration will be a time of spiritual prosperity greater than the nation has ever known. During this time, God will work a miracle that will change the fortunes for people forever (30:1–3, 8–10).

God is going to deal with their hearts—the very source of the problem. God promises to circumcise their hearts (30:6). Circumcision is the requirement God put on Abraham. It was one of the ways the Hebrews were set apart from the nations around them. Here, the idea of circumcision is used as an image of God claiming the people's hearts for Himself, marking them irrevocably. He will give them a new will to obey.

With this new heart they will experience the abundant blessing that comes from obedience. In fact, the ultimate goal of God's covenant with the Israelites is to bring about this new heart. God is at work in the lives of this nation, not just to give them a land, but to give them a heart that will obey Him (30:6; Jeremiah 31:31; Ezekiel 36:24–32).

According to verse 7, when this restoration happens, all the enemies of Israel will receive all the curses mentioned in this book.

📄 30:11–14

CHOOSE LIFE

According to verse 11, God's commands are not beyond the Israelites' ability to understand. Though the law has a heavenly origin, God clearly reveals it to Israel directly. Israel did not need a special interpreter before they could obey the law. For this reason, verse 14 says the word is very near. The people can speak it (it is in their mouth) and they know it (it is in their heart). When God laid out His will and His plan for the nation, He communicated it and recorded it in a manner for all to see, hear, and understand. The problem with their disobedience has nothing to do with the structure, form, communication, and recording of the law—the problem is with their hearts.

Take It Home

Paul quotes this passage in Romans 10:6–8. He makes the point that just as God revealed His law in a very clear way, and it was near them and accessible to them, so, too, Jesus came and fulfilled the law and revealed God's righteousness, and it is near to humanity in the same manner.

Our God is a speaking God who communicates to us rather than forcing us to find Him and force Him to speak. All that He does He puts out there to communicate to us in all clarity.

📄 30:15–20

THE CALL TO OBEY

The point of this passage is not the salvation of the souls of the nation. Instead, it is about the fellowship of these people with God. Genesis 15:6 makes it clear that a person is made righteous by faith. Deuteronomy 30:15–20 explains how a believing people can then have fellowship with God. For the Israelites, their full enjoyment of life depends on their obedience to God's Word. Though no one can be justified by the law, the people can be blessed under the law. The quality of their lives in the land is based on what they do with this law of God (30:15–16).

Critical Observation

Inherent in Deuteronomy 30 is the truth that humans cannot obey God's law without divine intervention, thus reaffirming the reality that without God circumcising the heart of humanity, no one can be right with God.

On the other hand, according to verses 17–18, anyone who disregards the law can easily be drawn back into idolatry (see also 29:18) which would bring catastrophic judgment into that person's life. In this way, the law serves the purpose of keeping the nation (as well as the individuals) in check and providing a barrier to unfettered sin.

So the life of the nation as they lived in the land is to consist of obeying the Lord. This obedience can be passed down from one generation to another. Parents who choose to obey the Lord are also making a significant choice for their children—they will be passing on to the next generation a heart of obedience (30:19).

Since the Lord is the One who gave life to Israel and provided all the blessings that they have and will have in the future, this chapter concludes by again urging the people to love the Lord, to listen to and obey Him, and to cling to Him (30:20). In fact, this is a key theme of the entire book of Deuteronomy.

DEUTERONOMY 31:1–29

TRANSITIONS

Setting Up the Section

Here, at the end of their journey through the wilderness and at the doorstep of the conquest, Moses prepares to step out of the way. He is now going to transfer leadership from himself to Joshua. Moses' priority is ensuring that the next generation places a priority on their relationship with God.

📖 31:1–8

THE TRANSITION FROM MOSES TO JOSHUA

Moses has been forbidden to enter Canaan because of an earlier act of unbelief (Numbers 20:1–13), but God's plan does not depend on any one human leader. Instead, God's plan depends only on God's power to fulfill His own promises to His people. Therefore, in light of God's past faithfulness, Moses charges the nation to be obedient and fearless.

There is nothing that they should be afraid of—God will make good on His promises.

After his strong charge to the people, Moses commissions Joshua with the same charge: Be strong and courageous! God will bring victory to this nation. Joshua is not the one responsible to take the land; he is the one responsible to lead the nation to be faithful to the God who will take the land for them.

📄 31:9–13

THE PUBLIC READING OF THE LAW OF GOD

Moses records God's law and then commissions the priests to ensure that it is read every seven years to the entire nation. The priests are to read the law during the Feast of Tabernacles. Entire families are required to attend this holiday, which means the most people possible will hear the reading. As a nation, they will be reminded of what God requires for them to remain an acceptable nation before Him.

Critical Observation

The reading of the law every seven years was important for two reasons. First, not everyone had a copy of the entire law in their homes. Therefore, it would be a time for the whole nation to hear the entire law read in its context.

Second, the celebration of the Feast of Tabernacles (with its tradition of the Israelites leaving their homes) would remind them of the exodus from Egypt and the forty years of wandering their ancestors experienced. This event is central to the theology of Israel as well as her history. Because of this, the people would hear the law within the context of God's deliverance.

📄 31:14–23

THE COMMISSIONING OF JOSHUA

The commissioning of Joshua begins rather ominously. After Joshua is called to the tent of meeting, God addresses both him and Moses. He tells Moses that the people are going to rebel after they enter the land. Their idolatry will bring on God's judgment (31:14–18).

In hearing God's revelation to Moses, Joshua is prepared for what will come. As a leader he will understand the full spiritual context of what is about to take place.

God commissions Moses to write a song to outline the rebellion of the people. This way, when the people rebel and run from God, the song will serve as a reminder and a point of accountability (31:19–22).

Demystifying Deuteronomy

In this account, God is clearly showing the Israelites their need for Him. Unfortunately, even in the face of this information, the people do not cry out to God for help.

God is making the point here that they need Him in order to set the stage for their eventual repentance. Even after they fall, they can return to God for deliverance.

Moses' song includes both the path of repentance as well as a warning of the judgment to come when the people fall away from their faith (31:19–22). God is fully aware of the tendency of the human heart to stray from Him and the extent to which these people will stray. Yet rather than rejecting the nation outright, He will use them and provide hope that they can have a changed heart (30:6).

In spite of this knowledge that the people will fall, the Lord formally commissions Joshua, giving him a charge to be strong and courageous and assuring him of success—God will be true to His plan.

31:24–29

THE PLACEMENT OF THE LAW AS A WITNESS

The Book of the Law is to be placed beside the ark, rather than inside of it. Only the Ten Commandments are placed inside (Exodus 25:16; 31:18). This placement of the law is a witness that the people are not going to follow this law. Though this is a harsh reality, it is also an expression of God's grace.

Take It Home

God will bring a Savior, One who will deal with the rebellion in the hearts of these people (30:6). Thus, this accountability—the placement of the law—is a beginning of God dealing with the people and their sin. It is only by knowing that they are sinners that they will be able to turn to God for forgiveness and redemption. As faithful as God is in revealing the sin of His people, He is equally as faithful in dealing with sin and overcoming it through Jesus Christ (Colossians 2:13–15).

DEUTERONOMY 31:30–32:52

THE SONG OF MOSES

Setting Up the Section

Deuteronomy 31:19–21 tells us that Moses' song is to be used to remind Israel of God's law within the context of God's deliverance. It will remind the people of their sin and rebellion and of the fact that their hearts are far from God.

📄 **31:30**

MOSES BEGINS

The account of Moses' song actually begins at the end of chapter 31. Based on the information given thus far, Israel's future seems gloomy. Yet, the consequence of the people seeing the seriousness of their spiritual condition is to place them in the right position to be delivered spiritually—deliverance greater than the physical deliverance they had experienced from Egypt.

Critical Observation

A true understanding of Moses' song must come within the context of Deuteronomy 30:6, a verse of hope in the midst of disappointing news. This verse tells that God is going to show the people of Israel their sin so that they can embrace the salvation that the Messiah is going to bring.

📄 **32:1–3**

THE THEMES

There are seven themes in Moses' song. These seven themes take us on a journey from the great goodness of God to the horrible sin of humanity to the grace and kindness of the Lord.

At the opening of the song, we are told that it is for everyone in the entire world to hear and learn from. In other words, these historical events reveal eternal and binding truth for all humanity. These words are to water the earth and give meaning for all creation, for the God of all creation is going to be declared to the entire world.

📄 32:4–9

A FAITHFUL GOD AND A FOOLISH PEOPLE

In verse 4, God is described as a rock and as faithful and just. This description is presented in contrast to humanity in verse 5. The faith of His people had become so skewed that they bore no family resemblance to their Father. Even with the deliverance God has already provided in a variety of ways, the people still rebel, highlighting how extremely foolish and faithless humanity really is.

📄 32:10–14

THE GOODNESS OF GOD

As this nation is growing and developing in some rather difficult circumstances, God is there. The metaphor of the eagle speaks of God's wise and loving parental care. Like an eagle, the Lord remains ready to catch them when necessary.

Demystifying Deuteronomy

In verse 13, the idea of getting honey and oil from the rock suggests that even the most barren places will become fertile. In the goodness of God, the people will be blessed in miraculous ways!

📄 32:15–18

FROM PROSPERITY TO IDOLATRY

Throughout the centuries, many lives have revealed that prosperity is often more dangerous for the faithful than adversity. In adversity, a person calls out to God as a way of life, while in prosperity it is easy to give lip service to faith but not make it a true priority. Israel (in verse 15, ironically referred to as *Jeshurun*, "the upright one") abandoned the Lord, their only hope for salvation, when they became prosperous. The mention of *kicking* builds on the metaphor of an animal kicking at its owner. It suggests the mindless nature and complete foolishness of Israel's rebellion against God.

The downfall of Israel took shape in idol worship. They actually made sacrifices to something that God created rather than to God Himself. Put in its proper perspective, this is demon worship (32:16)—pure evil. In verse 18, Moses compares God to both a father and a mother. Yet, in spite of His provision, the people scorn Him and His great love.

JUDGMENT

Israel's idolatry provokes God to anger, which He expresses in judgment. God's anger is not like the anger of humanity. Human anger is based on selfish emotions. God's anger, in this case, is based on His righteous indignation toward children who are unfaithful and perverse (32:20), who follow worthless idols and scorn the only way of salvation. The rebellion of the nation is such that they are leading countless generations into a path of destruction.

Demystifying Deuteronomy

In His righteous indignation, God withdrew His presence and judged Israel with a foreign nation (32:21). This means that while God may have provided protection to Israel from the attacks of surrounding enemies, because of Israel's lack of faithfulness, God would remove His protection. The consequences, then, would be the defeat of Israel and hopefully the repentance of the nation in light of that defeat.

God's judgment will touch every area of Israel's life. The devastation from the attacks of armies and plagues will be so great that Israel will almost be completely wiped out. Though the nation deserves to be wiped out, the Lord will not allow it. Why? Because her complete destruction will cause her enemies to question His sovereignty and power (32:22–27).

LACK OF DISCERNMENT

Even after all the signs of God's power, displays of God's holiness, and warnings of judgment, Israel continues unaware down her destructive path (32:28–29).

The evidence of God's supernatural judgment through other nations will be clear. Those coming against Israel will have such strength and power that only God could be behind them (32:30–31). This judgment could not be attributed to the gods of Israel's enemies. In fact, according to verses 32–33, the enemies who will execute God's judgment on Israel are as evil as Sodom and Gomorrah. God allows the worst of the worst to come against Israel so that the people can see how far they have fallen.

GOD'S JUSTICE AND MERCY IN JUDGMENT

Though the Lord will use Israel's enemies to execute His judgment, He will still hold those enemies accountable for their wickedness and repay them for their evil. God will use their evil to chastise Israel, but He does not condone that evil.

In bringing judgment on Israel, God will have compassion on them. The statement in verse 36 that God will judge His people is interpreted by some to mean that He will judge *for* them, or vindicate them. Yet, Israel will not experience God's compassion until they abandon all trust in their own efforts and in the false gods to which they have turned. In verses 37–38, Moses calls on Israel to turn for help to the false gods so that they can plainly understand that these gods cannot help them.

God's goal in judging Israel is not to extinguish the nation. Instead, it is to bring her to understand that there is no god besides the Lord. He wants Israel to understand that God alone has power over death and life (32:39). He is the only hope for humanity, the only power for salvation, and the only God to trust in for help and deliverance. When Israel comes to this realization, then God will take vengeance on her adversaries (32:41, 43). The turning point will be the nation's true repentance.

📄 **32:44–52**

MOSES' FINAL CHARGE

After reciting all the words of the song, Moses tells the people to consider them seriously. If the people will meditate on the certainty and severity of the judgment that the Lord will bring, this song could serve as a powerful deterrent for their rebellion. If they will repent of the sin that is in their hearts right then, God will forgive them. The threat of the Lord's discipline is a warning for them to turn from their wicked ways. This fear of the judgment set forth in the song would also enable them to teach their children the need to obey the words of this law (32:46).

At the close of chapter 32, Moses goes up to view the land that he had earlier in his life hoped to enter with his people. Because of his break with faith, the view from Mount Nebo is as close as he will get to Canaan.

Demystifying Deuteronomy

The breaking of faith God refers to in verse 51 is a reference to an incident in Meribah, in which Moses was instructed to speak to a rock to miraculously draw water from it. Instead Moses struck the rock and seemed to claim that he and Aaron were responsible for the miraculous water, rather than following God's specific instructions and letting Him get the glory for the incident.

DEUTERONOMY 33:1–29

THE BLESSING OF MOSES ON THE TRIBES

Setting Up the Section

The blessing of Moses given here, just before his death, is very important and common for that day. It was typical for a father to impart a blessing just before his death. Moses, leader of the Exodus and mediator of the covenant, served in a fatherly capacity for the nation. As they were being birthed into a nation, Moses was there to provide the earthly fathering that they needed.

📄 **33:1**

THE MAN OF GOD

In verse 1, Moses is referred to as the "man of God" (NIV). This is a term used throughout the scriptures to denote a man set aside to serve God. After this passage, the phrase is used in the Old Testament to refer to messengers of God (1 Samuel 2:27; 1 Kings 13:1; 2 Kings 4:7). It is also used in the New Testament in the same way (1 Timothy 3:16–17). Moses was not just a leader, but he was a servant of God, a man set apart for the purpose of leading people in the will and Word of the Lord.

📄 **33:2–5**

ALL BLESSING FLOWS FROM PRAISE

Moses begins this blessing with praise for the greatness of God, including a description of the Lord's appearance at Sinai when He gave the Ten Commandments (Exodus 19–20; Deuteronomy 33:1–2). Verse 2 is written in poetic language that describes the light of God shining on Sinai in the south, and then on Seir in the northeast, and then on Paran in the north. The idea is that God's law engulfed the land.

The fact that God came surrounded by angels (33:2) made the giving of the law not just a transaction, but a moment of worship.

Critical Observation

The giving of this law was more than just a moment when the glory of God shined upon the world; it was also a moment of love. This moment served to be the time when God's love came to the earth in the form of the revelation of His will and His heart. Thus, the response of all the followers of God was a response to this love.

The proclamation of the Lord's kingship over *Jeshurun* (a name for Israel; 32:15; 33:26) is a reference back to the nation's deliverance from Egypt and the giving of the law (when the leaders and the tribes assembled to receive God's commands). When God brought the law to the people, they gathered under His rule, and He became their official king. The giving of the law was then the event that ratified His kingship over the nation.

📖 33:6–25

THE BLESSING OF THE TRIBES

Moses pronounces a blessing on each tribe. The names of these tribes represent the son of Jacob from whom the tribe descends:

Reuben (33:6). The prayer for the tribe of Reuben to survive suggests that it will face some unique adversity that might bring a disaster. While this tribe, descendants of the firstborn son of Jacob, would have typically been in a position of honor, this is clearly not the case. Genesis 49:4 and Judges 5:15–16 reveal that the tribe of Reuben is not going to excel. The dishonor found its root in the affair Reuben had with Bilhah, his father's concubine (Genesis 35:22).

Judah (Deuteronomy 33:7). When the order of the tribes was given for the journey to Canaan, the tribe descended from Judah marched first (Numbers 2:9) and therefore was first in battle. Moses' blessing here is a prayer for Judah's military success through the power of God.

Levi (Deuteronomy 33:8–11). The tribe of Levi was set apart to care for the tabernacle and to provide priests to serve there. The Thummim and Urim are used by priests to cast lots, a method of receiving direction from God (some compare their use to throwing dice in order to leave the outcome out of human hands). Thus, the tribe of Levi was entrusted with the great work of mediating between God and humanity. At first, the faithfulness of Levi is praised because they are faithful at Massah, also called Meribah (Exodus 17:1–7). Then the tribe is praised collectively (Deuteronomy 33:9) for their faithfulness to execute God's judgment in the matter of the golden calf (Exodus 32:25–29). Moses' blessing here is a prayer for supernatural ability so that the Levites will use their skills in God's work.

Benjamin (Deuteronomy 33:12). Moses prays that this tribe will have security and peace through being shielded by the Lord. This prayer reflects Benjamin's special status as Jacob's youngest and particularly loved son (Genesis 44:20).

Joseph (Deuteronomy 33:13–17). Moses prays first for Joseph's material prosperity—that the crops will grow as they receive water from above and below. God wants this tribe to experience true earthly blessing.

Moses then prays for the military success of Joseph. This tribe is eventually divided into the two tribes named after Manasseh, Joseph's firstborn, and Ephraim, Joseph's younger son. Though Manasseh was the older son, Jacob gave Ephraim the blessing of the firstborn (Genesis 48:17–20). That is why Moses mentions Ephraim first and credits ten thousands to him, and only thousands to Manasseh (Deuteronomy 33:17).

Zebulun and Issachar (33:18–19). Zebulun and Issachar, mentioned together here, are also mentioned together in Jacob's original blessings over his sons (Genesis 49:13–15), as well as in the Song of Deborah (Judges 5:14–15). The prayer here is that these tribes will receive blessing in their daily lives and especially in their trade upon the sea. Though the

Canaanite territories assigned to these tribes apparently do not touch the Mediterranean Sea, Issachar is near the Sea of Kinnereth (Galilee), and Zebulun is only a few miles from the Mediterranean. What this probably means is that merchants traveled through both tribal territories with products from the sea and the coast, and the tribes benefited from the trade.

Gad (Deuteronomy 33:20–21). Even though this tribe held choice land east of the Jordan, they still fought valiantly in the conquest of Canaan. In this way the tribe of Gad carries out the Lord's will.

Dan (33:22). The image of Dan as a lion's cub implies a potential for great strength. The tribe has the possibility for doing great things. However, though the tribe could be strong, it remained timid, not reaching full potential. The tribe of Dan did not stay in the land allotted to them, but instead established a colony in the north. For this reason some say that Dan not only was timid, but also acted like a snake in taking land that did not belong to him (Genesis 49:17–18).

Naphtali (Deuteronomy 33:23). Naphtali's blessing describes the tribe's assigned land as extending southward to the lake, probably the Sea of Galilee. This was a fertile area. Thus this blessing is similar to Joseph's sons Ephraim, Manasseh (33:16), and Asher (33:24)—the tribe will enjoy material blessings from God.

Asher (33:24–25). The name *Asher* means "blessed, happy." This blessing will be great material prosperity. To bathe one's feet in oil rather than simply to anoint them is something only a person of extreme wealth can do. Thus the tribe of Asher will experience abundant prosperity. The bolts of iron and bronze indicate the tribe's military security will be outstanding.

📖 **33:26–29**

FINAL WORDS OF PRAISE

Jeshurun ("the upright one") is a name for Israel. Verse 26 honors the God of Israel as incomparable in power. He rides on the heavens and the clouds (33:26). Because God is eternal and a refuge for His people, His everlasting arms will protect Israel in times of trouble. God will destroy her enemy (33:27). Having such a wonderful and powerful God, the nation can walk in the full assurance that God will provide for them the promised land. They also can have the confidence that, once in the land, they can live in both safety and prosperity (33:28).

Take It Home

This chapter closes with a strong reminder of God's provision. Moses claims God as the Great Deliverer. With the descriptions given here, we are left with the clear idea that the God of Israel is worthy of our trust.

DEUTERONOMY 34:1–12

THE DEATH OF MOSES

Setting Up the Section

At the close of the book of Deuteronomy, Moses ascends to Mount Nebo as the Lord told him to do. Though Moses is not to lead the people into the land, God allows Moses to see the land.

34:1–4

A GLIMPSE OF THE PROMISED LAND

In verses 1–4, the places Moses sees from the mountain start in the north and follow to the south in a counterclockwise direction. Though one could not normally view the western sea (the Mediterranean) from Mount Nebo, God may have allowed Moses to supernaturally do so in order to see the great promise that was made years before.

God's mention of the oath (34:4) reminds Moses that He will still be faithful to His promise to the great ancestors of the Israelites—Abraham, Isaac, and Jacob (Deuteronomy 1:8; 6:10; 9:5, 27; 29:13; 30:20)—and bring Israel into her new land.

34:5–9

THE DEATH OF MOSES

Though Moses' inability to enter Canaan is a form of discipline for his act of unbelief at Meribah (Numbers 20:1–13), he still dies as a man of faith. This one act of rebellion is not the defining characteristic of his life and ministry.

God bestows an honor on Moses by being the One who buries him. Moses' last moments on earth were evidently spent in fellowship with God. The place of his grave is unknown today. In Jude 9 we learn that there might have been a supernatural struggle over the body of Moses. Moses' death, at the age of 120, was an ending of an era for Israel. It was time for a new beginning.

The typical mourning period for a loved one at this time was seven days (Genesis 50:10). But the Israelites mourn for thirty days after Moses' death.

After Moses' death, Joshua is empowered with the wisdom necessary to take Israel to the next step in experiencing the fulfillment of God's promise. Since this job is truly a spiritual job, Joshua will need the supernatural insight and power to carry out the will of God. According to verse 9, the Israelites accept Joshua's leadership, and in a sense, even this is an honor to Moses' leadership.

34:10–12

THE EPITAPH OF MOSES

Moses is unique among the prophets for his intimacy with the Lord and for his miraculous works. From his early days facing the king of Egypt with the plagues to the miracles of the desert such as speaking water out of a rock, Moses displayed the power of God. This becomes even more significant when you remember that early in Moses' life, when God called him to lead the people, he felt himself the least likely candidate for the job (Exodus 3:11–14; 4:10).

Take It Home

After Moses, the Israelites longed for another leader like him, and God did provide one. Hebrews 3:1–6 tells us that One came who was greater than Moses to bring a covenant even greater than the one given on Sinai. This new covenant would be one in which our hearts are made right with God (30:6)—and that leader is Jesus Christ.

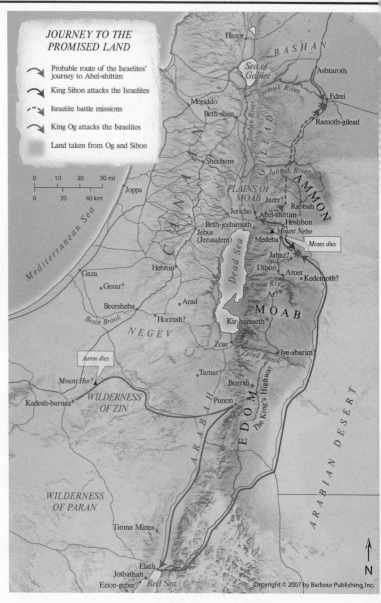

JOURNEY TO THE
PROMISED LAND

Probable route of the Israelites'
journey to Abel-shittim

King Sihon attacks the Israelites

Israelite battle missions

King Og attacks the Israelites

Land taken from Og and Sihon

0   10   20   30 mi
0   20   40 km

Hazor

BASHAN

Sea of
Galilee

Ashtaroth

Yarmuk River

Edrei

Megiddo

Beth-shan

GILEAD

Ramoth-gilead

Jordan River

Shechem

Jabbok River

AMMON

PLAINS OF
MOAB

Jazer?

Rabbah

Joppa

Jericho

Abel-shittim

Heshbon

Beth-jeshimoth

Mount Nebo

Jebus
(Jerusalem)

Medeba

Moses dies

Jahaz?

Dibon

Aroer

Kedemoth?

Mediterranean Sea

Hebron

Dead Sea

Arnon River

Ar?

MOAB

Gaza

Gerar?

Arad

Beersheba

Hormah?

Kir-hareseth

Besor Brook

NEGEV

Zoar

Iye-abarim?

Zered Brook

Aaron dies

Tamar

Bozrah

Mount Hor?

Kadesh-barnea

WILDERNESS
OF ZIN

Punon

ARABAH

EDOM

The King's Highway

ARABIAN DESERT

WILDERNESS
OF PARAN

Timna Mines

Elath

Jotbathah

Ezion-geber?

Red Sea

Copyright © 2007 by Barbour Publishing, Inc.

N

JOSHUA

INTRODUCTION TO JOSHUA

For centuries, the descendants of Abraham had anticipated possessing the land God had promised to the patriarch in the Abrahamic Covenant (Genesis 12:1-3; 15:5-8) and then reiterated to Isaac and Jacob. Joshua is the compelling history of the fulfillment of that promise.

AUTHOR

There is some tradition that claims Joshua as the author of this book. But the author is unknown, as is the date of writing.

PURPOSE

This is an account written to reveal God's faithfulness and how, by faith in God's promises, God's people can overcome and experience His life-changing deliverance.

OCCASION

The book of Joshua describes the conquest and possession of the land of Canaan. This is the land God had promised Israel through Abraham, Isaac, and Jacob. Here God fulfills that promise, though not exhaustively, since there still remains a rest for the people of God. Joshua describes the military triumph of God's people through faith and obedience. However, unlike most military histories, Joshua's focus is on the commander's Commander, the Captain of the Lord's host (5:15). Repeatedly, as Joshua's name illustrates ("Yahweh saves"), the book demonstrates that Israel's victories are due to God's power and intervention.

THEMES

The primary theme of the book of Joshua is God's faithfulness to His promises, that He has done for Israel exactly what He promised (Genesis 15:18; Joshua 1:2-6; 21:43-45). The events recorded in Joshua set forth God's special intervention on behalf of His people against all kinds of tremendous odds. The fulfillment of God's promises, as is evident in the birth of Isaac to Abraham and Sarah (Genesis 17:19-21; 21:1-5) and in possessing the land with its fortified cities, is the work of God, which cannot be accomplished without God's blessing no matter how hard one tries (see Romans 4).

HISTORICAL CONTEXT

Joshua is the history of Israel's conquest of the land of Canaan in fulfillment of God's promises for the people of Israel. In Joshua, the nation of Israel crossed over Jordan and took possession of the land God had promised them. If Moses is the symbol of deliverance, then Joshua is the symbol of victory. Joshua teaches us that faith is the victory that overcomes the world (1 John 5:4).

CONTRIBUTION TO THE BIBLE

God's Word continually shows our need of deliverance that only God can provide. This story reminds us of the absolute necessity of looking to God for salvation. The Israelites were brought into the promised land, which was an image of the eternal inheritance we now claim in the saving work of Jesus Christ. The book of Joshua portrays the rest that comes to the believer who experiences the blessings of salvation through a faith that overcomes the various trials, temptations, and difficulties of life that are faced in our three enemies: the world, the flesh, and the devil. The battle belongs to the Lord.

OUTLINE

THE COMMISSIONING OF JOSHUA

Setting Up the Section

In Joshua, we are introduced to the leadership of Moses' successor. Joshua is first mentioned in Exodus as a military leader fighting the Amalekites (Exodus 17:9–13). The book of Numbers reveals that he served as Moses' aide (Numbers 11:28). What better preparation could there be to lead the Israelites? Israel's preparation for taking control of the promised land proceeds out of God's commission and charge. Here we see God's people behaving well, responding to His revelation according to His will.

📖 **1:1–5**

THE CHARGE FROM GOD

God's powerful words of commission here are a direct result of the fact that His people, lead by Joshua, hear and respond to His charge. Apart from God's Word there is no chance for God's people to experience the blessings of either the old covenant (as seen here in the promised land) or of the new covenant—blessings of a rich life in the kingdom of heaven through Christ. Whenever anyone begins to turn away from God's Word through indifference or apathy, they are turning away from His power into defeat.

The commission of Joshua and the continuation of God's purposes for Israel happen immediately after the death of Moses. In many ways, Moses represented God's law as revealed atop Mount Sinai. The law was a guide, a measure that would be fulfilled by Christ. Thus, the conclusion of God's revelation of His standard (the law) and the death of that standard bearer (Moses) opens the scene for God to introduce the Israelites to a new leader and a new era as He delivers the promised land to their possession.

Demystifying Joshua

Joshua's name means "Yahweh is salvation." As the Hebrew equivalent of the name *Jesus*, Joshua typifies the saving work that would later come for all people through Jesus, whose saving life provides believers with redemption and the power to enter into the possession of our inheritance in Christ.

With the command to cross the Jordan, the Lord is saying, "get out of the desert and move on into Canaan." God's will is never for His children to languish in the wilderness. This command is repeated to the New Testament believer—take up your armor and trust God (Ephesians 6:10–17).

Take It Home

While the Christian life involves obedience to the principles and imperatives of the Word, it is more than just that. It is a faith relationship with God to be lived out in the power of the Spirit and in the light of the Word. The abundant Christian life is God's plan and will for every single one of us; it is only limited by our lack of availability to His constant availability to us. Every believer is blessed with every spiritual blessing and is a priest of God with abundant grace, available for every situation if we simply seek God in faith.

In verse 5, Joshua is given the promise, "no one will be able to stand up against you" (NIV), but this promise is also a warning. While the land is theirs for the taking, it would not be taken without conflict or battle. This is a wake-up call, a reality that must be faced: Life is full of battles and conflicts, even for God's people.

📖 **1:6–18**

THE CALL TO COURAGE

The issue before Joshua and the people is God's call to be strong and courageous. God is calling Joshua to a special yet difficult ministry, one with tremendous challenges and obstacles far beyond his own skill or abilities. In the same way, God has called each of us to ministry in some way—we are all gifted priests of God called to live out the gospel among those around us.

This passage reminds us that moral strength and courage come from faith in the sovereignty and provision of God. Courage is that quality of mind that enables people to encounter danger and difficulty with firmness and resolve in spite of inner fears (1 Corinthians 2:3; 2 Corinthians 7:5). Strength and courage come through recognizing and relating to God's pleasure (His will) and having a sense of God's calling and destiny (Joshua 1:1–2).

Joshua's courage is the direct result of knowing God's will (see Ephesians 5:9–10). Also, Joshua is reminded that he has already been prepared for this as the servant of Moses (Joshua 1:1). Regardless of the obstacles, Joshua is commanded to act on God's will by faith in the Lord's person, promises, and provision. Now Joshua begins to survey the land, size up the enemy, and prepare the people for battle.

In verses 10–15, the keynote is Joshua's immediate and obedient response, regardless of the obstacles that lay before them. There is a note of urgency, certainty, expectancy, and faith in Joshua's commands to the people. As God commanded, the new leader is taking charge and following the Lord's orders with confidence.

Joshua delegates specific tasks promoting the concept of the people of God as a team, which was first given to Moses in Exodus. This principle shows up repeatedly in the kingdom of God: Each person is needed and each person has a crucial role. The people are not only willing to obey, but they are willing to deal with any disobedience in their midst because of the demoralizing effect on others and the dishonor it brings to the Lord.

Take It Home

Israel got into the promised land the same way they got out of Egypt—with God as their deliverer. Likewise, we enter into the abundant life of Christ the same way we were delivered from wrath—by faith in the saving life of Christ. Just as we trusted in Christ and the accomplishments of the cross for redemption, so we must rely on God's salvation as the basis for our security and the foundation of our courage (Romans 6:4–11; Colossians 2:6–3:3).

JOSHUA 2:1–24

FAITHFUL PREPARATIONS

Israel's Spies	2:1–3
The Faith of Rahab	2:4–14
The Scarlet Thread	2:15–24

Setting Up the Section

Joshua and the people are called to accomplishments far beyond their ability. Regardless of these obstacles, Joshua, believing the promises of God, courageously moves ahead preparing to lead the Israelites into the promised land.

📖 2:1–3

ISRAEL'S SPIES

While Joshua has the promise of God's deliverance, he has not been given instruction on just how God plans to defeat the enemies they will face. As a wise military leader, he is simply gathering information concerning the layout of the enemy's defenses, the condition of their morale, and other important factors. Moreover, he is not to presume on the Lord. He is to trust the Lord implicitly; but in that trust, he is also to use the resources God gave him: the training, the men, and the wisdom he had gained.

Critical Observation

Jericho lay just five miles on the other side of the Jordan and was one of the most formidable fortresses in the land. Conquering this city would not only give them a strong foothold into the land, but it would literally split the forces of the Canaanites by hindering their communication and supply lines. This would have a further demoralizing effect on the rest of the inhabitants.

Rahab is mentioned eight times in scripture (Joshua 2:1, 3; 6:17, 23, 25; Matthew 1:5; Hebrews 11:31; James 2:25), and in six of these occurrences, her name is found with a specific descriptive noun—*harlot* or *prostitute*. To remove this stigma, some have argued that she was only an innkeeper. That is unlikely, but there is some evidence that inns in the ancient world doubled as brothels, so both could be true.

Very likely, Rahab's house is the only place where the men can stay with any hope of remaining undetected; plus they will be able to gather information. Rahab's house also offered an easy way of escape since it was located on the city wall (Joshua 2:15). This story illustrates God's amazing grace—how He accepts and forgives us not because of what we are or might be, but because of who He is.

Demystifying Joshua

The king may have assumed that the spies were staying with Rahab, but he would have had reason to expect that she would do her patriotic duty and turn the spies in. The ancient law code of Hammurabi contains a provision for putting prostitutes who harbor felons to death. And yet Rahab had faith in God's ability to deliver her against all odds.

2:4–14

THE FAITH OF RAHAB

Rahab is saved because she believes in the God of Israel (see 6:17; Hebrews 11:31; James 2:25). Hiding the messengers is an outworking of her faith. She has come to believe that the God of Israel is indeed "God of the heavens above and the earth below" (Joshua 2:11 NLT).

Rahab's faith, which gives her strong convictions about God, causes her to act to the point of putting her life on the line. She knew Israel would eventually attack the city and destroy it, and she wanted to be delivered and to be on God's side. She does not know much about Israel's God—His laws of righteousness or the way of salvation—but she knows He is God.

Was Rahab's lying justified? Most commentaries approve of her faith but disapprove of her lie. In essence, they approve of her hiding the spies, but not telling the lies. In 6:17 Joshua explains that Rahab is to be spared because she hid the spies, and she did this as an ally. The question of whether her lie was justified by God because it was a matter of warfare is debated by theologians. Obviously, her faith was recognized as sincere regardless of whether or not her lie was excused by the circumstances.

Rahab is confident in the Lord's power. Somehow she knew what had occurred at the Red Sea and that it was the product of the sovereign power of Israel's God. Rahab is not only concerned about herself but also her family (2:12–13). This attitude of concern demonstrates God's plan for evangelism—sharing the hope we have in the Lord with those closest to us.

The inhabitants of the land are terror stricken. Three times in this chapter, the word *melted* is used to describe the emotional condition of the people (2:9, 11, 24). Mentally and emotionally, they are defeated. God had already given the people of Jericho into their hands. Note the irony: The inhabitants are looking at Israel's God and shaking in their sandals. The Israelites, who have seen the mighty works of God over and over again, are looking at their problems instead of focusing on God and are terrorized into unbelief.

📖 **2:15–24**

THE SCARLET THREAD

Joshua and the men of Israel see the words and actions of Rahab as clear evidence of the sovereign providence and blessing of the Lord. This passage demonstrates God's concern and work to deliver each person who calls on Him (2 Peter 3:9). The story also demonstrates that the only thing that can hinder us in doing the will of God and fulfilling our calling is our own unbelief. Our faith should lead to action and ministry to and for others. Rahab reaches out to both the spies and to her household (John 1:35–51; 4:28–29, 39).

From this passage, we see that God's mercy and grace is powerful enough to overcome even His own wrath. Rahab was an Amorite, and according to the Law of Moses there is to be no pity or covenant with any inhabitants—only judgment (Deuteronomy 7:2). Yet through her genuine faith, Rahab becomes an exception and an archetype of God's purpose to save anyone who comes to God in faith to partake with Israel in the blessings of the kingdom.

Take It Home

The story of Rahab echoes the deliverance we have seen of God's children before. In the days of Noah, there was safety and refuge for those who entered into the door of the ark. In Egypt, there was safety and refuge for those who were gathered behind the doors that were sprinkled with the blood of the Passover lamb. The scarlet thread is a picture of Christ's redemptive work on the cross. For you and me, there is safety and refuge from eternal judgment—only if we enter the right door: Jesus Christ alone (see John 10:9).

JOSHUA 3:1–17

CROSSING THE JORDAN

Setting Up the Section

Life in a fallen world necessitates our need for strength from above, even for God's chosen people. The battle is really the Lord's, and this is what Israel is being taught in this chapter. With their hopes high, they prepare to confront the challenges ahead.

📖 3:1–6

CAREFUL PREPARATIONS

Aside from the miraculous way the river is crossed, the most important feature of this chapter is the ark of the covenant. Its prominence is stressed in the number of times it is mentioned in chapters 3 and 4 (nine times in chapter 3 and seven times in chapter 4) and by the nature of the commands and statements given in its regard.

The ark represents the person and promises of God. It points to the fact that, as the people of Israel set out to cross the Jordan and invade and possess the land, they must do so not in their own strength, but in God's. Indeed, it is God Himself going before them as their source of victory.

In verse 5, Joshua commands the people to consecrate themselves in view of the wonders God would work among them on the next day—not exactly the preparations we might expect from a military standpoint. But God's ways are not our ways. For God's people, spiritual preparation is the vital element; for it is being rightly related to God that brings the power of God on our work and ministry.

Demystifying Joshua

Consecrate means "to set apart, prepare, or dedicate." Here it has reflexive meaning, "to prepare yourselves." This word is often used (in Exodus and Leviticus) in connection with cleansing of sacrifices, washings, and offerings. It underscores the need for God's people to deal with their own sin. It sets them apart for the Lord and His purposes. When there is a lack of consecration, we hinder the power of God. And there is even more included here—the people are preparing themselves for a miracle. Israel is to *expect* God to work wonders.

The consecration of Israel reminds us of God's holiness and the cleanliness He insists on in His servants. God is absolute holiness, completely set apart from sin. He is a holy God who cannot have fellowship with sinful man or allow sin in His presence without a solution to the sin problem. For believers, God's call for consecration demonstrates the necessity for cleansing through confession. To experience God's power, protection, and deliverance, we need to prepare our hearts and deal with the known sin in our lives through confession (Exodus 19:10, 22; Joshua 7:13).

This command also reminds us of the necessity of understanding our purpose as God's people along with a commitment to God and His purpose. It means the Israelites are to set themselves apart to Yahweh to cross the Jordan so they can enter the land, defeat the enemies, and become a testimony to the nations (Exodus 19:4–6).

📖 3:7–13

THE PROMISE OF SAFETY

These verses reinforce the concept of grace. They show that crossing the Jordan and dispossessing the enemies (as in all aspects of our salvation and sanctification) is the work of God. The things we do in consecration are not works of righteousness that merit God's favor or overcome our enemies. Rather, the acts of consecration (like confession) remove the barriers to God's power and to fellowship, and so prepare our hearts to receive God's grace; they build our faith so we will put our feet in the water, cross over, and go up against the enemy.

To be effective, leaders need the right credentials—solid biblical training under people of God who truly know His Word. So it is time that God establishes Joshua as His representative to guide the nation (3:7). It is significant that it is God who does the exalting (4:14). The natural tendency is to exalt ourselves, but Joshua, in reporting God's communication to him, says nothing about this promise of being exalted. Instead, he focuses their attention on the fact that it is the living God who is among them, and it is He and He alone who will dispossess the enemies of the land (3:10).

Since the priests carry the ark of the covenant, and since the ark represents God's person and power, they alone are to take it to the edge of the water and stand still. What do we gather from this? It reminds us of our part in the plan of God. We must learn to step out in faith and obedience to the principles and promises of scripture. (This passage reminds us of the words of Moses in Exodus 14:13–14, when the Israelites are hemmed in with the Red Sea in front of them and Pharaoh and his chariots behind them.)

God's people are reminded to focus on hearing the words of their Lord (Joshua 3:9; Romans 10:17). We learn here that the authority of leaders among God's people needs to be the scripture rather than their personality, charisma, or whatever happens to appeal to people. The ark of the covenant helps the Israelites focus on the fact that it's God's battle.

📖 3:14–17

PASSAGE BY GOD'S POWER

After breaking camp, as instructed, the priests carrying the ark of the covenant lead the way and walk to the Jordan, which is swollen over its banks. This must have been a fearful sight; but resting in the presence of God, they step into the waters. Immediately, a miracle occurs.

Many insist that this is no miracle since the event can be explained as a natural phenomenon. Earthquakes on record have caused the high banks of the Jordan to collapse and dam up the river for extended periods of time, however, never during flood season. Admittedly, God could have employed natural causes such as an earthquake and a landslide, and the timing would have still made it a miraculous intervention. But considering all the factors involved, it seems best to view this occurrence as a special act of God brought about in a way unknown to humans. The most important point about the event, however, is that it is to remind the people of the crossing of the Red Sea when God opened up a path. This would have clearly communicated that the God of power who was with their fathers against the Egyptian enemy is still with this next generation.

Crossing the Jordan at flood stage with two million people has several immediate results: God is magnified and Joshua is exalted (3:5). God's people are energized and motivated, and the people of the land, the Canaanites, are terrorized (just as in 1:9 and 5:1). God is indeed giving His people the promised land. Providentially speaking, He had already done so (1:2–6; 2:9), but the people of the land were not going to simply lie down. The inhabitants of the land would resist with all the resources at their disposal.

Crossing the Jordan meant two things for Israel. First, they must be totally committed to going against armies, chariots, and fortified cities. But then, if they are to be successful, they must also be committed to a focused walk of faith in Yahweh rather than, as they had done in the wilderness, a walk according to the flesh and their own resources.

Take It Home

For believers today, crossing the Jordan represents passing from one level of the Christian life to another. It is a picture of entering into spiritual warfare to claim what God has promised. This should mean the end of a life lived by human effort and the beginning of a life of faith and obedience.

JOSHUA 4:1–24

LEST WE FORGET

Setting Up the Section

God is often wisely concerned over our proneness to forget His faithfulness. Here we see His reminder for the Israelites by building a physical monument to their crossing of the Jordan.

📄 4:1–7

PREPARED TO REMEMBER

Exodus 15 describes a relevant story in the history of God's people—how in only three days the Israelites, although they had just seen and sung of the mighty works of God, are quick to forget God's faithfulness. Rather than having confidence in God, we read of their grumbling (Exodus 15:24). The memorial of stones in this passage serves to promote encouragement and reverence in all Israel and for all time (4:6, 7, 24); in the context of the Israelite's former forgetfulness, we see God's great wisdom.

Critical Observation

The name *Gilgal* means "a circle of stones." Every time Israel returns to Gilgal, they will see the circles of stones and remember what God has done to roll away the waters of the Jordan. The very site of the stones was to be an encouragement, but also a reminder of the sovereign power of the Lord over nations and creation so they might fear the Lord forever and remain faithful to their purpose in the plan of God.

📄 4:8–24

SIGNIFICANT STONES

The memorial is significant for many reasons. It is a permanent sign to future generations (4:6–7, 21–23). In two places in the chapter, covering five verses, parents are reminded of their responsibility to communicate God's Word and His calling to their children, generation to generation, whenever they ask about the stone monument. Parents dare not and cannot abdicate this to others. God charges parents with this privilege and responsibility. Finally, the stones are a testimony to other nations (4:24). Here, God is again reminding Israel of her purpose as a nation of priests (Exodus 19:4–6; 1 Peter. 2:5, 9–11).

Take It Home

Christians are living stones of a holy temple, living memorials of the power of God (1 Peter 2:4–5). But we, too, face the threat of forgetting the Lord by forgetting our pilgrim character through preoccupation with the world. All of God's children are regularly called to do things that form memorials of the saving grace of God such as assembling together, partaking of the sacraments, meditating on scripture, praying, and fellowshipping with other believers.

JOSHUA 5:1–15

CONSECRATING THE PEOPLE

Setting Up the Section

This chapter bridges the crossing of the Jordan and the beginning of the military campaigns. Israel needed a preparation of heart and willingness to submit to God's directions that they might experience His power and overcome the enemy.

📖 5:1

THE CONDITION OF CANAANITES

The Canaanites are, in essence, already defeated. They are fearful of the nation of Israel because of the mighty works of God. God's people need to recognize and understand that the Lord is mightier than all their enemies (John 16:33; 2 Corinthians 2:14). God calls us to be strong in the Lord and in the strength of His might (Ephesians 6:10). The Lord leads Israel through a number of important experiences to spiritually fortify and prepare them for battle.

📖 5:2–10

RENEWING THE COVENANT SIGNS

As a nation, this is the second time a group circumcision is observed among the Israelites, the first being while the older generation was still in Egypt. Circumcision was not unique to the Israelites. For instance, it was an Egyptian practice with religious connotations reserved for the priests and upper-class citizens. In associating it with God's covenant, however, the Israelites gave significance to circumcision that other nations did not.

The renewal of the rite of circumcision is necessary again because none of the men born after they came out of Egypt had been circumcised—that generation of men had died. Circumcision symbolized their faith that God would enable them to posses the land. At Gilgal the people are to remember God's covenant promises and past deliverance in order that they might live as His people in the days ahead.

This instance (5:10) is only the third Passover God's people have kept. The first was in Egypt (Exodus 12:1–28), and the second was at Mount Sinai (Numbers 9:1–5). By partaking of the Passover, they reexperience their deliverance and redemption out of Egypt and look forward to other victories—to the defeat of the Canaanites and also to the victory to come in Christ's work on Calvary.

THE CAPTAIN OF THE LORD'S ARMY

The Passover stands for God's deliverance out of Egypt. The promised land speaks of their new beginning, their new life as the people of God delivered from judgment into the place of blessing.

The manna had begun as a provision during a time of God's judgment of the people's disobedience when they rebelled and failed to believe God's promises. But now the new generation had left the wilderness by faith in the power of God. Now they are able to appropriate the blessings of the land and taste the goodness of the Lord.

For forty years, manna had served as God's special supply for His people in the wilderness, even after their acts of rebellion and unbelief. Israel's feasting on the fruits of the land is a demonstration of faith and a lesson from the Lord of the saving life of God through fellowship with Him. After eating of the land, the manna is no longer necessary because their time of wandering in the desert is over—the people are coming into the promised land.

The blessings of the promised land are only a foretaste of what is to come. Experiencing God's blessings leads to a two-fold expectation: Through fellowship and faith, there is always more for us to taste of the goodness and mercy of God in this life (1 Peter 2:1-3), but this is only a taste of richer and more abundant blessings that await us in eternity as the people of God.

In verse 13 Joshua looks up and sees a man armed with a sword. Joshua's question (of whose side this man is on) expresses his concern as well as his courage. It reveals a mind-set that poses a threat to his effectiveness in the service of the Savior—the tendency to see the battles we face as *our battles* and the forces we face as forces marshaled *against us*. From the commander's answer, we learn (with Joshua) that the Lord is there with the armies of heaven to secure Jericho.

Joshua needs to acknowledge God's claim over him for God's purposes.

Certainly, the battle is a joint venture between God and the people of Israel under Joshua's leadership as appointed by the Lord (1:1-9), but Joshua must be following the Lord, submitting to His authority, taking orders from Him, and placing the battle in His hands.

The Lord reminds Joshua of God's personal presence and His powerful provision. Joshua responds how each of us should respond when confronted with God's power—in worship and submission. He quickly gets the picture after being confronted by the divine commander; he is reminded of a truth he heard Moses declare many years earlier when they stood on the banks of the Red Sea. "The Lord will fight for you; you need only to be still" (Exodus 14:14 NIV). Joshua learns afresh the truth that David will learn and declare when facing Goliath: This is the Lord's battle (1 Samuel 17:47).

Critical Observation

God is not present to fight our battles or help in our causes when we get in trouble as though He were a genie in a bottle. The battle is His, and our role is that of soldier-servants: We are here to serve Him, do His will, follow Him, and depend on Him completely. The warfare of God's people is a holy calling, but it's also a divine undertaking accomplished by those who humble themselves under the mighty hand of a present and powerful God (1 Peter 5:6–7).

Joshua's worshipful response to this figure shows this is a vision of God Himself. If this was only an angel, he would have repelled Joshua's worshipful response. Joshua is reminded here that he is merely the leader of God's army for whom God abundantly supplies the most important kind of armor—the armor of God (Ephesians 6:10–18).

Take It Home

Joshua had an encounter with the very revelation of God. It was an encounter that lifted a great burden from his shoulders. Like Joshua, we need to go into battle mindful of the Lord and mindful of His Word, which must guide our thoughts, direct our actions, and fortify our hearts. As we look over the battles in our own lives, we must look up and see the Commander of the Lord of Hosts, in awe of our glorious guide.

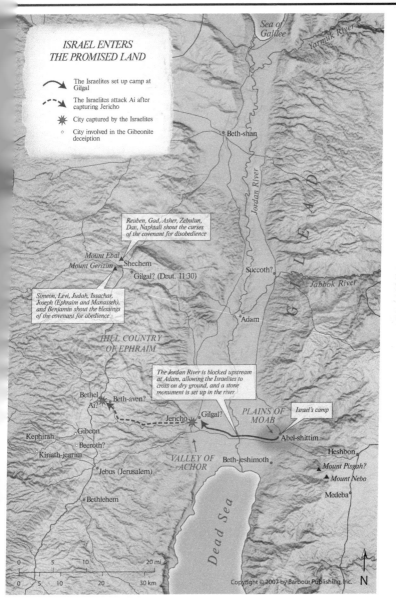

ISRAEL ENTERS THE PROMISED LAND

→ The Israelites set up camp at Gilgal

⇢ The Israelites attack Ai after capturing Jericho

✳ City captured by the Israelites

○ City involved in the Gibeonite deception

Sea of Galilee

Yarmuk River

Beth-shan

Jordan River

G I L E A D

Reuben, Gad, Asher, Zebulun, Dan, Naphtali shout the curses of the covenant for disobedience

Mount Ebal
Mount Gerizim — Shechem
Gilgal? (Deut. 11:30)

Succoth?

Jabbok River

Simeon, Levi, Judah, Issachar, Joseph (Ephraim and Manasseh), and Benjamin shout the blessings of the covenant for obedience

Adam

HILL COUNTRY OF EPHRAIM

The Jordan River is blocked upstream at Adam, allowing the Israelites to cross on dry ground, and a stone monument is set up in the river

Bethel
Ai?
Beth-aven?
Gilgal?
Jericho
PLAINS OF MOAB
Israel's camp

Kephirah
Gibeon
Beeroth?
Kiriath-jearim
Jebus (Jerusalem)
VALLEY OF ACHOR
Beth-jeshimoth
Abel-shittim
Heshbon
Mount Pisgah?
Mount Nebo
Medeba

Bethlehem

Dead Sea

0   5   10   20 mi
0   5   10   20   30 km

Copyright © 2007 by Barbour Publishing, Inc.

N

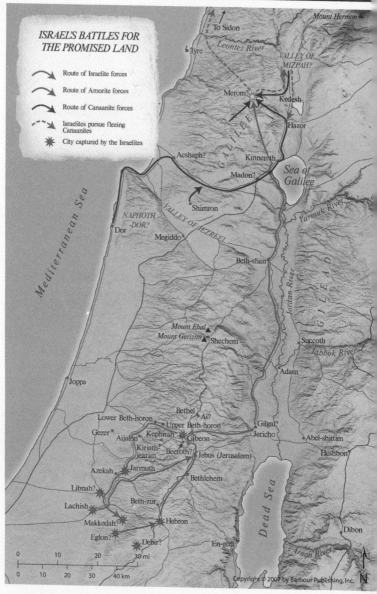

ISRAEL'S BATTLES FOR
THE PROMISED LAND

→ Route of Israelite forces

→ Route of Amorite forces

→ Route of Canaanite forces

-→ Israelites pursue fleeing
    Canaanites

✳ City captured by the Israelites

Mount Hermon

To Sidon

Leontes River

VALLEY OF
MIZPAH?

Tyre

Merom?   Kedesh

GALILEE   Hazor

Acshaph?   Kinnereth

Madon?   Sea of
Galilee

Shimron   Yarmuk River

NAPHOTH
-DOR?

VALLEY OF JEZREEL

Dor

Megiddo

Beth-shan   Jordan River

GILEAD

Mediterranean Sea

Mount Ebal
Mount Gerizim   Shechem

Succoth

Jabbok River

Joppa

Adam

Bethel   Ai?

Lower Beth-horon

Upper Beth-horon   Gilgal?

Gezer   Aijalon   Kephirah   Gibeon   Jericho

Kiriath-   Beeroth?   Abel-shittim
jearim   Jebus (Jerusalem)

Azekah   Jarmuth   Heshbon

Libnah?   Bethlehem

Lachish   Beth-zur   Dead Sea

Makkedah?   Hebron

Eglon?   Debir?

En-gedi   Dibon

0   10   20   30 mi

0   10   20   30   40 km   Arnon River

N

Copyright © 2007 by Barbour Publishing, Inc.

JOSHUA 6:1–27
VICTORY AT JERICHO

Setting Up the Section

God guides the Israelites into a miraculous victory with an unlikely strategy.

📄 **6:1–7**

THE PLAN FOR VICTORY

The directions given to Joshua by God for the conquest of Jericho obviously seem strange, but only if we fail to think in biblical terms of the life of faith and mankind's inherent inability to accomplish God's plan on our own. Before the Lord outlines His plan, He graciously assures Joshua of victory. Victory is always by the Lord's hand, and we should expect it to be something that bypasses dependence on human strength and ability.

The words *have given* (6:2) describe a future event or action as having already been accomplished. Future victory was already assured by the promise of an omnipotent, faithful, and immutable God. God's plan for victory will serve to teach Israel and God's people for all ages. Though we have human responsibilities in tearing down the strongholds raised up against the knowledge of God, our victory is dependent on two things: God's power and faithfulness to His plan.

Critical Observation

The number seven is used eleven times in this chapter. Seven signifies perfection or completion, which reminds us that God's plan is always perfect and cannot be improved upon (Romans 11:33–36; 12:2; 1 Corinthians 1:18). Further, the number seven shows that the conquest is part of a spiritual exercise designed to set the people apart (sanctify them) for the Lord as a holy people who belong to a holy God. Because of the significance of the number seven to creation and the Sabbath, and the fact they were entering into their inheritance, it also signifies the beginning of a new order and the land as a picture of the believer's rest in the Lord (Hebrews 4).

📄 6:8–21

THE PATH TO VICTORY

The statement about the men being able to charge straight ahead (6:20) calls our attention to the fact that they are able to charge in from all around the city. The whole wall around the city collapses with the exception of the portion where Rahab's house is located. Some interpreters claim that an earthquake caused the destruction. If so, it was a miracle of timing and location since the camp at Gilgal (a little more than a mile away) and Rahab's house remain intact.

We should not forget that these instructions and the events of this chapter are preceded by a number of things God used to prepare the people to believe and obey Him. Israel had been prepared to trust the Lord by the events of the first chapters and their consecration to the Lord, especially in chapter 5. Spiritual preparation is fundamental to our ability to appropriate God's strength in exchange for our weakness.

The passage does not tell us why they are to be silent (6:10), but perhaps it illustrates and teaches the principle of being silent before God and resting in Him (Exodus 14:14; Psalm 46:10–11).

Take It Home

Hebrews 11:30 says that the walls of Jericho fell down by faith. In spite of the taunts that were perhaps hurled down at them from the walls as they marched silently around Jericho, they were willing to look foolish for the Lord. He was their source of strength. If we want to overcome our obstacles, we must submit to God's way by faith (Galatians 5:5).

Joshua does not unfold the entire plan at first, but day by day gives the people instructions. Each day they go out and march silently around the city. Though nothing seems to happen, they do not murmur or complain or question Joshua's instructions. They simply obey, day after day, until the seventh day when they give the great shout and the walls come tumbling down by their faith in the mighty hand of God (Hebrews 11:30). This reminds us that the Lord often works slowly. We want immediate deliverance, but the Lord often tests our faith and in the process builds our character and our relationship with Him so we find the Lord to be what we really need (James 1:2–4).

📄 6:22–27

THE PROMISE FULFILLED

In these final verses, we see some marvelous facts about God and His dealings with people. First, they demonstrate God's faithfulness to His Word (James 1:17). The promises to Rahab are kept—she and her family are delivered. While it is not stated, evidently that part of the wall on which Rahab's house was built did not collapse. Second, they demonstrate God's grace and mercy. God's love and plan of salvation are open to anyone who calls on His name (John 3:16; Romans 10:11–13; 2 Peter 3:9).

The prophecy against any who would seek to rebuild Jericho (6:26) demonstrates God's severity and the surety of His Word. This prophecy came to be fulfilled in the days of Ahab (1 Kings 16:34), keeping with God's faithfulness to keep His promises. Jericho was occupied sporadically after its destruction, but never to the previous degree.

JOSHUA 7:1-26

THE AGONY OF DEFEAT

Setting Up the Section

The distance between a great victory and a terrible defeat is one step and often a short one at that. Ai is the next objective in the path of conquest because of its strategic location.

7:1–5

DISOBEDIENCE AND DEFEAT

This chapter reminds us of the reality of the ever-present threats and contrasts of life—victory is always followed by the threat of defeat. Never is the child of God in greater danger of a fall than after a victory (1 Corinthians 10:12).

Jericho has been placed under a ban, a phrase which comes from the Hebrew word *herem*, meaning "a devoted thing, a ban." The verb form, *haram*, means "to ban, devote, or destroy utterly." Basically, this word refers to the exclusion of an object from use or abuse, along with its irreversible surrender to God. So, to surrender something to God meant either devoting it to the service of God or putting it under a ban for utter destruction.

The problem facing the Israelites as a nation is not their enemies as much as their own unfaithfulness. The Lord holds the whole camp of Israel accountable for the act of one man, and He withholds His blessing until the matter is dealt with. This does not mean that the rest of the nation is sinless, but this sin is of such a nature (a sin of direct disobedience and rebellion) that God uses it to teach Israel and remind them that they are a community, a family, a body—like the church is today. Sin contaminates the whole assembly—like yeast in dough (1 Corinthians 5:6).

Nothing escapes the omniscience of God, especially sin (Numbers 32:23). God sees the sin in our lives and desires for us to deal with it, not hide it. Even though the Lord died for our sins and stands at God's right hand as our advocate and intercessor, God does not and cannot treat sin in our lives lightly (James 4:5–6).

Critical Observation

There is an irony of the defeat of Ai. The name itself means "ruin," so it is being contrasted with the powerful city of Jericho. Jericho falls easily because God fights for obedient Israel, whereas Ai, the dump, defeats them because of Achan's sin.

The defeat at Ai demoralizes God's people. It creates misgivings and a lack of hope in the Lord. Rather than examine their own lives as the source of their defeat, they begin to doubt the Lord. People are quick to blame, make excuses, and hide, but they often fail to honestly examine their own lives.

📖 7:6–9

THE DISMAY OF JOSHUA

Joshua's dismay shows us his humanity and encourages us in our own failures to know that God will still accept us if we turn to Him for forgiveness. God can greatly use us if we will trust Him. Failure is not the end—often it is a test. Most leaders fail God at some point but refuse to continue lying in the dust. Failure and repentance teach the human heart a more ample conception of the grace of God. We learn that God is slow to anger and abounding in love, even when we are not. Defeat and failure often enable people to grow in faith.

📖 7:10–15

GOD'S DIRECTION

While the Lord understands and sympathizes with our problems and fears, and while humbling ourselves before the Lord is always needed, He never condones our being prostrate in despair or excuses us from appropriating His grace and moving out in obedience. Instead He calls us to turn back to Him.

The consequences of unconfessed sin are weakness and an inability to serve and live for the Lord. We each have the capacity to live victoriously for the Lord, but the ability to do so always depends on fellowship with the Savior in the power of the Spirit; we must walk in the light (1 John 1:5–9).

God calls for a restoration to fellowship and faith in the power of God (Luke 22). Joshua is to call their attention to the sin of someone taking things that are under the ban, which is also the cause of their failure in the battle against Ai. As the Lord had emphasized to Joshua, he is to call the people's attention to both the cause and the consequences of the sin.

📖 7:16–26

LEARNING FROM SIN

As 1 Corinthians 10 reminds us, what happens to Achan is recorded for our warning and instruction. Achan's sin was a familiar one. He saw, he coveted, and he took. It was the same with Eve and with King David, and it is the same with us.

As with Satan and Eve, Achan is dissatisfied, impatient, and self-reliant. He is trusting in his own strategies to get what he wants. Ironically, God is in the process of taking Israel into the land filled with abundant blessings. Yet Achan does not trust or believe in God's power to give him every good thing. As with Ananias and Sapphira, Achan is put to death to exemplify the seriousness of sin and to strike the fear of God into the hearts of the people.

Had Achan voluntarily cast himself on the mercy of God, his life might have been spared, as in the case of David. When Achan sins, the blessing and strength of God is halted, and the nation is met with discipline and failure. But once the sin is dealt with as the Lord commanded, by His grace, the blessing and strength of God resume.

Take It Home

Our failure to find contentment in the Savior and His love and grace is surely the cause of a great deal of our own self-made misery and sinful behavior (Matthew 6). Jesus defined the pursuit of the details of life at the expense of seeking first the kingdom of God and His righteousness as a simple matter of not truly trusting in God's supply. The issue is one of having too little faith. Known sin in one's life creates a barrier between one and God. Sin involves seeking from other things what only God can give. So, we seek contentment in the Lord (Philippians 4:12–13).

JOSHUA 8:1–35

VICTORY AT AI

The Battle   8:1–29
The Covenant Renewed   8:30–35

Setting Up the Section

Often God engineers defeat before He engineers victory. Sometimes success comes through the back door of failure. In this chapter we again see the grace of God and the truth of restoration. Defeat never has to be the end.

📖 8:1–29

THE BATTLE

God's new revelation to Joshua is meant to both encourage him and give him directions for victory. God uses significant words to encourage God's people—the same ones He used with Moses at Kadesh-barnea, as he sent out the twelve spies (Deuteronomy 12:21). These are also the words Joshua heard from Moses forty years later (Deuteronomy 31:8) as he turned over the reins of leadership. Joshua hears similar words directly from the Lord as He commissions him to lead the people into the land (Joshua 1:9). Joshua uses these same words to encourage the nation in the face of their enemies, and they are used on three other occasions when Judah faces the enemy and terrible odds (Joshua 8:1; 10:25; 2 Chronicles 20:15, 17; 32:7). These words remind us that God is a God of comfort and that He wants to encourage us through His Word.

With God's blessing assured through words of comfort, a few specific directions are given: Don't make the same mistake twice. Though the primary cause of the defeat at Ai is Achan's sin, a secondary cause is underestimating the enemy, overestimating themselves, and presuming on the Lord (7:3–4). By trusting Him, God promises they can turn a place of defeat into a place of victory.

Still, the basis of victory is the same: Just like at Jericho, victory at Ai will come by the power of God. The irony of God's blessing is that the spoils of Ai and its livestock can now be taken by Israel. As the firstfruits of the land, Jericho has been placed under the ban, but this is not the case with Ai. Achan's dissatisfaction actually causes him to miss precisely what he longs for and much more.

With the battle at Ai, we are reminded that we should not expect God to work the same way always. We need to be open and sensitive to the various ways God may lead. As the sovereign God of the universe, He is never limited to one particular method to accomplish His purposes.

The strategy for the capture of Ai is ingenious (8:3–9). The plan works like clockwork (8:14–22). Thus Israel, out of their failure, comes not only to a second chance but to a great victory along with some much-needed lessons. Though we should never seek to fail, failure can be the back door to success; for God is willing to forgive and restore us if we will deal with our sin appropriately and sincerely.

📄 8:30–35

THE COVENANT RENEWED

Instead of further pursuing the military campaign following the victory at Ai, Joshua leads the Israelites on a spiritual pilgrimage for a special time of worship. Moses had commanded it (Deuteronomy 27:1–8) because of what this event would stand for in the lives of the Israelites. This counterintuitive strategy illustrates the principle of first priorities: Our capacity in life is always dependent on our spiritual capacity and orientation to the plan of God.

Joshua leads the entire nation—men, women, children, and cattle—to the place specified by Moses, the mountains of Ebal and Gerizim. This is a march of about thirty miles and evidently is not difficult or dangerous because they pass through an area that is sparsely populated. These mountains are located in the geographic center of the land. This place represents all the land, both at the time of entrance into Canaan and also when Joshua's leadership comes to a close (24:1).

Critical Observation

The place where Joshua led the people had outstanding acoustical properties, kind of like a natural amphitheater, and one person standing on one mountain could be easily heard by someone standing on the other mountain. Mount Ebal stood for cursing, and Gerizim stood for blessing. These mountains formed a huge object lesson. What happened to the Israelites in the land was going to depend on where they lived, as it were—on Mount Ebal, in disobedience and under the curses, or on Mount Gerizim, in obedience and under God's blessing.

When there is obedience to the law of God, there is victory. But when there is disobedience, the result is defeat. We are reminded in this object lesson of God's grace and provision that obedience brings blessing and disobedience brings cursing.

At Mount Sinai, God gave the Ten Commandments and the judgments, and He also gave the ordinances, the sacrifices. The altar here is for those who acknowledge their sin and come not as righteous, but as sinners to the place of sacrifice. The altar, constructed of uncut stones without any human workmanship (8:30–31), is a negation of humanism and salvation by works. It shows that human beings can add nothing to the work of God for salvation or for spirituality. It is by God's work that we are saved.

Take It Home

The law pointed Israel to those moral statutes that are so vital to justice and order within nations. But it did more. It demonstrated the holiness of God and man's inability; it showed how sin separates people from God. Through the tabernacle, the sacrifices, and the priesthood, it pointed forward to a suffering Savior, the Lamb of God, who must die for humanity's sin that we might have a relationship with God and be His people in a fallen world.

JOSHUA 9:1–27

THE PERIL OF WALKING BY SIGHT

Setting Up the Section

This passage describes the danger of failing to commit to the Lord, the peril of prayerlessness, and the peril of walking by sight—making decisions on the basis of how things appear rather than trusting in God for guidance. As we have seen, Israel's failure at Ai was to a large degree the result of failing to consult the Lord.

9:1–2

THE ALLIANCES AGAINST ISRAEL

The record given here is typical of Satan's strategies. Powerful alliances begin immediately to form in both the north and the south of Canaan. Where tribal warfare had gone on for years, suddenly deadly enemies come together in alliances as they unite against the invasion of God's people into the land.

Critical Observation

When righteousness becomes aggressive and bent on an objective, it has a way of uniting the forces of righteousness and the enemies of righteousness. It happened this way when Jesus Christ launched His earthly ministry. His aggressive ministry of healing, preaching, and the confrontation of sin galvanized His own followers; but it also welded together three groups who had formerly been enemies—the Pharisees, the Sadducees, and the Herodians.

It appears that all the city-states in mountainous regions join forces against Israel as a means of keeping Joshua and his army from attacking one city at a time, as had been done with Jericho and Ai. In resisting Israel, however, these kings are resisting God. Their stubborn rebellion against God is an eloquent testimony that the sin of the Amorites had reached its full measure.

9:3–17

THE DECEPTION OF THE GIBEONITES

Not all are willing to openly go against Israel in view of Israel's victories. The Gibeonites, which include a league of cities (9:17), concoct a clever ruse designed to deceive the Israelites and hide their true identity—a typical strategy of Satan, the deceiver. They evidently somehow know that God had commanded the Israelites to totally destroy all the inhabitants of the land.

Their claim is that they are impressed with the great things Joshua has done, and so they want a treaty allowing them to live because they are not of the land of Canaan.

The Gibeonites play on the Israelites' sympathies by appearing as weary travelers who have been on a long journey. They also play on their egos and their sense of pride. They insist they came from a great distance to show their respect for the power of the God of the Israelites and want to be allowed to live as the servants of Israel. Caught off guard, Joshua and the leaders of Israel listen to the ruse of the Gibeonites.

The primary mistake here is a failure to seek counsel from the Lord. The Israelites should have sought direction from the Lord through the Urim and Thummim. Here we see the peril of presumption through prayerlessness. It is always a mistake for us to lean on our own wisdom or judgment and make our own plans apart from God's direction.

📖 9:18–27

THE DECISION OF THE LEADERS

The text tells us that once the ruse is discovered, the people grumble against their leaders because they judged them to be responsible. Though the Israelites erred by leaning on their own understanding rather than consulting the Lord, they honor their agreement with the Gibeonites. To break the covenant would dishonor God's name and bring down His wrath.

While they could not go back on their pledge, the Gibeonites had deceived them, so a punishment fitting their sin must be prescribed. First, Joshua rebukes them for their dishonesty and then sentences them to perpetual slavery. In the ruse of the Gibeonites, they had offered to be the subjects of the Israelites (9:8, 11). By this they are merely offering to become Israel's vassals. In return they expect Israel, the stronger of the two, to protect them from their enemies (10:6). Their plan backfires and they become woodcutters and water-bearers for the Israelites, especially in relation to the tabernacle service. In God's grace, this turns out to be a great blessing.

The very thing the Gibeonites hoped to retain—their freedom—was lost. But the curse eventually becomes a blessing. It is on behalf of the Gibeonites that God later works a great miracle (10:10–14). Later, the tabernacle of the Lord will be pitched at Gibeon, and the Gibeonites (who may have been later known as Nethinims) will replace the Levites in temple service (Ezra 8:20). That is the amazing way the grace of God works. God not only forgives, but in many cases He actually overrules our mistakes and brings blessing out of sin.

The Gibeonites have the privilege of being brought close to the Lord on a regular basis. It is interesting that in later years, when the Israelites go into idolatry, the Gibeonites are still standing at the altar where the true God ordains that sacrifices should be made for sins. As a result of what they have seen God do for Israel, they become convinced, like Rahab, that Israel's God is the true God. Like Rahab, they become loyal believers.

Take It Home

As Christians, we are involved in deadly spiritual warfare with a power far superior to our own strength. To be delivered from our opponent and his nefarious schemes, we must clothe ourselves with our spiritual armor as given us in Christ. The offensive weapons given to us by the Lord are the Word of God and prayer. Without the Word and prayer, we are sitting ducks. When God's people are victorious or prosper, it seems Satan doubles his efforts in attacks against them. Be ever on your guard! (Read 1 Samuel 12:23; Proverbs 3:5–6; 1 Corinthians 10:12; Ephesians 6:10–18.)

JOSHUA 10:1–43

DESTRUCTION OF THE COALITION

Setting Up the Section

During Israel's campaign and victory over the southern portion of Canaan, something miraculous happens that provides Joshua with a great military opportunity for a quick victory over a number of enemies at once.

📖 10:1–5

THE AMORITE COALITION

The defection of the Gibeonites is cause for great alarm for three reasons: (1) It is discouraging to see such a large city surrender to the enemy, (2) without Gibeon the southern coalition is severely weakened, and (3) they constitute a fifth column to fight with Israel in time of war. Though it has no king, Gibeon is like a royal city; it is just as strong and influential as any city-state (11:12).

📖 10:6–15

MIRACULOUS DELIVERANCE

Faced with the armies of the coalition and certain destruction, the Gibeonites send a messenger to Joshua asking for help based on their treaty with Israel. Humanly speaking, this is the perfect opportunity for Joshua to get rid of the Gibeonites. Yet Joshua is a man of integrity who honors his word and does not consider that an option. The Israelites had given their word and are duty bound to honor it. Plus, the situation now provides a unique military opportunity to defeat and destroy several armies at once.

The fact that God now gives this promise might suggest that Joshua had inquired of the Lord and had received this answer and promise. With all these kings coming together, there was surely a certain amount of concern in Joshua's heart. The situation was urgent, and God's word of encouragement and His promise of victory were certainly needed.

This passage provides an excellent example of the interplay between the work of God and the work of humanity in achieving victory. Here a man's efforts and God's sovereign intervention cooperate with the clear emphasis on the fact that it is the Lord who gives the victory. God gives us responsibilities and talents to serve Him, yet ultimately, we must understand that victory is the Lord's.

The Canaanites worshiped gods in the image of natural forces. What a shock when it seems that their gods, in which they have placed their faith, are helpless against the God of Israel, who sends a hailstorm to defeat them.

This battle includes the greatest of four miracles found in the book of Joshua (10:12), often called "Joshua's long day," or "the day the sun stood still." It is noon, and the hot sun is directly overhead when Joshua utters his prayer. The petition is quickly answered by the Lord. Joshua prays in faith and a great miracle results. The record of this miracle has been called the most striking example of conflict between scripture and science because, as is well-known, the sun does not move around the earth causing day and night. Instead, light and darkness come because the earth rotates on its axis around the sun. Why, then, does Joshua address the sun rather than the earth? He is using the language of observation; he is speaking from the perspective and appearance of things on earth.

Demystifying Joshua

Obviously, this was a unique day in the history of creation. Views concerning this phenomenon fall into two categories. The first assumes a slowing or suspending of the normal rotation of the earth so that there were extra hours that day. God did this so that Joshua's forces could complete their victory before the enemy had a night for rest and regrouping. The Hebrew for *stood still* (10:13) is a verb of motion, indicating a slowing or stopping of the rotation of the earth on its axis. The second category includes views that assume no irregularity in the rotation of the earth. One view argues for the prolonging of daylight by some sort of unusual refraction of the sun's rays. While the details of how it took place are not described in scripture, what is made clear is that God did something completely amazing to give the Israelite armies a complete and decisive victory.

📄 10:16–43

FURTHER VICTORIES

The five kings and their armies have left the safety of their fortified cities to fight Joshua and his army out in the open, which gives Joshua a great advantage. He is determined to keep them from escaping to the safety of their walls, which will prolong the campaign against that portion of the land.

Joshua's thinking of human responsibility and tactical wisdom combines with his faith in the One who ultimately delivers victory. Our need is to keep our eyes on Him, to obey

Him, and above all, to trust in His strength rather than in our own. This will usually mean expending great effort, as we see Israel doing here, all the while knowing that the Lord is also at work to enable and to fight for us. Most of us learn, early in our Christian experience, that we do not just face one enemy. We face a coalition of evil forces that have banded together in an attempt to destroy us. Those enemies are commonly called the world, the flesh, and the devil.

Together the world, the flesh, and the devil make an unbeatable combination—or they would be unbeatable, if not for the saving intervention of God. Without God, victory against such an alliance is impossible. With God, victory is assured. Joshua was a man who knew God above all else; the impressive results are told in this history.

Take It Home

Joshua and the Israelites take possession of their God-given inheritance, but not without having to go up against hostile forces. The Christian life is precisely like this. In Christ we have been given every spiritual blessing (Ephesians 1:3). In Him, we are complete (Colossians 2:10), but the appropriation of those blessings requires faith in the accomplished work of Christ, along with personal effort through the disciplines of godliness—things such as prayer, Bible study, meditating on God's Word, and regular fellowship with other believers for encouragement.

JOSHUA 11:1–23

THE CONQUEST OF THE NORTH

Setting Up the Section

Joshua has a decisive victory over the south of Canaan. Now the rulers of the cities in the north have become scared. Although earthly rulers are quick to devise plans to stop Israel, they underestimate the power of God being on one's side. The victory He promised Israel will be realized, even if the battle is long and grueling.

📖 11:1–5

AN ATTEMPT TO STOP ISRAEL

King Jabin believes the only hope for the kingdoms in north Canaan is to unite into one powerful army to fight off the coming Israelites. This strategy provides yet another opportunity for God to demonstrate that it is His power and His plan that will prevail. Strategically, it allows Joshua and the Israelites to fight a collective army rather than having to go through the work of taking each city one at a time.

The threat of annihilation forces the kings of the north into an unlikely partnership. Prior to Israel's imminent threat, the kings of the north were hostile to each other and had no alliances. This new united force made an impressive army—militarily speaking, they have a distinct upper hand. The text uses hyperbole to describe the numbers—soldiers as numerous as the sand on the seashore and horses and chariots in great numbers—suggesting that the army is a formidable, overwhelming enemy for the worn-out Hebrews to face.

Demystifying Joshua

Josephus, a Jewish historian of the first century AD, estimated that this northern alliance included 300,000 infantry soldiers, 10,000 cavalry troops, and 20,000 chariots. With such a huge army, it would appear from outside observation that Joshua and his army had good reason for fear.

11:6–15

GOD'S PROMISE FOR VICTORY

As the remaining Canaanite forces gather and take position, Joshua is moving, too. The Israelites are not staying in one place waiting for the battle to come to them. They are marching directly toward Merom, a five-day trek from their home base. It is during this journey that God speaks to Joshua and reminds him again that God will deliver provision and victory. The promise God gives Joshua echoes what He has been saying to Joshua from the very beginning of his time as the leader of Israel: "Do not be afraid; your enemies will be delivered to you" (1:9; 8:1). Joshua's courage flows from faith in the power of God to deliver the promised land to His people.

Not only is Israel going to see this army delivered over to them, but God even tells Joshua specifically to cripple their horses and burn their chariots. These acts may seem brutal, but they send a strong message to the Canaanite kings. Not only have the Israelites defeated their spectacular force, but they destroyed their hope and resources for future attacks. Destroying these weapons holds a lesson for Israel as well: not to depend on superior weaponry, but on the Lord.

Through Israel's conquest of the north, God sends a signal both to Israel and the world that He is the One who provides victory, and His victory is complete and thorough. Never again will these people be able to use their horses to attack God's nation.

Demystifying Joshua

Hazor alone among the northern cities is both seized and burned. This city was by far the largest and most prominent city of ancient Palestine (200 acres in size, compared with Megiddo at 14 and Jericho at 8). Hazor was also ruled by King Jabin—the instigator of the alliance among the northern cities. It was strategically positioned at the center of several branches of an ancient highway which led from Egypt to Syria, Assyria, and Babylon. Because it was the hub of a trade route, Hazor was a very wealthy city. If Hazor could not escape the power of God, the remaining cities would be forced to acknowledge their own vulnerability to the Israelites.

📖 **11:16–23**

GOD'S VICTORIES REVIEWED

With the victory in the north, the formal end of the conquest occurs. Before giving the record of how the land is distributed among the tribes, the author reviews Israel's triumphs in Canaan. He includes a description of the conquered geographic areas (11:16–23) and a list of the defeated kings (chapter 12). This is done to make sure that everyone knows and understands the great work that God has done. Reviewing God's provision builds faith and serves as a reminder of God's blessings.

The battles fought by Joshua and his troops ranged over lands that stretched from border to border, from south to north, and from east to west (11:16–17). The entire land was covered in Israel's amazing conquest. Understandably, it takes time for Israel to gain victory through this vast geography. Conquest of the enemy was neither easy nor quick. Even though God promised them victory, His people were still required to participate, work, and struggle along the way.

One amazing fact is that during the entire conquest, amidst all their confrontations, only one city, Gibeon, sought peace and salvation. The rest were so given over to their depravity that God led His people to take them in battle. Remarkably, even when faced with the ultimate, supernatural power of God, the Canaanites were willing to die rather than submit to God's will or ask for mercy.

Critical Observation

Forty-five years before, the Israelites failed to enter the land for fear of giants—the Anakites Numbers 13:33). Under Joshua, those fearful enemies were almost completely destroyed. Only a few remained in Gaza, Gath, and Ashdod.

The final verse of this chapter (11:23) concludes a major section in Joshua—the conquest. This verse looks backward to where the people have come and forward to where they must go. Even though there are still areas that need to be secured, the victory is now decisive. The battles in the north are the end of this rigorous war schedule.

JOSHUA 12:1–24
KINGS CONQUERED

Setting Up the Section

The list in this chapter is the only complete list of the kings Israel conquered. This list is a testimony to the power of God to accomplish His purposes, overcome earthly powers, and provide for His people in a magnificent manner.

📄 **12:1–6**

THE RECORD OF MOSES

The conquest of the promised land does not begin with Joshua—it began with Moses. It is important to recount the deliverance of God under the leadership of Moses. What Joshua records here are the victories Israel had—over Sihon and Og—under Moses' leadership on the east side of the Jordan. These were important victories because they signified the beginning of Israel establishing itself as a God-empowered powerhouse. Additionally, they remind us just how long ago—more than a generation—this battle for the promised land had begun.

Sihon was the king over a piece of land about ninety miles south to north from the Arnon Gorge at about the midpoint of the Sea of the Arabah (today called the Dead Sea) up to the Sea of Kinnereth. Og ruled over a piece of land extending north from Sihon's northern boundary for about sixty miles (Numbers 21:21–35; Deuteronomy 2:24–3:17). This territory was given to the tribes of Reuben and Gad and the half-tribe of Manasseh (Numbers 32; Joshua 13:8–13).

📄 **12:7–24**

THE RECORD OF JOSHUA

The sixteen kings of southern Canaan who the Israelites defeated under Joshua's leadership are listed first (12:9–16). This is followed by the list of the fifteen kings of northern Canaan (12:17–24). Not only is this list impressive because of the number of kings, but it serves to highlight the power of God to carry out His promises.

For the Israelites, these kings' names bring back a flood of memories of specific experiences, faces, and events from battles they had participated in personally or from the stories that had been passed down to them from generation to generation. Imagine how hearing a list of names at a graduation ceremony can flood the graduates with memories of the individuals they know who are crossing the stage. This list does much more. It is as poignant and moving as the reading of a list of names at a war memorial service; this list is a memorial to the goodness of God.

Critical Observation

Consider the number of kings who reigned in the small region which would be Israel: thirty-one kings in a land approximately 150 miles from north to south and 50 miles from east to west. This may seem strange considering the nation-states we are familiar with today. However, these kings reigned over city-states and were more like governors or mayors over cities than kings of a nation.

In addition to the significance of the list of names, Joshua calls out the land itself. While the geography of this region is not something many of us have experienced first-hand, the promised land had been traversed by the nation of Israel. When Joshua mentions the hill country, the western foothills, the Arabah, the mountain slopes, the desert, and the Negev, the people had literally walked over those various areas and they could picture precisely what God's provision included. Indeed, this land is the backdrop for their nation's history. These are the same hills and valleys that Jesus and His disciples will travel through, the same territory that Rome will conquer, and later still, the Muslims. It is a setting that has significance not just to the generation of Israelites that had fought alongside Joshua, but for all generations to come.

These kinds of lists remind the people that their victory in the Lord does not come without tremendous cost—indeed thirty-one conquered kings represent a vast swath of humanity whose lives were completely interrupted and destroyed so that Israel might be given the inheritance the Lord had promised to Abraham. This list reminds the people of a crucial truth: There is no one more powerful than God, and no one can stand in His way.

Take It Home

The list in Joshua 12 was a great reminder for the Israelites of where they had been, who God had helped them overcome, and His enduring faithfulness in the face of thirty-one formidable enemies. We all benefit from being reminded of how God has taken us out of the wilderness of our unbelief and into the promised land of a rich life in Christ. Take a few moments to reflect on the enemies that God has allowed you to defeat during your journey as His child. How has He changed you and enabled you to conquer sins and grow in grace? Write down your vanquished enemies by name and keep the list to remind you of God's faithfulness and provision and just how far you've come.

JOSHUA 13:1–33

THE DIVISION OF THE LAND

Setting Up the Section

This chapter deals with an exciting time for the Israelites—the distribution of the land. After four hundred years in bondage in Egypt, forty years of wandering in the desert, and years of long hard fighting, they now are able to enjoy and possess the promised land.

📄 13:1–7

THE COMMAND TO DIVIDE THE LAND

Joshua is now growing old. God changes his title, and Joshua becomes more of an administrator for the nation of Israel rather than a military leader. The land has to be assigned to the various tribes, and Joshua is instructed to oversee these important transactions.

To many people this section of the book of Joshua, with its detailed lists of boundaries and cities, seems boring to read. Keep in mind that this is not just some boring list of boundaries; instead, it is the complete and literal fulfillment of the promise of God. When God gives a promise, He fulfills it perfectly and literally. As you read this section, do not forget that God is a promise-keeping God.

We know from later in the text that Joshua dies at the age of 110 (24:29). Given the timing of events between this point and his death, he probably is at least 100 at this time. Because of his age, it is important that Joshua begin the distribution of the land. Even though there are some military threats still facing Joshua, he must begin the distribution and encourage the people to begin settling and enjoying the land.

The land that remains to be taken is described from south to north and includes Philistia, Phoenicia, and Lebanon (13:5–6). All this land is now to be allotted to the nine and a half tribes because God promised to drive out all the enemies (13:6).

📄 13:8–33

THE SPECIAL LAND GRANT

In verses 8–13, Joshua confirms the provision and land division that had already been done by Moses on the east side of the Jordan. The tribes of Reuben, Gad, and the half-tribe of Manasseh, possessing large herds of cattle, had been anxious to settle in the rich grazing lands of the Jordan River valley. They are given this privilege only after their men agree to fight alongside their brothers to win Canaan proper (Numbers 32).

The text provides a survey of the area of Transjordan (13:9–12). It is interesting to note that Geshur and Maacah (already mentioned in 12:5) are not defeated by the Israelites.

It is not stated as to why, but it is something that was a present reality for the original readers of the book. These countries were located east and northeast of the Sea of Kinnereth (the Sea of Galilee).

We are told that the tribe of Levi receives no specific territory of land (see 13:33; 14:3–4; 18:7). Instead, the Levites receive forty-eight towns with pastureland for their flocks and herds (14:4; 21:41) as Moses had specified (Numbers 35:1–5). God wanted to make sure that the Levites were set aside as servants of Him and therefore, freed from the cares of the land. They are given cities to raise their animals and provide housing for their families.

Joshua emphasizes more than once that the tribe of Levi did not acquire any land (13:33, 14:3–4; 18:7). The reason for the repeated reminder of this is that it highlights why God set them aside. The Levites were given the important task of managing the worship of God. The tribe of Levi served particular religious duties for the Israelites and had political responsibilities as well. In return for their special calling and service, the landed tribes were expected to give 10 percent of everything they had (a tithe) to the Levites. The tithe is known as the Maaser Rishon, or Levite Tithe.

Reuben (as we see in 13:15–23) receives the territory previously occupied by Moab, east of the Dead Sea. The tribe of Gad inherits the portion in the center of the region, in the original land of Gilead (13:24–28). The allotment to the half-tribe of Manasseh (13:29–31) is the rich tableland of Bashan, east of the Sea of Kinnereth.

Demystifying Joshua

In Genesis 35:22 and 49:3–4, as he was dying, Jacob had uttered prophecies regarding his sons. His prophecy about his firstborn, Reuben, was intensely emotional and judgmental. According to Hebrew tradition and law, the firstborn is entitled a double portion of land (Deuteronomy 21:17). Yet his father's dying prophecy was that neither he nor his tribe received it, because he had defiled his father's bed by sleeping with his father's concubine. As Joshua is dividing the land up, more than four centuries later, Reuben's punishment is passed on to his descendants. The right of the firstborn passed over to his brother, Joseph, who received two portions, one for Ephraim and the other for Manasseh (Genesis 48:12–20).

JOSHUA 14:1–15
CALEB'S PORTION

Dividing the Land   14:1–5

Caleb's Request   14:6–15

Setting Up the Section

This chapter describes the process by which the land is distributed to the rest of the nine and a half tribes. The first inheritance is given to Caleb. This is fitting because Caleb, along with Joshua, is one of the only two left from those who are freed from Egypt, and they had been the only two who believed all along that God was powerful enough to give the land to Israel. Here, Caleb gets his reward.

Demystifying Joshua

After the Israelites first escaped Egypt, they traveled across the desert to the border of Canaan and sent twelve spies (one from each of the twelve tribes) across the border to do reconnaissance. Caleb and Joshua were two of the twelve spies and were the only two who brought back a good report. Rather than being fearful of the task ahead, Joshua and Caleb encouraged the people to believe that God would help them conquer the land.

Unfortunately, the people were not convinced, and because of their lack of faith they wandered for forty more years before reapproaching the border for entry. During that forty years, the generation that originally left Egypt died out except for Joshua and Caleb, the only two who made it across the border (Numbers 13:1–14:38).

📖 **14:1–5**

DIVIDING THE LAND

The beginning of this chapter introduces how Joshua is going to the divide the remainder of the promised land. The explanation is repeated regarding the dealings with the Reubenites, the Gadites, the half-tribe of Manasseh, and the arrangements for the tribe of Levi (13:14, 33; 18:7). The method by which the land is to be distributed is by lot (14:2; 18:3; 19:51).

It is important to note that the Lord had instructed Moses that each tribe was to receive territory proportionate to its population, while the casting of lots would serve to determine the land's location (Numbers 26:54–56). To cast a lot meant that dice from the breastplate of the priest were used. They were thrown on the ground, and if a certain combination emerged, then God's will would be known (Exodus 28:30; Numbers 27:21).

📖 14:6–15

CALEB'S REQUEST

When the time for distribution arrives, the tribe of Judah, receiving the first portion, assembles at Gilgal. Before the lots are cast, Caleb steps forward to remind Joshua of a promise the Lord had made to him forty-five years earlier: "I will give him and his descendants the land he set his feet on, because he followed the Lord wholeheartedly" (Deuteronomy 1:36 NIV).

Caleb then reviews the highlights of his life and makes his request. It is important that Caleb stand up at this point—not just so he will get the land, but so all will remember the lack of faith in their forefathers set in contrast to the great hand of deliverance of God. This moment speaks volumes about how the hand of God provides and rewards His faithful servants.

The autobiographical story continues as Caleb reminisces about God's faithfulness to him over many years (14:10–11). Caleb bears testimony that God kept him alive the past forty-five years as He had promised. Caleb was given two divine promises: one, that his life would be prolonged, and the other, that he would someday inherit the territory he had bravely explored near Hebron.

Demystifying Joshua

Caleb's remarks provide important information to help us determine the length of the conquest of Canaan by the Israelites. Caleb states that he was forty years old when he went to spy the land (14:7). Then he adds that the years Israel spent wandering in the wilderness lasted thirty-eight years. Finally, at the time of the conquest, Caleb was eighty-five years old. That tells us that the conquest lasted seven years. This is confirmed by Caleb's reference (14:10) to God's sustaining grace for forty-five years since Kadesh-barnea (thirty-eight years of the wanderings plus seven years of the conquest).

Caleb concludes his speech to Joshua with a very important request: that he and his family be given the same section of land whose inhabitants had struck fear into the hearts of the ten spies so many years before. This was the inheritance he desired. Imagine how meaningful it must have been to see his faith come to fruition forty-five years later. He wants that land as a testimony of God's power and his own faith.

In order to take possession of this particular portion of land, Caleb still has some battles to win. Yet even at eighty-five, he feels as strong and confident in the Lord as he did years before. Thus, Caleb is ready to fight the Anakites at Hebron and take that city for his own inheritance. His faith is steadfast and sincere, and he wants to see God deliver that land to Israel.

A historical note explains that the previous name of Hebron was *Kiriath Arba* (14:15). Arba was a giant among the Anakites, a nation of giants. Yet, although these giants scared most of Israel, they were taken down by God through Caleb, and thus Hebron was renamed. The giants proved no match for God or the faith of His servant Caleb.

Take It Home

The examples of Caleb's faithfulness and God's provision remind us of how mysteriously God often works in the lives of His children—and it also underscores the fact that divine timing is not always what we might expect (2 Peter 3:8). God requires that our hearts be in the right place even when His plan involves years of waiting. In our journey of faith we are often asked to expect good things from God, but the when and the how are not always made clear to us as quickly. Isaiah 40:31 reminds us that "those who trust the Lord will find new strength" (CEV). As you learn to wait on God's provision faithfully, remember to, like Caleb, claim His strength along the way.

JOSHUA 15:1–63

LAND FOR THE TRIBE OF JUDAH

Judah's Land	15:1–12
Caleb's Portion	15:13–19
The Towns of Judah	15:20–63

Setting Up the Section

After Caleb's allotment, Joshua now turns to the distribution of the land for the tribe of Judah. Judah receives the largest portion because they are the largest tribe. In the distribution of the land to Judah, there are some things already spoken by Jacob that have a remarkable bearing on this tribe.

📄 **15:1–12**

JUDAH'S LAND

The great patriarch Jacob had prophesied several specifics concerning his sons. In regard to Judah, Jacob had predicted that his tribe would grow to be strong and fierce because they would be surrounded by their enemies (Genesis 49:8–9). With the land they are given, Judah's tribe is surrounded by the Moabites to the east, Edomites to the south, Amalekites to the southwest, and the Philistines to the west.

Jacob also noted that Judah would be a place flowing with wine and milk (Genesis 49:11–12). The placement of this land is ideally suited for vineyards and cattle. In fact, it was from this region that the spies cut down the huge cluster of grapes (Numbers 13:24).

Jacob also made it clear that Judah was to be a royal line (Genesis 49:10). This prophecy can be understood in two ways. Most immediately, it looks for the rise of kingship in Judah, namely David and his descendants. Also, it looks forward to the coming of the Messiah.

With the allotment of this tribe we begin to see the fulfillment of what Jacob said years ago. If you were looking at the boundaries of this land on a map, you would see that the territory conquered by Joshua in his southern campaign is included in Judah's inheritance (Joshua 10:1–43).

📖 15:13–19

CALEB'S PORTION

This passage is unique in its position. In fact, it seems a bit out of order. It is here, either in anticipation of what will happen later (Judges 1:12–15), or the Judges passage is a flashback to this event. If it is in anticipation of a future event, it is probably included here by the author to bring completeness to the land distribution.

Included in Judah's portion of land is the city of Hebron (Kiriath Arba; 14:15). This city has been granted to Caleb. Caleb has to drive out the Anakites in order to take possession of his land, specifically their three leaders: Sheshai, Ahiman, and Talmai (15:14). These three kings are mentioned earlier (Numbers 13:22) as having been at Hebron when Caleb and the other spies were sent by Moses to scope out the land forty-five years earlier. Do you see the way that God works? Caleb is able to attack and drive out the kings that should have been driven out by a previous generation—a very redemptive victory indeed.

After his victory over Hebron, Caleb turns his attention to the nearby city of Debir (10:38–39; 11:21). Caleb puts an offer out to his men—whoever helps him take this city will be given his daughter Acsah's hand in marriage. Othniel captures the city and he receives Acsah as his wife. Othniel is part of the Kenizzite clan, and he is also Caleb's nephew (15:17), which keeps the land in the family. Othniel is later one of the twelve judges whom God uses in delivering the Israelites from foreign oppressions during difficult years ahead (Judges 3:9–11).

According to the text, Acsah urges someone to seek a piece of land from Caleb. It is not entirely clear who she is asking, but it seems that she is asking her husband, Othniel, to acquire a piece of land for them. This is the second time someone has specifically requested a portion of the land (15:18–19)—ironically, the first had been Caleb. This account is set apart from the rest of the text, forming an aside to the main story.

The text moves abruptly to a conversation between Acsah and Caleb. The father asks his daughter what she wants, and she adds two more things to the land: a blessing and some springs. Natural springs would give her and her new husband the resources to prosper. The Negev is noted as being a place where there is little water. The blessing that she seeks is the special favor of God upon her so that she will truly prosper in the land. Her father, Caleb, complies.

Critical Observation

Many interpret this as a sign of a woman of faith who was seeking what was best for her family. Others have suggested that her request was presumptuous, even greedy. Whatever your opinion of her boldness, this is a very unique moment, and it shows the extreme amount of passion that existed for the Israelites regarding the land. Here was a couple who had fought to conquer the land (and win each other) and then who persisted in expecting God to give them good things.

📄 **15:20–63**

THE TOWNS OF JUDAH

God is clearly providing for each tribe as He promised. But there is one thing in the list that seems to be a contradiction; the number of towns in the Negev is said to be twenty-nine (15:32), but thirty-six are listed (15:21–32). The reason for the difference is that seven of these towns were separated out later and given to Simeon's tribe (19:1–7).

It is interesting to note that Judah inherits well over one hundred cities and occupies almost all of them with little difficulty. The only city that is difficult for them to possess is Jerusalem. The distribution for the tribe of Judah ends on a dark note: Judah could not remove the Jebusites, who were living in Jerusalem (15:63). Was this lack of victory because they simply weren't strong enough, or was it because they failed to trust God? Joshua does not say. Unfortunately, the Jebusites will prove to be a snare for Israel later.

JOSHUA 16:1–17:18

EPHRAIM AND MANASSEH

Setting Up the Section

Years before, while Joseph was away in Egypt, he had two sons: Ephraim and Manasseh. When his father Jacob discovered Joseph was not dead (Genesis 48:21), he included these two children in the blessing of the promised land. In his joy, Jacob brought Ephraim and Manasseh into his direct inheritance. Thus, they were considered heads of tribes with their uncles (Joseph's brothers).

📖 16:1–4

THE SONS OF JOSEPH

The boundary line for the sons of Joseph began in the east, near Jericho, which was north of Judah's boundary. Ephraim's territory does not butt up against Judah, because sandwiched in between Ephraim and Judah is Benjamin. The territory given to Ephraim in Canaan is in many respects the most beautiful and fertile. They are centrally located and have a wonderful piece of land.

The borders outlined here are for the tribes of both Manasseh and Ephraim. The text is giving us the overall picture of what both tribes receive. This overall picture gives us a clearly defined southern border—the area that makes up the southern part of Israel.

Demystifying Joshua

The unified treatment of the two Joseph tribes ends (15:1–4), completing the common southern boundary that separated them from the southern tribes of Benjamin and Judah. From this point on, the boundaries are given for each of Joseph's son's tribes individually, almost foreshadowing how significant this southern border would soon become. The southern border is significant because it marked a real geographical division between the north and south, which already had significant cultural and political ones. It is noteworthy that even at this early stage of being a landed nation, God's people were experiencing some divisions. These divisions surface with a vengeance during the reign of David before Israel and Judea split into two separate nations. You can see in the scriptures where Judah is distinguished from Israel, even before there had been an official split (2 Samuel 2:9–10; 3:10; 4:1). It's possible that hints of this division were already at play when the author was writing the history.

LAND FOR EPHRAIM

The specific allotment for the tribe of Ephraim is located immediately north of the territory to be assigned to Dan and Benjamin. The allotment of Ephraim stretches from the Jordan to the Mediterranean and includes the sites of some of Joshua's battles as well as Shiloh. Shiloh is the sacred place where the tabernacle will remain for close to three hundred years. To foster unity between the two tribes, some of Ephraim's towns are located in the territory of Manasseh (16:9).

Just like the men of Judah, the men of Ephraim do not completely drive out the Canaanites from their region. In fact, they greedily keep the Canaanites around as forced laborers. This provides a labor force for free and fostered economic growth—for a season. Moses had warned the Israelites against failing to drive out the Canaanites (Deuteronomy 20:15–18). Ultimately, this decision proves to be a fatal mistake for the tribe of Ephraim. In the time of the judges, the Canaanites rise up and enslave the Israelites.

LAND FOR MANASSEH

Half of the tribe of Manasseh had settled in the Transjordan region (13:29), while the other half settled in Canaan proper. Machir is Manasseh's firstborn (Genesis 50:23; Numbers 26:29). His descendants represent the half-tribe of Manasseh that had already received a separate portion east of the Jordan, in Gilead and Bashan (Joshua 13:29–31). The rest of Manasseh's allotment is west of the Jordan. The remaining heirs settle in Canaan proper and are given the territory north of Ephraim, extending from the Jordan River to the Mediterranean Sea (17:7–10).

Machir had been given land in Gilead and Bashan. The text refers to him as a "man of war" (17:1); many years later, the same fighting streak would be ascribed to Machir's descendants in Gilead (Numbers 32:39). A portion of Manasseh's descendants inherit the lands east of the Jordan, and this fact forms the backdrop for understanding why the rest of Manasseh's descendants receive their inheritance west of the Jordan (17:2).

The allotment to Manasseh's other descendants was to be west of the Jordan. All six sons are named, and we learn later that all are descendants of Gilead (Numbers 26:30–32). For these six male descendants of Manasseh, Jewish tradition allows them to inherit the land with no problem. Yet one descendant, Zelophehad, a great-great grandson of Manasseh, had already died with no male heirs.

In fact, Zelophehad had five daughters, but no sons. Hebrew culture demands that the inheritance go to the son, not to the daughter. This is because women entered into a new family when they were married and were not able to own land or receive inheritance. The Lord declared that because their father died without any sons, the daughters could receive his inheritance (Numbers 27:1–11). The only requirement is that they not marry outside the tribe so that the land would not switch out to another tribe.

These girls go to the high priest Eleazar (Aaron's son; 24:33), who with Joshua and the tribal leaders oversee the allotments to the tribes (19:51). These five women receive their portion within the territory of Manasseh. This incident shows God's concern for the rights of women at a time when most societies regarded them as mere chattel. God was committed to being fair with the entire tribe—men and women. God's faithfulness to the women reminds us that a custom should never be held to such a degree that it hurts the very people it was intended to protect.

Critical Observation

The daughters' names and Zelophehad's genealogy are carefully recorded (17:3) to show the legal legitimacy of their claim. It was important to keep all the division of the land legal to prevent any misunderstandings or misinterpretations arising from confused identities in the future. The details with which the tribes' boundaries and cities are recorded extend down to the inheritance for individuals because this was God's gift to the whole nation. The daughters presented their case to Eleazar, the priest, and Joshua precisely for this reason. With their approval, no one could take this land away from this family.

This text reinforces the point stated that daughters could—and indeed did—inherit land, under the conditions mentioned (Numbers 27). Their portion was fair and allowed this line of Manasseh to be cared for in the new land. Manasseh's actual inheritance is outlined, but just general boundaries are given (17:7–10)—including a few cities that outline the boundary list properly. Two cities in its boundary description became Levitical cities: Shechem (17:2, 7; 21:21) and Taanach (17:11; 21:25).

Several cities located in the tribes of Issachar and Asher are given to Manasseh (17:12–13). Apparently it is considered necessary for military purposes that these cities be held by a strong tribe. The sons of Manasseh, like the Ephraimites, however, choose tribute over triumph: Rather than driving out the Canaanites, they enslave them. This proves to be a major issue for Israel in the future. Going outside God's instruction can be deadly.

📖 17:14–18

THE COMPLAINT

In this passage, the sons of Joseph speak as one (16:4 and 17:14). These two tribes are discontented with their allotted territory, challenging Joshua for more land. The episode unfolds through two verbal exchanges between Joshua and the tribes (17:14–15, 16–18). This is the fourth narrative of people wanting to talk about land.

Joshua handles their complaint with skill. He challenges them to clear the trees and settle in the forested hill country (17:15). He suggests that they combine their energies to drive out the Canaanites (17:18). This shows how much land there is yet to possess. Joshua's advice is wise—if they need more land, then they should clear out land from the forests where the Perizzites and Rephaites live. In short, there is more land; they just need to possess it.

This complaint evidences a degree of arrogance and greed in the Joseph tribes' confrontation with Joshua. Compare this attitude with the tone of Caleb (14:6–12) and the daughters of Zelophehad (17:4). In both instances, the requests are made based on the

Lord's promises. The sons of Joseph had no promise to appeal to. Instead, they were just dissatisfied with what God had provided for them. At the heart of this is more than just a complaint against Joshua—it's a complaint against God.

The response of the sons of Joseph further reveals their hearts. They say that the entire hill country is not enough and that they fear the Canaanites. Thus we see that their faith is weak. God had promised to give them the land and told them to trust in Him as their deliverer. At this point, the sons of Joseph are not trusting in God. Joshua agrees that they should have more land, but that they must take the hill country and drive out the Canaanites.

Take It Home

The sons of Joseph had a remarkable lack of faith. Their pride backed them into a corner and the result was fear. The point to see here is that without faith in God, it is impossible to take the promised land. The ten spies learned this in Numbers 13 and 14, and now the sons of Joseph are learning the same lesson. What are the things that frighten you? How can you learn to trust God, unlike the sons of Joseph, to provide all you need?

JOSHUA 18:1–28

THE ALLOTMENT OF THE REST OF THE LAND

The Nation Prepares to Settle	18:1–10
The Allotment for Benjamin	18:11–28

Setting Up the Section

The context of chapter 18 is very simple. There are still seven tribes that need to receive their allotment. The story now reaches a turning point in the land distribution lists for the nation of Israel. The nation is now moving to Shiloh. It is at this new location that the Tent of Meeting is mentioned for the first time in the book. The Tent of Meeting is going to be set up in a place where the presence of God will be close to the center of the entire nation.

📖 **18:1–10**

THE NATION PREPARES TO SETTLE

Prior to this point, Israel's central encampment in the land appears to have been at Gilgal, near Jericho. It is at this camp where the nation observes several ceremonies (4:19–20; 5:2–12) worth commemorating. Now the people are moved about fifteen miles northwest of Jericho to Shiloh. This place will remain an important Israelite religious center for several hundred years. In fact, it will remain the center of religious worship until the taking of Jerusalem by David (2 Samuel 5–6).

The tabernacle was a large portable tent where the presence of God dwelt when the Israelites were in the wilderness. In it was the ark of the covenant as well as other holy items that were to be kept clean and sacred. It was made of fine boards that were covered with layers of fabrics according to specific instructions given to Moses by God (Exodus 26).

Demystifying Joshua

Joshua calls the land "a land which the God of your fathers has given you" (18:3). The phrase "your fathers" refers to the patriarchs of Israel: Abraham, Isaac, and Jacob. This expression, "the God of your fathers," was an important one, for it had a rich history in Israel. God used it with Moses at the burning bush (Exodus 3:13). Moses used it often in Deuteronomy when he would speak to the people (1:11; 4:1; 6:3; 21:1; 27:3). This is the first time we see it in Joshua, and it reminds the nation of the historical importance of this moment. God had made a promise a long time ago that He has now fulfilled (Genesis 12:7; 15:18–21; 26:3–4; 28:4, 13; 35:12).

To begin the process of dividing the rest of the land, Joshua instructs that three men from each of the seven remaining tribes be appointed as surveyors. The role of these surveyors will be to travel throughout the land and record its description (18:4). They are to write down their findings. This is highlighted three times (18:4, 6, 8); God is making sure that all generations will know the land division.

The previous allotments are reviewed to remind the remaining people how God has provided for all the people of Israel (18:5–7). The Lord was with the nation, not only in the tabernacle, but also in the casting of lots for the remaining allotments. The Levites' special inheritance is important, so Joshua mentions it again. He will make sure that those set apart for God's service are cared for and given everything they need.

📖 18:11–28

THE ALLOTMENT FOR BENJAMIN

Of the seven remaining tribes, Benjamin's allotment is given in the most detail (eighteen verses). This is probably because Benjamin's geographical location is between Judah on the south and Joseph (Ephraim) on the north.

Benjamin's northern boundary is the same as the Joseph tribes' southern boundary (16:1–4). Every place mentioned in this passage is found already in 16:1–5, except for the desert of Beth Aven. Beth Aven is between Jericho and Bethel, but its exact location is not fully known. Benjamin's southern boundary is given in the most detail in this passage. This is no doubt because it is bordered by Judah. Judah is the most prominent of all the tribes.

Critical Observation

Several of the cities mentioned in Joshua's lists have the same name as others. Therefore it is important not to confuse the cities. Ophrah (18:23) is also found in Manasseh (Judges 6:24; 8:27). Ramah (18:25) is also found in Asher's northern border (Joshua 19:29), in Naphtali's territory (19:36), and in Simeon's territory (19:8). The name *Ramah* means "height," and for this reason it is not unreasonable that several cities shared that name. Mizpah (18:26) is found in Judah (15:38). Gibeah (18:27) is also found in Judah (15:57).

JOSHUA 19:1–51
THE REST OF THE LAND

Allotment for Simeon	19:1–9
Allotment for Zebulun	19:10–16
Allotment for Issachar	19:17–23
Allotment for Asher	19:24–31
Allotment for Naphtali	19:32–39
Allotment for Dan	19:40–48
Joshua's Allotment	19:49–51

Setting Up the Section

Joshua is now ready to allot the rest of the land to the remaining tribes. God deals with each tribe according to their lot.

📖 19:1–9

ALLOTMENT FOR SIMEON

The tribe of Simeon's inheritance is unique because they are not given an independent allotment, but rather receive land scattered within Judah's allotment. Judah's portion was more than they needed (19:9). Simeon's tribe was small relative to Judah's (1 Chronicles 4:27).

Jacob's prophecy describes why Simeon does not inherit any land. Simeon and Levi are brothers who were bent toward violence. Both men committed acts of violence against the inhabitants of Shechem, when they annihilated every man in the city while the men were recuperating from circumcision (Genesis 34:24–30). Simeon and Levi's landless status is a punishment for their taking violent, personal vengeance against the men of Shechem.

Critical Observation

The tribe of Levi is favored by the Lord. They received a special inheritance far greater than Simeon's. Forty-eight cities throughout the land were all components of their inheritance (chapter 21). One possible reason God deals with these two tribes differently is that the Levites vindicated themselves in the episode involving the golden calf. When Moses discovered the golden calf, he called those who believed in the Lord to follow him, and only the Levites responded (Exodus 32:26). Moses then told the Levites to kill the offenders among them, which they did, killing about three thousand people. Therefore, Moses blessed the Levites and declared them to be set apart to the Lord (Exodus 32:27–29).

Simeon's cities fall into two groups: thirteen cities in the southern portion, the Negev (19:2–6), and four additional cities—two in the Negev and two in the western foothills, the Shephelah (19:7). One additional city in the far south is mentioned (19:8) for a total of eighteen. It is not long before Simeon loses its individual identity as a tribe, as the scattered people become incorporated into the tribe of Judah. As this incorporation begins, many in the tribe of Simeon migrate north to Ephraim and Manasseh (2 Chronicles 15:9; 34:6).

📖 19:10–16

ALLOTMENT FOR ZEBULUN

Zebulun's lot is cast third, and it is the first of five small tribes in the north whose territories are now listed. The text provides very few details about the inheritance of these five smaller tribes beyond standard boundary and city lists for each. Zebulun was a small tribe whose territory nestled between Issachar, western Manasseh, Asher, and Naphtali. According to Jacob's prophecy, Zebulun would live by the seashore and become a haven for ships. In this text we see that Zebulun is assigned land in lower Galilee. This land extends to the Mediterranean Sea, forming an enclave in Issachar's territory.

Demystifying Joshua

The city named *Bethlehem* mentioned here is not the same as the one in Judah—famous for being the birthplace of the Messiah (Judges 17:7; Ruth 1:1; 1 Samuel 16:1; Micah 5:2; Matthew 2:1). Rather, it is in Zebulun, the site where Ibzan, the judge, is buried (Judges 12:8–10). Three cities within Zebulun's boundaries later became Levitical cities: Jokneam (Joshua 19:11; 21:34), Nahalal (19:15; 21:35), and Daberath (19:12; 21:28).

ALLOTMENT FOR ISSACHAR

Issachar is the second small tribe in the north, in the region of Galilee. Its boundary description consists of only three cities (19:22), and its city list contains thirteen cities. Issachar's general location is clear: It is north of western Manasseh, east and south of Zebulun, west of the Jordan, and south of Naphtali.

ALLOTMENT FOR ASHER

The tribe of Asher's territory lay in a long, narrow strip in the far northwest. The land is bordered on the west by the Mediterranean Sea and the tribe of Zebulun, and on the east by Manasseh's western boundary. This territory, by virtue of its position, serves as a major land of protection from northern coastal enemies (including, for example, the Phoenicians). By the time David is king, this tribe had lost much of its significance. One significant fact connects this tribe to the Messiah; Anna, the prophetess who blesses Jesus, is from this tribe (Luke 2:36–38).

ALLOTMENT FOR NAPHTALI

Naphtali receives the rich, forested land in the heart of the Galilee region. Asher is to the west, Zebulun to the south, and the Jordan River and eastern Manasseh to the east. This region does not play a highly significant role in the Old Testament period. Yet in the New Testament, this is the region where Jesus centers His Galilean ministry. It is in this region where Jesus fulfills the prophecy of Isaiah (Isaiah 9:1).

Naphtali's allotment includes a list of fortified cities (Joshua 19:35). To be fortified means that these cities were built up with strong fortresses and surrounding walls. This layer of protection was necessary, because a branch of an international trade route from Egypt to Mesopotamia ran through the territory of Naphtali. The city of Hazor guarded a section of that important route. Because of these well-protected cities, the tribe of Naphtali enjoys periods of prosperity, especially when Israel's kings are strong.

ALLOTMENT FOR DAN

The final lot is cast for the tribe of Dan. The Danites' territorial allotment is in the south, abutting Judah and other tribes. Yet they are listed in this chapter with the northern tribes in Galilee. They are unable to take their own land, so they move north and attack the city of Leshem, which is opposite of the northern part of Naphtali, and settle there (Genesis 49:17; Judges 1:34; 18). Thus they are included among these smaller tribes with allotments in Galilee, because this is where they eventually settled.

JOSHUA'S ALLOTMENT

Caleb's inheritance is settled first (14:6–15); Joshua's is last. Joshua evidently wanted to make sure that his work had been accomplished before he would take what belonged to him. He allows all of the land to be distributed and takes from what is left over. In no way does he exercise his position for selfish gain; his choice of land demonstrates his humility.

Joshua asks for Timnath Serah, a region that promised to be difficult to settle because of its rugged mountainous terrain. The region is within the allotment of his own tribe of Ephraim. Joshua could have taken land in the fairest and most productive area of Canaan, but he did not. Instead, he chooses an area that may otherwise have been overlooked and builds from the ground up. Joshua had an amazingly wide skill set. He is a wise military leader, a fair chief administrator, and now we see that he is also a skilled builder.

God grants Joshua his own personal inheritance. Both of the faithful spies, Caleb and Joshua, have not only entered the land, but they both also receive special portions in it. Yet only Joshua is given his own city. No other Israelite receives any inheritance in this way—not even Caleb. Joshua is an extraordinary leader who is blessed by God.

The most difficult work has been accomplished; the land has been conquered, and the regions have been distributed. All that remains is the marking out of cities for the Levites and the establishment of cities of refuge. Now that the greatest work is behind them, the people are finally in possession of the promised land. Their faithful and powerful God has made good on His promise to their forefathers (19:51).

JOSHUA 20:1–9

CITIES OF REFUGE

A Place of Grace	20:1–6
Cities of Refuge	20:7–9

Setting Up the Section

God knows that all murder should not be treated in the same manner; thus He commands the Israelites to set up cities of refuge for people who have accidentally killed another person.

A PLACE OF GRACE

The instructions governing the cities of refuge are based upon legislation established by Moses. In the Pentateuch, the Israelites were instructed that six cities should be established within their nation as cities of refuge, where a man could flee if he accidentally kills someone (Exodus 21:12–14). The all-knowing God of the Israelites recognizes that people are often victims of the fallen world in which they live. These cities provided a place where people could flee if they had accidentally murdered someone—they were establishments of grace and mercy in a nation where murderers were normally condemned to death.

The Israelites were instructed to select six cities, three on each side of the Jordan (Numbers 35:9–29). Thus Moses had established three cities for the tribes east of the Jordan (Deuteronomy 4:41–43). He had also given instructions that the same should be done with three cities west of the Jordan (Deuteronomy 19:1–10). By establishing these cities, the law is making distinctions in degrees of guilt. God's law recognizes that motive or intention set some murders apart from accidents, and He makes gracious provisions for such cases.

A man who flees to one of these cities is to state his case before the elders of the city. The elders have the power to return him to his original city and into the hands of the blood avenger (Deuteronomy 19:12). When the refugee's story is credible, innocence is presumed, and the refugees are able to live in the city under the protection of the elders. The refugee is to remain in this city until he has a chance to make his case and defend his innocence, and also until the reigning high priest dies (20:6). Then he is free to return home with no fear of being executed. There is still a consequence for the accidental killing—refugees are bound to their city of refuge—yet their lives are spared.

Demystifying Joshua

Some suggest that refugees had to wait for the death of the high priest before returning home, because the high priest represented the sacrificial system and his death atoned for the sins of the manslayer. No ransom was to be accepted for a murderer or for a manslayer (Numbers 35:30–31). In this rule, God allowed for there to be proper justice (one life for another) for the death. The justice of Old Testament law was taken even further by Jesus Christ in His famous Sermon on the Mount, when He called believers to sacrifice themselves, turn the other cheek, and love their enemies for the sake of the gospel (Matthew 5:38–42).

📖 20:7–9

CITIES OF REFUGE

No place in the land was more than a day's journey from one of these cities of refuge. All six of these cities are mentioned again in the next chapter, since they also were Levitical cities. Despite their importance here and in the Pentateuch, however, they do not appear again in the Old Testament. The six designated cities were located on both sides of the Jordan River. On the west side were Kedesh in Galilee, Shechem in Ephraim, and Hebron in Judah. The cities on the east side were Bezer in the south, Ramoth in the region of Gilead in the tribe of Gad, and Golan in the northern territory of Bashan in Manasseh's tribe.

Take It Home

God takes justice very seriously—consider the example He made of Achan (chapter 7). Yet He is also abounding in love and aware of the challenges that are present in this world. The God of the Old Testament is often considered harsh and unloving, and yet this is the same God who sends His Son to make the ultimate sacrifice for sinful people. This passage reminds us that the God of the Bible is the same throughout all time. As you consider the grace and mercy exemplified in these cities of refuge, consider how God has called you to give grace and mercy to those refugees that come into your world. Also, remember that Christ's standards of justice call each of us to follow His example and sacrifice vengeance for mercy as a means of witnessing the gospel to our enemies.

JOSHUA 21:1–45

CITIES FOR THE LEVITES

Setting Up the Section

The Levites are not to possess land but are to be given cities and pasturelands to raise their families and care for their cattle (Numbers 35:1–8). They are to be set apart to the Lord for the service to God.

📖 21:1–3

THE FINAL TASK

The last act of distribution is now taking place. Because the Levites are not given an allotment of their own territory, they are scattered (like Simeon's tribe; see 19:1–9). The Levite's inheritance is the honor that they have been set apart to serve God. The call to service is a gift greater than wealth or territory, and the Levites are reminded here to treasure what God has already blessed them with so abundantly.

The leaders of the tribe of Levi claim the towns that had been promised to them by Moses. These forty-eight towns with pasturelands, including the six towns of refuge, are now assigned to the Levites and are the final act of laying claim to the land.

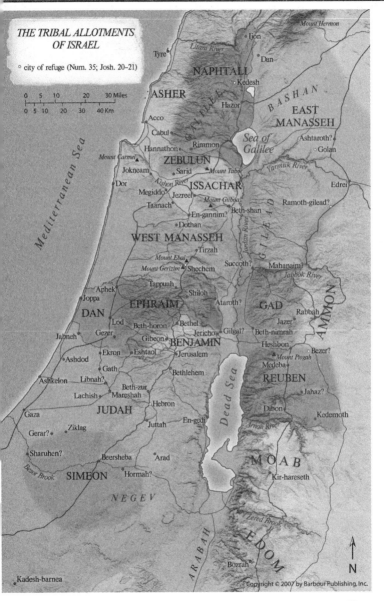

THE TRIBAL ALLOTMENTS
OF ISRAEL

∘ city of refuge (Num. 35; Josh. 20–21)

0 5 10   20   30 Miles
0 5 10   20   30   40 Km

Copyright © 2007 by Barbour Publishing, Inc.

📖 21:4–42

PROVISION FOR GOD'S SERVANTS

The distribution takes place according to the three main branches of the tribe of Levi. These three main branches correspond to Levi's three sons: Kohath, Gershon, and Merari. This detail is included to show the reader that not one aspect of God's promise is missed. Every clan of every branch receives what was promised—God does fulfill His promises. This should give us great hope as we consider the future promises waiting for us in heaven (1 Peter 1:3–9; Revelation 19–22).

Thirteen towns for the Kohathites are listed first (21:8–19). Nine are in the territory belonging to the tribes of Judah and Simeon. Hebron is listed as a city of refuge because the Levites are responsible for these cities. Ten more cities, including Shechem (another city of refuge), are listed (21:20–26). These cities are assigned to the other branches of the Kohathites in Ephraim, Dan, and western Manasseh. The priestly cities fall primarily within the southern kingdom of Judah. It is in the southern region where the temple will be built in Jerusalem, so it makes sense for the Levites to be nearby.

Critical Observation

To understand the distribution described here, it is important to be reminded of the history of the Levites. The tribe of Levi was cursed by Jacob (Genesis 49:5, 7) for their senseless murder of the Shechemites (Genesis 34). God overruled this curse in Levi's descendants to preserve their tribal identity and make them a blessing to all Israel, because the Levites stood with Moses when the rest of the tribes desired to worship at the feet of the golden calf (Exodus 32:26). God was also pleased with Phinehas (a Levite and Eleazar's son) because he vindicated God's righteous name in the plains of Moab (Numbers 25).

To have the Levites dispersed within the land is a great blessing for the nation. The Levites are to instruct Israel in the law of the Lord, to maintain the knowledge of His Word among the people. The blessing of this inheritance allows the nation to have the constant reminder and the continual discipleship of the way of God. God is, in essence, sending His ministers all throughout the land to build up, protect, and equip all generations in the way of the Lord.

No one in Israel lives more than ten miles from one of the forty-eight Levite cities. This means that every Israelite has access to one of God's men who could shepherd the people. Keep in mind that for the nation to stay in the land, they must obey God (Leviticus 26). God provides the shepherd and leadership that the people need to obey the Lord.

📖 21:43–45

GOD'S FAITHFULNESS

God was, as He always is, faithful to His promise. Not one aspect of God's promise to the nation of Israel is unfulfilled. Looking back to the beginning of the Israelites' journey out of Egypt, through the wilderness years, and now into the conquest and possession of the promised land, Joshua is impressed by the theme that resonates through each experience in the nation's history: God always keeps His promise. God had kept His promise to give Israel the land, rest from their wanderings, and victory over their enemies.

Critical Observation

Though God had fulfilled His promises, every corner of the land was not yet in Israel's control. God had told Israel they would conquer the land gradually (Deuteronomy 7:22). Additionally, God's faithfulness does not guarantee that the people will not walk away from Him in the future. The unfaithfulness of Israel is not dependent in any way on the faithfulness of God. Even though Israel would fail God in the future, God remained faithful.

JOSHUA 22:1–34

HOME TO THE EAST

Service	22:1–8
Misunderstanding	22:9–20
Seeking Peace	22:21–29
Peace Preserved	22:30–34

Setting Up the Section

As the eastern tribes returned home and got settled, something occurred that almost disrupted the unity of the nation. The eastern tribes acted so inappropriately that a civil war almost overtook the newly formed nation. In the midst of this tension, God protected the nation and taught them some serious lessons about true worship.

📄 **22:1–8**

SERVICE

The eastern tribes of Reuben, Gad, and the half-tribe of Manasseh have served the rest of the nation and fought alongside their brothers. Now it is time for them to return to their land. Joshua praises them for their efforts and for their commitment to their promise—to fight with the rest of the nation before they took their land (Numbers 32; Joshua 1:16–18; 4:12–14). They had been faithfully fighting for seven years, and during this time they had been away from their family and their homes. These men are being honored for their service.

Leaving for home, the men from the eastern tribes take with them much of the spoils from the enemy. They are instructed to share the spoils with those who remained at home to care for and protect the land (22:8). The rule that is being established here surfaces again in the history of the Israelites (1 Samuel 30:24). The principle is that those who serve in support of war but who do not actually do the fighting are able to share in the full spoils of war. Support roles are of equal importance.

The returning soldiers are given six commands by Joshua before they leave: First, be very careful to keep the commandment and the law. Second, love the Lord your God. Third, walk in all His ways. Fourth, keep His commands. Fifth, cling to Him. And finally, serve Him with all your heart and all your soul. The message is that just because their military commitment to God is complete, their spiritual commitment is not. In exchange for their service, God promised that they will be allowed to stay in the land to the east. God desires for His people to have a heart to work and fight for Him and love and serve those around them (Micah 6:8).

22:9–20

MISUNDERSTANDING

As the eastern tribes return to their new home, the realization hits them that they will be separated from their brothers on the other side of the Jordan. This creates fear of what this separation might cause them. The mountains that surround the river rise to heights above two thousand feet. The Jordan Valley is a huge trench, five to thirteen miles wide. When it is hot, this valley becomes impassable. Thus, the Jordan River creates a difficult barrier that truly does separate the eastern tribes from the rest of Israel. The eastern tribes become afraid that this separation will cause the next generation to be excluded from the worship of the Lord.

The solution to this problem is to build a huge altar, one that can be seen from a great distance. This will keep the worship of God front and center for all generations. The eastern tribes erect such an altar on the Israelite (western) side of the Jordan River. The motive that drives these men is the fact that they prioritize the worship of God, and they know that the true basis of their unity is their common worship of the one true God.

The act of building this altar is interpreted as an act of apostasy. The rest of the tribes of the western side of the border meet at Shiloh. This is significant because this is where the one true altar is located. It is here that they decide to go to war against the armies of the eastern tribes. They conclude that this new altar is rebellion against God. From their perspective they believe that the others have set up a second altar of sacrifice contrary to the Mosaic Law (Leviticus 17:8–9).

The western tribes believe that if their brethren are going to mock God and set up an alternate place of worship, then they will go to war to defend the integrity of worship. As difficult as this must have been, the rest of the tribes are prepared to go to war against their own brothers. Eleazar's son, Phinehas, is passionate for the Lord (Numbers 25:6–18). He heads a force to confront the eastern tribes.

God has always treated rebellion with severe consequences, and the leaders know that obedience to Him is very important (Joshua 22:20). Phinehas warns the people of the eastern tribes that they are in jeopardy because of apparent rebellion. He then offers a solution to the problem: If the land east of the Jordan is defiled because of this altar, the western tribes will make room for their brethren on their side of the Jordan. They take the holiness of God seriously enough to relocate these two and a half tribes in order to help them walk with God.

SEEKING PEACE

Notice that the eastern tribes do not fight back or act in a defensive manner. Rather, the eastern tribes respond with humility to the charge that the altar they erected is in rebellion against God. They present their hearts before God as a witness and they swear twice by His three names—El, Elohim, Yahweh (the Mighty One, God, the Lord), strongly stating that if their act was in rebellion against God and His commands then they deserved His judgment. Despite their initial misunderstanding, we see in this account that both tribes handle this situation correctly—with humility and a willingness to listen.

The eastern tribes make it clear that they are fully aware of God's laws governing worship. The point of this altar is not to replace the place for burnt offerings, but instead it is intended to show all generations that the eastern tribes have the right to worship God with the western tribes; in short, they are a part of the community.

Critical Observation

Every generation loses the heart and the understanding of the first generation. Inevitably the battle wounds, lessons, and wisdom of the past must be relearned again and again by the younger people. It is important to make sure that things are in place to help protect future generations, to remind them of history's lessons. It is not unreasonable to assume the next generation will have a breakdown because pride and conflict are sewn within the sin nature that all humans carry around in them.

God ordains the law that all Israelite males are to appear at the sanctuary three times a year (Exodus 23:17). Thus, what they erect is not necessary. This law preserves the unity of all the tribes if followed. God had already anticipated this problem and put in place a way of avoiding it. The bigger concern of this altar would have been that rather than driving people to the real altar at Shiloh, it would replace it; though this was not the heart of those who erected it.

PEACE PRESERVED

The explanation of the eastern tribes is fully accepted by Phinehas and his delegation. Indeed, this response causes the western tribes to rejoice and praise God. Phinehas expresses joy and thankfulness that no sin has been committed and that the wrath of God is not going to be called down upon their eastern brothers.

Take It Home

Look for God's solution rather than picking your own fight. Sometimes things appear one way and yet turn out to be another. We don't always interpret the people around us appropriately, so it is important to seek understanding and peace before launching into conflict. Israel learned a lesson about listening. What appeared as a separation was really an act of unity. One person can do one thing to keep unity, and someone else may interpret it as an act of separation and rebellion. God's children need to commit to communication.

JOSHUA 23:1–16

JOSHUA'S CHARGE

| Be On Your Guard | 23:1–8 |
| Disobedience Has Consequences | 23:9–16 |

Setting Up the Section

Joshua ends with his farewell address. His parting words express his deep concern for a potential danger emerging in Israel—a growing complacency on the part of Israel toward the remnants of the Canaanites. Joshua feels compelled to warn the people that obedience to God is essential to His blessing, including enjoying all the fruits of the land.

📖 23:1–8

BE ON YOUR GUARD

Some years after the end of the conquest and distribution of the land, Joshua summons Israel's leaders, probably to Shiloh where the tabernacle is located. This gathering serves a very serious and solemn purpose—to warn the leaders of the dangers of not taking God and His commands seriously.

Joshua has one theme that he repeats three times: God has been faithful to Israel, so Israel must serve and obey Him all the days of their lives (23:3–8, 9–13, 14–16). There is no more important message for followers of God in any age. God must be taken seriously, obedience must be a way of life, and sin must be treated as an abomination to the Lord.

Joshua reminds the people that their enemies have been defeated solely because the Lord had fought for them. The battles that they fought were the Lord's, and God provided the victories. Scripture tells us repeatedly that every good and perfect thing we have is from God (James 1:17).

Joshua reminds the leaders that the Lord will push the Canaanites, who are still scattered throughout the country, out of the land entirely if they rely on God. God remains committed to creating their nation if they rely on His strength, and He has promised to enable them to carry out the task of taking full possession of the land.

All leaders are called to establish for the next generation what God has taught them. Joshua passes on to the next generation the very words that he was instructed with at the beginning of His time as leader of Israel: Be strong and courageous and careful to obey (1:6–9). Courage and obedience are the virtues that led to the success of conquering Canaan, and they are no less essential now (22:5). Joshua is also concerned about Israel's conformity to the people around them. For this reason, he forbids all contact and marriage with these nations. Joshua knows that his people will walk away from God if they become engaged with the nations around them.

This is the very definition of complacency—once a person becomes comfortable with sin, it becomes easier to fall headlong into a sinful way of living rather than remaining sensitive to the Spirit of God. Knowing this, Joshua wants to make sure that the leaders take obedience to God seriously.

📄 23:9–16

DISOBEDIENCE HAS CONSEQUENCES

To make sure that they understand the seriousness of this, Joshua reminds the leaders that God will not tolerate a nation that mingles with the sin of the Canaanites. God is faithful, but if the Israelites unite themselves with the Canaanites in sin, God will not bless them with His strength.

At the heart of Joshua's message is the reminder of the faithfulness of God and the command to love Him with all their hearts (22:5). The type of love that Joshua speaks of requires diligence and watchfulness. The Israelites must keep an eye on their hearts, because they are in the presence of corruption.

Take It Home

This is true for all of God's followers. Believers must remember that loving the things of this world is the same as loving what God has sent His Son to transform. God loves sinners for the express purpose of changing them—not keeping them in their state of depravity, but bringing them into right relationship with Him. To use the grace and mercy of God to pursue sin is to treat God with contempt.

Israel's greatest danger was not military; it was spiritual. The key to the success of Israel was not in their strength but in how dedicated they were to the will and glory of God. This is true for us today as well.

JOSHUA 24:1–33

THE COVENANT RENEWED

Setting Up the Section

Joshua's last meeting with the people takes place at Shechem. In this significant city, Israel's covenant with God is renewed.

📖 24:1–13

GOD'S WORDS REVIEWED

Shechem is the place where Abraham first received the promise that God would give his seed the land of Canaan. Abraham responds by building an altar to demonstrate his faith in the one true God (Genesis 12:6–7). Jacob, too, stops at Shechem on his return from Paddan Aram and buries the idols his family had brought with them (Genesis 35:4). After the Israelites complete the first phase of the conquest of Canaan, they journey to Shechem where Joshua builds an altar to Yahweh, inscribes the law of God on stone pillars, and reviews these laws for all the people (Joshua 8:30–35).

Critical Observation

The location is one of importance, because this spot symbolizes the covenant that God made with Israel. Consider what would be in this location: The stones on which the law had been written were still there reminding people of their theological heritage and that their calling as a nation serves something higher than just being a nation. They serve the one true God to whom all the glory for their victory is owed. This place had been dedicated as the spot for worshiping the Lord and remembering His holiness.

Joshua is reminding the people what God Himself has said. In other words, this is God speaking to the people, reviewing with them what He has done and reminding them what lies at the heart of their covenant. First, He brought them out of Ur of the Chaldees (24:2–4). Then, they were delivered out of the bondage to Gentile worship and brought to the land of blessing. Next, they were brought out of Egypt (24:5–7) and into Canaan (24:8–13). Again, they were delivered from the bondage and slavery of the Egyptians and brought to the freedom of the promised land.

God uses "I" eighteen times to underscore that these good things, these amazing deliverances and victories, were performed by Him and not the Israelites. God is the

One who pulled them out of every mess, out of every conflict, and out of every problem. God is the One who delivered them from all of their trials and the One who brought them into the land flowing with milk and honey.

Any greatness, prosperity, or blessing that Israel ever received was not by her own effort but through God's grace and power. From the first call of Abram, to the conquest, to the present moment, everything they have and all that they are is because of God's good mercies.

THE RESPONSIBILITY

Israel must fear the Lord and serve Him. Joshua personalizes this command, saying that whatever the leader's choice is in regard to serving God, his own mind was made up. He declares, "But as for me and my household, we will serve the LORD" (24:15 NIV).

The initial response of the people is good. They are still so close to the time of the conquest that they despise the very thought of forsaking God. They had the firsthand experience of being delivered by God.

But Joshua is not at all satisfied with their verbal commitment. He knows the human heart and how people can easily be led astray, and he knows how deceptive sin can be. He is quite aware that an emotional commitment made at a moment in time does not mean as much as it might appear. Joshua bluntly declares to the Israelite leadership that they are not able to serve the Lord. He is a holy God and a jealous God. He will not forgive their rebellion and their sins.

Joshua does not mean that God is not a God of forgiveness. He means that God is not to be worshiped or served lightly. To forsake Him deliberately and to serve idols will be willful sin against God, and to sin in this manner under their circumstances will be unforgivable under the law (Numbers 15:30). This type of sin will result in disaster. Again the people respond to Joshua's probing words, earnestly reaffirming their purpose to serve the Lord.

Joshua speaks a third time and calls Israel to serve as witnesses against themselves if they do turn aside from God. The people immediately reply "yes." Joshua then speaks a fourth and final time, coming again to the point he had mentioned at the beginning—that they must get rid of their idols. They have already begun the slow and steady slide to disobedience. Joshua challenges them to prove their sincerity by their works and get rid of the idols. It is interesting to note that without the slightest hesitation, the people shout, "We will serve the LORD our God. We will obey him alone" (24:24 NLT).

There can be no mixing of allegiance to God with idol worship. Every generation has to make this decision in life—*Will we be completely committed to God, or will we adopt the practices of the nations around us?* Every individual today must also make a strong commitment to serve the Lord above anything or anyone else.

24:25–28

THE REMINDER

Joshua makes a covenant with the people this day. He writes down their agreement in the book of the law of God, which is probably placed beside the ark of the covenant (Deuteronomy 31:24–27).

As a final reminder, Joshua also inscribes the statutes of the covenant on a large stone slab, which is set up beneath the oak at this sacred location. Joshua says that the stone is a witness to this covenant. It bears the words of the covenant for all generations to see.

All of this again underscores the seriousness with which God is to be taken. Fast-forward to the book of Micah, and one will see the great cost the nation pays for completely rejecting God.

24:29–33

GOD KEEPS HIS PROMISE

Three burials—each of them in Ephraim—mark the close of the book of Joshua. First it is recorded that Joshua dies at the age of 110 years. He is buried in his own town (19:50). No greater tribute can be paid to him than the fact that he is called the servant of the Lord. Such should be the highest goal of every person who lives.

The burial of Joseph's bones is also recorded. Joseph's dying request was that he be buried in the promised land (Genesis 50:25). Moses, knowing of this request, took Joseph's bones with him in the Exodus (Exodus 13:19). Finally, Joseph's remains, which had been embalmed in Egypt more than four hundred years earlier, are laid to rest in Shechem (Genesis 33:18–20; 50:26).

The third burial mentioned is that of the high priest Eleazar, son and successor of Aaron. These burials testify to the faithfulness of God. Joshua, Joseph, and Eleazar once lived in a foreign nation where they received God's promise to take His people back to Canaan. Now all three are laid to rest within the promised land. God kept His word to these men, just as He had kept His promise to the Israelites.

Take It Home

The responsibility to serve God is a great gift, not a burden. The call to the Israelites to serve God comes after the great blessings of life, freedom, and autonomy. Our service is a response to His love, kindness, and mercy. Therefore, God's call in our life, like the command of Joshua, should be seen as the only appropriate response to the gift of freedom. God is faithful with all of His children to the end.

JUDGES

INTRODUCTION TO JUDGES

The book of Judges gets its name from its main characters: the people God graciously selected to save ancient Israel from itself. It tells the stories of colorful and imperfect individuals with charismatic qualities God uses to break the yoke of oppression that Israel experienced, time after time, as a result of its own sinfulness. Through these types of saviors, God calls His children back to Himself.

AUTHOR

Although Samuel was traditionally thought to be the author of Judges, no one knows who put it together. Experts say it could have been a single author, because the material is well-shaped into a coherent whole; or there may have been more than one compiler.

PURPOSE

Judges is a compilation of selected independent stories, mostly centered on one individual. But there is one overall message: Israel's repetitive cycle of sin, and God's consistent and merciful response.

THEMES

In Judges we see Israel's continual cycle of unfaithfulness:
1) Obedience to the law of God
2) Moral complacency
3) Moral compromise as a result of their complacency
4) A falling away from their faith and religious roots
5) Oppression from other nations as their weakening faith results in a weakened nation
6) Deliverance from these consequences and a temporary return to faith

It is in the deliverance that God provides at the turn of each cycle that reveals His righteousness, mercy, and long-suffering nature. The individuals God chooses, though certainly imperfect deliverers, can be seen as temporary models of the great deliverance that will one day come through Jesus, the perfect and permanent deliverer of the people of God.

HISTORICAL CONTEXT

Judges is known as one of the books of the "former prophets," and it reveals God working throughout the history of His people. The book covers approximately 350 years, from the time of Joshua's death until the rise of Samuel, the last judge before the kings of Israel begin to lead as the formal monarchy is established.

The era that Judges recounts is a period of transition—from the conquest of Canaan in the latter part of the thirteenth century to the beginning of the monarchy with King Saul, perhaps in 1020 BC. There is a direct correlation between the decisions Israel makes during these centuries and her downfall later.

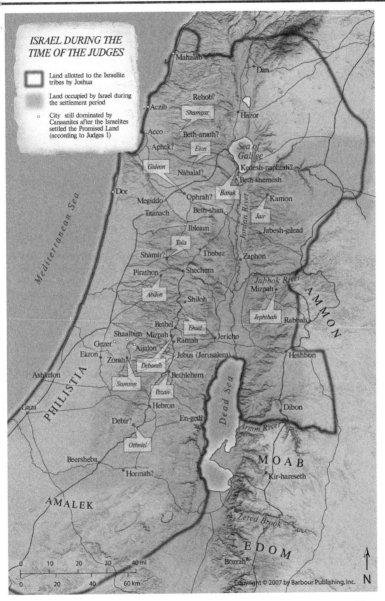

ISRAEL DURING THE
TIME OF THE JUDGES

☐ Land allotted to the Israelite
   tribes by Joshua

☐ Land occupied by Israel during
   the settlement period

○ City still dominated by
   Canaanites after the Israelites
   settled the Promised Land
   (according to Judges 1)

Mahalab
Dan
Rehob?
Aczib
Shamgar
Hazor
Acco
Beth-anath?
Aphek?
Sea of Galilee
Elon
Gideon
Nahalal?
Kedesh-naphtali?
Beth-shemesh
Dor
Ophrah?
Barak
Kamon
Megiddo
Beth-shan
Jair
Taanach
Jabesh-gilead
Ibleam
Tola
Thebez
Zaphon
Shamir?
Pirathon
Shechem
Jabbok River
Mizpah
AMMON
Abdon
Shiloh
Jephthah
Rabbah
Bethel
Ehud
Shaalbim Mizpah
Ramah
Jericho
Gezer
Aijalon
Heshbon
Ekron
Zorah?
Jebus (Jerusalem)
PHILISTIA
Deborah
Ashkelon
Bethlehem
Samson
Ibzan
Hebron
Dead Sea
Gaza
Debir?
En-gedi
Othniel
Arnon River
Beersheba
MOAB
Hormah?
Kir-haresheth
AMALEK
Zered Brook
EDOM
Bozrah

Mediterranean Sea
Jordan River

0 10 20 30 40 mi
0   20   40   60 km

N

Copyright © 2007 by Barbour Publishing, Inc.

JUDGES 1:1–36

AFTER JOSHUA

Initial Faithfulness   1:1–21
Theological Geography   1:22–36

Setting Up the Section

The era in Israel's history described in this book occurs after Joshua, Moses' successor, had led the Israelites into Canaan and begun the process of conquering the land assigned to each of the twelve tribes that make up the nation of Israel. Judges then describes the occupation of Canaan. The accounts here track the growing consequences of the people's compromises as they fail to obey God faithfully and completely in this process.

📄 1:1–21

INITIAL FAITHFULNESS

Judges begins with several short accounts of victory by the Israelite tribe of Judah. This tribe (from which the royal line of King David eventually will descend) is called to lead the battle into Canaan.

Critical Observation

The tribe of Simeon mentioned in verse 3 would have lived in close proximity to the tribe of Judah. Simeon was given territory within the boundaries of the southern kingdom, taking land out of Judah's territory (Joshua 19:1–9). This connectedness to Judah, while it may have had advantages, also meant that the tribe of Simeon lost some of its distinct identity. Many trace this loss back to the curse that Jacob put on his son Simeon, the ancestor of this tribe, in Genesis 49.

In verses 4–7, we're told of the destruction of ten thousand men. This count of ten thousand is more of a representative number than an actual head count. The destruction includes Adoni-Bezek (lord of Bezek). While their treatment of Adoni-Bezek seems extreme, it also has a sense of justice. He is receiving the same kind of treatment that he often dished out—for instance, rendering his victims unable to run or bear weapons. Adoni-Bezek dies in Jerusalem.

According to verse 8, Jerusalem is set on fire; but the Israelites did not occupy the city at this time. Eventually, of course, Jerusalem will become the capital city of the Israelite territory of Judah. The day will come when King David, a descendant of Judah, will rule from there.

Kiriath Arba is mentioned in verse 10. This name means "the city of Arba." It is so named because Arba was the great man among the Anakim who spawned a population of giants (see Joshua 14:13–15). This same city later came to be known as Hebron, a city mentioned often throughout the Israelite monarchy.

Critical Observation

Caleb, mentioned first in verse 12, is one of the twelve spies who, forty years earlier, entered Canaan on reconnaissance to report back to Israel before they entered the land. Of the twelve spies, only Joshua and Caleb believed that God could and would give them the land He had promised. As a result of their faith, these two men were the only two of the spies who actually entered Canaan (Numbers 14:21–24).

In verses 11–15, Othniel, to win his bride, destroys a great city of wickedness. Caleb, the father figure, gives the bride to his nephew and grants them a land of peace. The bride seeks a blessing, an outpouring of water, from the father.

Moses had persuaded some of his father-in-law's (Jethro) family to come with him to the land of promise. Those who believed and followed Moses came through his line of Levi and found a place to flourish in the land of Judah (1:16).

Hormah in verse 17 means "placed under the ban, totally destroyed." If this utter destruction described in verse 17 is done according to God's decree (see Deuteronomy 20:16–18), then it is considered a whole burnt offering to the Lord. Simeon may be mentioned, because this time (as opposed to his actions in Genesis 34) he is faithfully bringing God's wrath to bear.

In verses 19–21, Judah takes several Philistine cities and the hill country; but he cannot take the valley due to the strength of the Canaanites' iron chariots. Judah initially takes Jerusalem (also called Jebus), which is in the land given to Benjamin, but Benjamin is not able to drive out the Jebusites living there. In the end, they allowed these pagans to dwell with them.

In both of these cases, only a partial victory is obtained. This is significant in that it represents only a partial obedience to what God told the tribes to do. The land was supposed to be claimed for God entirely. Any non-Israelites who remained there should have been incorporated into the worship of the Israelite God Yahweh rather than taken on as simply co-inhabitants.

Demystifying Judges

The lessons of the book of Judges are taught not through a systematic recounting of theology, but through stories. These stories teach us about a purity of faith in the midst of a culture that is often in opposition to that faith. They also teach us that victory has nothing to do with the size of the enemy, but rather with the size of our faith in the promises of God.

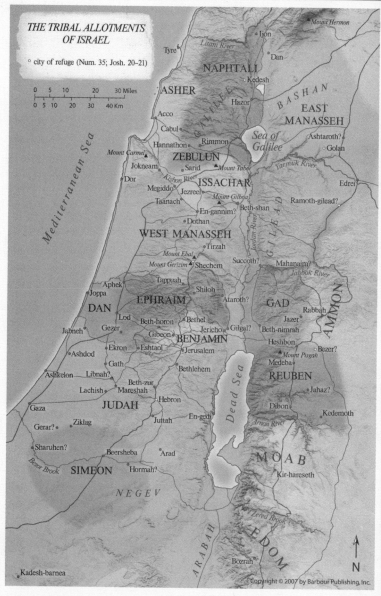

THE TRIBAL ALLOTMENTS
OF ISRAEL

○ city of refuge (Num. 35; Josh. 20–21)

0   5   10   20   30 Miles
0 5 10 20   30   40 Km

Mount Hermon

Tyre
Litani River
Ijon
Dan

NAPHTALI
Kedesh

ASHER
Hazor
BASHAN

EAST
MANASSEH

Acco
Cabul
Rimmon
Hannathon
Sea of Galilee
Ashtaroth?
Golan

Mount Carmel
Jokneam
ZEBULUN
Sarid
Mount Tabor
Yarmuk River

Dor
Kishon River
ISSACHAR
Edrei

Megiddo
Jezreel
Mount Gilboa
GILEAD

Taanach
En-gannim?
Beth-shan
Ramoth-gilead?

Dothan

WEST MANASSEH
Tirzah

Mount Ebal
Succoth?
Mahanaim?
AMMON

Mount Gerizim
Shechem
Jabbok River

Tappuah

Aphek
Shiloh

Joppa
EPHRAIM
Ataroth?
GAD
Rabbah

Lod
Beth-horon
Bethel
Jazer
Beth-nimrah

DAN
Gezer
Gibeon
Jericho
Gilgal?

Jabneh
BENJAMIN
Heshbon
Bezer?

Ekron
Eshtaol
Jerusalem
Mount Pisgah

Ashdod
Medeba

Gath
Bethlehem
REUBEN

Ashkelon
Libnah?
Beth-zur
Jahaz?

Lachish
Mareshah
Hebron

Gaza
Dibon
Kedemoth

JUDAH
Juttah
En-gedi
Dead Sea
Arnon River

Gerar?
Ziklag

Sharuhen?
Beersheba
Arad
MOAB

SIMEON
Hormah?
Kir-hareseth

NEGEV

ARABAH

Zered Brook
EDOM

Kadesh-barnea
Bozrah

N

Besor Brook

Mediterranean Sea

THEOLOGICAL GEOGRAPHY

In the description in verses 22–36, the author of Judges provides a verbal journey across the land. Here we see pragmatic victories and theological compromises made by the tribes. These compromises are spelled out in a list of progressive failures. Seven times in these verses, the tribes are charged with not driving others out. The significance of this is that by not driving out the inhabitants, the Israelites leave themselves open to the influence of other religions. As the rest of Judges plays out, that influence is a crucial factor in the faith of the nation.

In verses 22–26, spies are sent to Luz (Bethel), and they find help from within. But this time (unlike the story of Rahab in Joshua 2:1–13; 6:17), when the city is taken, the saved family does not repent and join Israel, but flees and sets up another pagan city.

Manasseh does not drive out the Canaanites but puts them under tribute, clearly against the Lord's commands (see Exodus 23:32). Ephraim and Zebulun act similarly (Judges 1:27–30). In this way, these tribes have not only ignored God's commands, they have put themselves at risk spiritually by allowing the current religions to still be practiced. Keep in mind that Israel was not yet a monarchy. Rather than being guided by the kings, they were still governed by religious leaders. The religious health of these tribes was in direct correlation to their political health.

In verses 31–33, Asher and Naphtali allow the previous inhabitants to dwell among them. What this means is that the Canaanites predominate these lands. Rather than Asher and Naphtali allowing the Canaanites to live there under each Israelite tribe's dominion, this situation is closer to the other way around. This is a great evidence of weakness for these tribes.

The tribe of Dan is forced to live in the mountains. The wickedness of this tribe is revealed in much more detail in chapters 17–18.

JUDGES 2:1–3:6

VICIOUS CYCLE

Yahweh's Judgment	2:1–5
Generation to Generation	2:6–15
Spiritual Adultery	2:16–3:6

Setting Up the Section

At this point, though God had commanded them to enter the land and drive out any peoples there that refused to follow Yahweh, the Israelites are convinced that their half attempts and compromised efforts in claiming their territories are justified and, in fact, represent practical victories. They are at least in the promised land, and they are settling down. The story of the Exodus, the mission the people set out upon, and the amazing works God performed seem to be a distant memory.

📖 2:1–5

YAHWEH'S JUDGMENT

The angel of the Lord is specifically charged to bring judgment upon sinful Israel (see Exodus 23:20–23). The charges in this passage suggest that this angel visitor is the Lord Himself, probably a preincarnate visitation of Jesus.

Critical Observation

There are several events in the Old Testament in which an angelic visitor seems more like an appearance of Jesus than simply an angel. You can observe some other visitations like this in the accounts of Hagar (Genesis 16:7–12) and Abraham (Genesis 22:15–16).

The Lord had been with the children of Israel at Gilgal (Joshua 5), where the next generation had been circumcised, signifying their transition into the same covenant that God had made with Abraham—one that was sealed with the act of circumcision (Genesis 17:10–14). Now, at Bochim (or Bokim, which means "weepers"), they grieve over the fact that they had not stayed true to that covenant.

God had brought the people out of Egypt. Enemies with iron chariots were no match for Him. God had made good on His promises, but the Israelites made covenants with the Canaanites, defying the Lord's command (see Exodus 23:32). It also appears that they did not tear down the idols that already existed in the land, even in cities where they had some control (Judges 1:33), again disobeying the Lord (Exodus 34:13).

The result? In rejecting the Lord's commands, what the Israelites may have thought would be pleasures in their new lives in Canaan would become deep thorns in their sides. True mourning can produce comfort (Matthew 5:4), but it is unclear whether it occurs at this place. On the one hand, it appears the Israelites repent—they offer up sacrifices, acknowledging their sin and need for an atonement. Unfortunately, if there is true repentance, it does not get passed on to the next generation.

📄 2:6–15

GENERATION TO GENERATION

The passage from 2:6 to 3:6 is a second introduction of sorts, picking up from the end of the book of Joshua. The theme emphasizes the ongoing spiral—of compromise to faithlessness to slavery to God's deliverance—that defines the period of Judges in the history of the old covenant.

⌂

Take It Home

Joshua is buried in a place called "Portion of the Sun" in some translations. This may be reminiscent of one of God's great works during Joshua's conquest of Canaan when He made the sun stand still during the great battle at Gilgal (Joshua 10). Joshua was a great leader for the Israelites. His faithfulness influenced all the elders of his generation. His life is a reminder that the faithfulness of one person can have a great impact upon a family or a nation.

In stark contrast to the life of Joshua is the generation that follows after his death. In the historical review found in Judges 2:10–15, it is clear that the basic failure of Israel is that they do not pass on to their children the stories of the Lord nor the loyalty He requires of them. Faithfulness only lasts as long as one generation if it is not passed on to children.

The consequences of Israel's disobedience are devastating. After their great journey and the building of the tabernacle, carrying it with them to every camp, here when they settle in the land, they seem to forget God's presence. They had been commanded in Deuteronomy 6:4–9 to keep God's commands ever before them, even placing them on their hands, foreheads, and doorposts. It is evident from this account, and much of the book of Judges, that the people did not fashion a life for themselves in this new land that followed those guidelines.

📄 2:16–3:6

SPIRITUAL ADULTERY

Later in the life of Israel, the prophet Jeremiah describes the people as those who had given up living water for their own broken cisterns, faulty water-catchers dug into the earth (Jeremiah 2:13). Certainly the roots of that accusation can be seen here in the Judges description of a nation that is departing from their faith for a life that does not support the values that had provided them their roots.

As expected, this angers God. However, this godly anger does not produce thoughtless rage from the Lord. He is faithful to His Word. He promised that if His children worship Him solely and properly, their fruitfulness would be supernatural, as would their strength against any enemy (Leviticus 26:1–13). And if they do not keep this covenant with Him, He promised the very consequences the tribes were beginning to experience in Judges (Leviticus 26:17; Judges 2:15).

Judges 2:16–19 describes a terrible cycle. God's children do not listen to judges God raises up for them. Instead, they spiritually prostitute themselves to other religions such as Baal worship. Then they *groan*, a word used before only in Exodus 2 and 6, under oppression. Each time, the Lord raises up a man to judge and deliver them again, but once he dies, the people quickly fall again into spiritual adultery. And unfortunately, each generation of Israelites falls more deeply into this cycle than the one before.

Critical Observation

The gods Baal and Ashtoreth, mentioned in verse 13, were the male and female counterparts of the representation of the power of nature. These two powers interacted (had intercourse, thus the sexual rituals included in Baal worship), and the fruit of their union was considered creation. Adherents to the worship of these deities believed religious orgies in the temples would motivate Baal and Ashtoreth to once again bring forth better crops in the land. These false deities were seen as hard taskmasters, as Psalm 106:34–42 describes.

Many times when God's judgments come into play, the very means of compromise becomes the means God uses to chastise His children (2:20–23). This is not merely the impassioned rage of God, but probably an ordained means of revealing humanity's sin in terms that are easily accessible.

Though they seem to say two different things, there is no contradiction between Judges 2:22 and 3:2. This generation has indeed not experienced war in the way the previous generation had (those who were first entering the land). Perhaps because of that, this generation has grown too quickly accustomed to having the Canaanites and their idols around. But it is also true that God used the battles with the Canaanites as a form of consequences for the Israelites, reminders that they needed God's power and presence.

Demystifying Judges

The judges were deliverers of Israel. This was their life's work. Their position was not hereditary (in most circumstances). While some believe the judges had legislative authority, much like elected officials today, there is not strong evidence that this is the case. Their special work was to act as avengers for Israel—being anointed to destroy God's enemies and deliver His people. In this way, they foreshadowed the redemptive work of Jesus Christ.

JUDGES 3:7–31

OTHNIEL AND EHUD

The First Judge	3:7–11
The Second Judge	3:12–30
Shamgar	3:31

Setting Up the Section

We now turn to the first of two stories of exemplary judges: Othniel and Ehud. The story of Othniel is given to us without much detail. In this simple story, we see the sovereign goodness and grace of God in both His chastisements and in His deliverance. The story of Ehud is a violent comedy, but also in some ways a picture of the gospel.

📄 **3:7–11**

THE FIRST JUDGE

The first evil mentioned in verse 7 (intermarrying when God specifically instructed the people not to) draws the Israelites into the second and more visible evil—forgetting God and worshiping idols. It is not that the people simply worshiped and served Baal, but they forgot about God. This forgetting was a sin. But, while the people may forget their God and their covenant with Him, God does not forget. Thus, the people experience consequences of this breaking of their spiritual covenant.

In the Hebrew, the name listed in verse 8, *Cushan-Rishathaim, king of Aram Nahariam,* is a play on words. Roughly, it means "the Cushite of double-wickedness, king of Syria of the double-river." This attack described here is from the north.

In this case, since the people do not want to follow God, He is sending them back, giving them over to their sin. Interestingly, this is also the place where one day, further down the line in Israel's story, Assyria and Babylon will come and take the people into exile, one that will be far worse than their famous bondage in Egypt. Through these eight years of subjection to a foreign power, the Israelites have an opportunity to experience life without God, since they seem to be choosing that life, after all.

As expected, the children of Israel cry out to God, who raises up a deliverer: Othniel. Othniel's victory is due to the work of the Spirit (3:10). The result of this victory is a full generation of rest (which most likely indicates a rest from war): forty years, until Othniel dies.

📄 **3:12–30**

THE SECOND JUDGE

After Othniel dies, Israel falls away from the God of their salvation once again and faces some ironic twists of circumstances that should draw their attention back.

According to verse 12, through God's hand, Eglon, king of Moab, overpowers Israel. He takes Jericho (the City of Palms) and forces Israel to pay tributes to him. These tributes may very well have been the firstfruit sacrifices, first harvests of crops and herds, which should have been rendered to the Lord.

Joining Eglon are the people of Ammon and the Amalekites. After they conquer the Israelites, it is eighteen long years of oppression before the Israelites meet their next deliverer.

Demystifying Judges

The Moab and Ammon people-groups are descendants from Lot, Abraham's nephew. Thus, they are distant relatives of the Israelites. These groups had a dark history. After the destruction of Sodom and Gomorrah, which had been Lot's home, he and his family were displaced. His two daughters conspired together, got their father drunk, and conceived children with him. The son born to Lot's oldest daughter became the ancestor of the Moabites. The younger daughter's son was the ancestor of the Ammonites (Genesis 19:31–38).

The Amalekites, who also partnered with Eglon, were sworn enemies of God and Israel. Exodus 17:8 describes a time when Israel defeated Amalek, but here in Judges 3 the roles are reversed.

Ehud, a Benjamite introduced in verse 15, is a left-handed warrior. He is also trusted by Eglon to present the required tribute. Ehud makes a dagger for himself and hides it on his right thigh. As unexpected as this might be, Ehud's unconventional actions have only just begun.

The stone idols mentioned in verses 19 and 26 either refer to the altar of stones built in Gilgal in Joshua's day (Joshua 4:20) or to idols placed there by Moab.

This shrewd deliverer takes advantage of his situation to bring about the salvation of his people from the tyranny of Eglon. This is not the act of an individual in a domestic dispute. Ehud is at war, and Eglon is an unlawful king in Israel's homeland. Ehud leaves the rest of his people and deals with the head of the enemy himself. He declares that he has a word from God and then drives the dagger into Eglon where it disappears, leaving the Moabite king helpless in a scene that becomes a mockery at Eglon's expense. Having crushed the political head of the enemy, Ehud summons his army and leads them to victory, killing ten thousand.

The day began with a tribute to an enemy king and ended with that kingdom routed and ashamed, and the people of God set free.

📖 **3:31**

SHAMGAR

In what can seem like a strange and out-of-place addendum, this story ends with a single verse about another judge, Shamgar. Although we know little of his story now, he was apparently well-known in the days of Deborah, the one female judge mentioned in this book (chapters 4–5).

Shamgar's name reveals that he was most likely not an Israelite, but a convert to the Lord. Apparently, this farmer-turned-warrior was a big surprise to his Philistine opponents.

Because the account following Shamgar's in chapter 4 still mentions Ehud, it may be that Shamgar's listing here doesn't relate to a linear time line. But we cannot know for sure when Shamgar's defeat of six hundred philistines took place. His weapon of choice, an oxgoad, was a long, thin tool, taller than a man when held upright. Among other uses, the tool probably had one end whittled to a point to be used to keep oxen moving along.

Take It Home

The Spirit of God was given to Othniel, Israel's temporary deliverer, in a limited way; but to Christ, the once-for-all deliverer, God's Spirit will be given without limits (see John 3:34). Othniel's victory was only partial (in time and space), but Christ's is, and will be, complete in eternity (see Isaiah 11:1–5; 42:1–4). Only in the Spirit-anointed Christ can we be strong against our enemies (Ephesians 6:10–13). The Spirit makes the preaching of the Word effective. The Spirit makes our work and prayers effective. The Spirit gives us strength to triumph over our sin.

JUDGES 4:1–24
DEBORAH AND JAEL

Jabin Again	4:1–3
Deborah, the Mother of Israel	4:4–5
Obey Your Mother	4:6–10
Another Battle, Another Woman	4:11–24

Setting Up the Section

In the account described in this section, a woman raises a man to lead an army against the enemy of Israel. Then a second woman completes the victory by crushing a wicked leader.

📄 4:1–3

JABIN AGAIN

When the Israelites continue their cycle of spiritual downfall—again—God lets them fall into the hand of a wicked king called Jabin. This may have been a title instead of a personal name, much as the Egyptians called their kings Pharaoh.

Jabin's commander, Sisera, cruelly oppresses the Israelites in Harosheth of the Gentiles. This area, in the north, is the land of Zebulun and Naphtali, north and west of the Sea of Galilee. Sisera commands nine hundred iron chariots, the same tools of battle that Judah had feared generations before according to 1:19 (4:2–3).

📖 4:4–5

DEBORAH, THE MOTHER OF ISRAEL

During Jabin's twenty-year rule, Deborah, a prophetess whose name means "bee," acts as a judge in Israel. According to verses 4–5, she held court under a tree. Deborah stands out simply because of her gender. It is unusual (though not unheard of) in this era in the history of Israel to find a woman filling the role of prophetess or judge. Though Deborah may be unlikely, she is effective in her role, providing a way to deliver her people by calling Barak.

Critical Observation

The image of trees is a significant one in the Bible. Trees were a source of comfort and shade. They provided not only shelter, but sometimes food as well. They are often included in important biblical events and images. Humanity was first judged at a tree, and that judgment is paid by a Savior who hangs on a tree. The tabernacle is pitched under a great tree where the Book of the Law of God was kept (Joshua 24:26). It was a place that represented a gate to heaven, a place of righteousness and justice, and (later) a place of healing and food (Revelation 22:2). In this chapter, Deborah judges under the Palm of Deborah, and Jael's husband moves away from the Lord and pitches a tent under a great tree.

📖 4:6–10

OBEY YOUR MOTHER

Barak is most likely a Levite from the northern city of Kedesh and therefore a priest of some sort. Barak's faith is tested as Deborah pronounces the command of the Lord. The plan, with no contingencies for the cutting edge iron chariots and the great army they will face, is a great test for Barak.

📖 4:11–24

ANOTHER BATTLE, ANOTHER WOMAN

Deborah's response to Barak's struggle to believe is a rebuke, but a gentle one. Barak does believe, raises up an army of ten thousand, and leads them to victory (more details are revealed in chapter 5). He is included in a list of faithful ancestors in Hebrews 11 as an example to follow.

According to verses 17–22, Jael's husband, Heber the Kenite, has moved away from his fellow Kenites' alliance with Israel and made peace with Sisera. Apparently Jael, whose name means "goat," does not approve. When she recognizes the fleeing Sisera, she courageously deceives this enemy of the Lord into coming into her tent, where she offers him milk (perhaps goat's milk) and then slays him. Then she faces up to Barak and shows him her handiwork—an honor Barak was told would not be his.

We have already seen with Ehud that deception and killing are not unlawful in times of war. Deborah, the prophetess of God, commends Jael (5:24–27) with a blessing similar to that given to Mary in Luke 1:28. Others have condemned Jael for disobeying her husband. But her story illustrates where the lines of matrimonial submission are to be drawn. A wife is to submit to and honor her husband, but when times of crisis and real choosing are required, she must side with the Lord.

JUDGES 5:1–31

THE SONG OF DEBORAH

Setting Up the Section

In chapter 5, Deborah and Barak praise God for His victorious strength. They exalt those who keep their word and serve the Lord in battle, and chastise those who fall back in their comfortable religion. They contrast the true and living God with Baal, the false god, and mince no words in describing the violent victory of the righteous and the violent debauchery of the fallen.

📖 5:1–9

PRAISE TO THE LORD

God is blessed when kings and their people choose to follow Him. Deborah recalls the battle from Mount Tabor in terms reminiscent of the historic coming of the Lord to Mount Sinai (compare Exodus 19:9–19 and Judges 5:4–5). The song recalls threatening scenes of normal life before the arrival of Deborah, a mother of Israel (5:7). And following this maternal motif, Deborah does bring new life to the nation of Israel.

📖 5:10–12

SPEAK! AWAKE! SING!

Verses 10–11 are somewhat obscure but appear to be summoning all of the people—the rich and the poor, men in arms and the common people at the watering places. All are to recount the righteous acts of God and thus stir one another up to serve God by coming down to the gates of the city. Deborah is to awaken the people with her song of deliverance (her prophecy of the Lord's promises), and Barak is to then call upon and lead a remnant, those who will believe the promises and obey the commands (5:12).

Critical Observation

Though Deborah's song celebrates those who came to fight, it is clear that the Lord does not need help to win a battle. God's assistants are not the point of this account. The point is that in a time of crisis and judgment, such as the fight against Sisera, events often conspire to test the people involved to see who is on the Lord's side.

📖 **5:13–23**

THE WORK OF MEN AND THEIR GOD

Deborah praises those who respond in faith and join the battle (5:13–15, 18), and she mocks those who are too comfortable, too busy, or too frightened to fight (5:16–17, 23).

Also, according to the song, Baal is impotent compared to the true Lord of the stars and clouds (5:20–21). This mention of stars and clouds may be a dig at the Canaanite astrologers. We have no record of the village of Meroz, cursed in verse 23.

📖 **5:24–31**

A TALE OF TWO WOMEN

Verses 24–31 celebrate the story of Jael, the Kenite woman who assassinated Sisera. In contrast to Meroz, Jael shows more zeal, courage, and faith. Jael refuses to compromise with her husband, and when the Lord grants her the opportunity, she serves Him honorably. Conversely, Deborah's words toward Sisera's mother are a form of mockery toward the woman for sitting and wondering why her son has not returned home (5:28).

Take It Home

Like Deborah, we applaud faithfulness, bravery, and obedience, and shun apathy, schisms, and hypocrisy. But most importantly, we acknowledge that it is God who wins the battle and stands as final judge. It is God who has led forth His captives and who crushes His enemies. More than anything else, this leads us to bless His name for His great mercy.

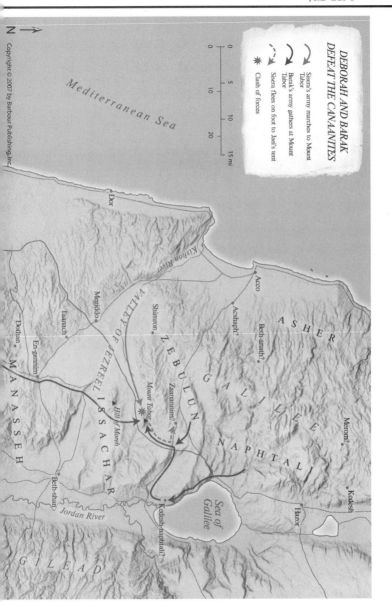

DEBORAH AND BARAK
DEFEAT THE CANANITES

Sisera's army marches to Mount
Tabor
Barak's army gathers at Mount
Tabor
Sisera flees on foot to Jael's tent

* Clash of forces

N →

Mediterranean Sea

0   5   10   20   15 mi

Copyright © 2007 by Barbour Publishing, Inc.

Dor

Kishon River

Acco

Megiddo

Taanach

VALLEY OF JEZREEL

En-gannim

Dothan

M A N A S S E H

Beth-shan

Jordan River

G I L E A D

I S S A C H A R

Hill of Moreh

Mount Tabor

Shimron

Zaanannim?

Z E B U L U N

Acshaph?

Beth-anath?

A S H E R

G A L I L E E

N A P H T A L I

Kedesh-naphtali?

Sea of
Galilee

Merom?

Kedesh

Hazor

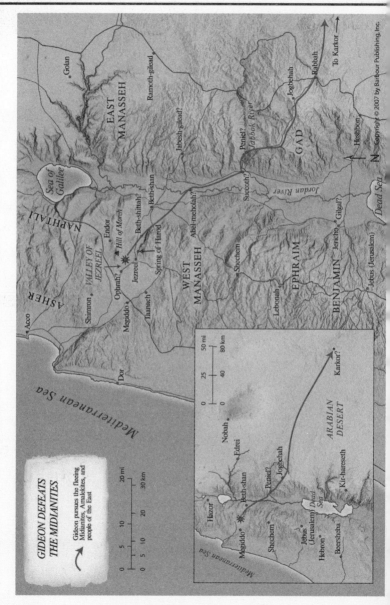

GIDEON DEFEATS THE MIDIANITES

→ Gideon pursues the fleeing Midianites, Amalekites, and people of the East

Copyright © 2007 by Barbour Publishing, Inc.

JUDGES 6:1–40

THE CALL TO GIDEON

Setting Up the Section

The cycle of falling away from faith, becoming oppressed, and then praying for deliverance starts again. This section begins the literary center of Judges, involving Gideon and his idolatrous son, Abimelech; and it emphasizes the central issues: the worship of Baal and the Lord's kingship over His covenant people.

📄 **6:1–6**

TERRIBLE OPPRESSION

Doing evil is a phrase used in the book of Judges to refer to idolatry. Israel strays again, which brings the typical consequences—the nation weakens, and the people have to leave their homes and hide in caves as foreign invaders come in and wipe out their crops and livestock. When Israel lives according to God's laws, they live under God's blessing—the Israelites get to reap what others sow (Joshua 24:13). On the other hand, when the Israelites live in disobedience, others reap what Israel has sown (Deuteronomy 28:29, 31). And true to form, in verse 6 we are told that Israel finally cries out to God again for deliverance (6:6).

📄 **6:7–10**

OBVIOUS WORDS

Before He sends them a deliverer, God sends them a prophet. This unnamed prophet, in essence, prepares the way for the deliverer. This prophet does not bring new prophecies; he declares what has been forgotten. Verse 10 again makes clear that the main problem is not oppression, but false worship, false gods, and disobedience to the Lord.

6:11–13

GOD IS WITH YOU

The angel of the Lord appears at the foot of a tree—sometimes translated as a *terebinth*, or *oak*. Gideon is threshing in a winepress, trying to hide what little wheat his father has from the marauding band. All of this symbolism points to a lack of communion with God.

The angel declares that the Lord is with Gideon. Because God is with him, Gideon will be a valiant warrior. Gideon's response is one of faith, for he acknowledges that the oppression is from the hand of God.

6:14–16

THE PROMISE OF STRENGTH AND VICTORY

The source of Gideon's might, according to verse 14, is that God is sending him. Gideon is dumbfounded at this idea. He is of the weakest clan in a half-tribe of Israel, he is the least in his father's house, and he is down in an empty winepress threshing wheat like an ox. In the history of Israel, however, there have been other situations in which a younger (and thus weaker in position) son was chosen: Abel over Cain, Isaac over Ishmael, Jacob over Esau, Joseph over his ten older brothers. Strength comes from God's appointment of a person rather than his or her human rank or glory.

The Lord rewards Gideon's humility with yet a third promise. Because God is with him, Gideon's victory will be total. Moses was considered the meekest man in the old covenant, and like Moses, Gideon now asks for a sign.

6:17–24

THE SIGN OF RESTORED COMMUNION

Why does Gideon choose this sign? What is his nagging question? It is this: Is God with us? Have we been reconciled to Him? Only then can we have confidence that He will deliver us. So he prepares an offering (a modified peace offering), and the fire that consumes it leaves no room for doubt—Gideon has been with God.

Critical Observation

Having witnessed a picture of Israel's atonement, one might expect Gideon to be filled with joy. Instead, he is scared to death: No one sees the Lord and lives. This sounds so strange to us; we no longer have a sense of terror in the awesomeness of God. But many would say that if there is nothing terrifying about God's holiness, then there is really nothing amazing about His grace.

Here, having received this sacrifice, God declares peace with Gideon. Gideon builds a memorial-altar, which is visible for generations to come, reminding the people of God's judgment and God's peace. In much the same way today, the ritual of the Lord's Supper is a contemporary reminder of God's judgment and peace through Jesus Christ.

📖 6:25–27

CLEANING HOUSE FIRST

Gideon's first task is to tear down an altar to Baal, which apparently is on his father's property. This task by itself reveals that Gideon grew up in an idolatrous home.

The second bull (which may be a sacrifice representing Gideon and his family) is seven years old (which may correlate with the seven years of oppression). The bull may have been considered sacred in Baal worship, which may add even more significance to this choice for a sacrifice. Gideon was instructed to use the wood of idols for the altar and to make the sacrifice publicly. Every connection between the outside oppression and the internal idolatry is to be declared. Notice that Gideon is not chastised for his fear of the mob and his decision to do this during the night. Apparently obedience is required, but boldness is optional (John 3:2; 19:39).

📖 6:28–32

JERUBBAAL

The morning after Gideon's sacrifice, everyone knows what has happened. Baal's altar is wrecked, Lady Asherah's pole is now ashes, and Joash's prize bull has been sacrificed as a sign of the Lord's favor. The men of the town demand that Joash turn over his son, but Joash, in biting sarcasm, reveals that his household is now following Gideon and the Lord. Then, Gideon's father renames him *Jerubbaal*, the Baal-fighter.

Critical Observation

The delivering judges in this book are types of our great Deliverer, the Lord Jesus Christ. On the cross, Christ made a mockery of all the false gods that lay a claim over the people He came to redeem (Colossians 2:15). And in Christ, our victory comes when His work continues through us: We are promised final and complete victory over all idols and sin (Romans 16:20; Philippians 1:6). We must tear down our idols (Colossians 3:5–7) not in our own strength, but by the same Spirit that came upon Jerubbaal, the Baal-fighter (Romans 8:12–14).

📖 6:33–35

AN ANOINTED ONE

In verses 34, the Spirit is imparted to Gideon. The idea is that the Spirit is "put on him" like clothing. Here we see also a pattern—a sacrifice for sin and the gift of repentance, followed by the equipping of God's people by His Spirit to finish the work which was already definitively accomplished by God in the sacrifice. Gideon is now clothed as a new man, re-created after the image of God. He calls upon the people of God to battle. The Midianites have come again, but this time God has sent messengers who gather the people back to Himself, back to the battle at hand.

Demystifying Judges

The Midianites have a long history with the Israelites. Where did they come from? This people group actually descended from Abraham (like the Israelites), but the Israelites were descended from Isaac, Abraham and Sarah's son. The Midianites were descended from Abraham and his second wife Keturah.

It was the Midianites who bought Joseph from his brothers and sold him as a slave in Egypt. Generations later, Moses married a woman who was a Kenite, a subset of the Midianites. Her Kenite father was Moses' father-in-law and advisor.

The Midianites were severely routed under Moses in Numbers 31. Here in Judges, some two hundred years later, the tables are turned. God is now using the Midianites as a judgment upon Israel.

📖 6:36–40

PUTTING OUT A FLEECE

To understand the prophetic meaning of these signs, it is important to keep the context in mind. Gideon has faith in God, but it is weak. His very need for the confirmation of the fleece reveals that. There is a battle about to take place between the Lord (who has been perceived as weak) and Baal (who has been perceived as strong). The Midianites are used to fighting; the Israelites are used to hiding. It will take a miracle. Does the Lord intervene in miraculous ways? And can Israel trust Him this time? How much does Gideon believe this?

The dew and fleece may represent Gideon being anointed and then, through him, all of Israel being blessed. As to miracles, the triune God of scripture is eternally active in His providence of all things.

Take It Home

Should we "put out the fleece" like Gideon? At one time, the ability to ask God for a miraculous sign was a function of only the prophets and apostles. It validated their ministry and gave a sign to the people that they were in fact speaking the very words of God (2 Corinthians 12:12). When Gideon asked for his sign from God, however, it was the request of a weak faith, not the sign of a strong faith.

Our faith needs to be more than asking God to reveal Himself in a miraculous way over and over. While God does do miracles still today, we don't depend on these miracles alone to validate our faith. We are also encouraged by the community of other believers, truthful Bible teaching, and meaningful rituals like the sacraments of baptism and the Lord's Supper.

JUDGES 7:1–8:17

GIDEON'S BATTLES

Setting Up the Section

The theme of weakness in people and strength in God is paramount to the story of Gideon's battle over the Midianites, foreshadowing what the apostle Paul taught in 2 Corinthians 12:9–11: that God's strength is made perfect in our weakness.

📄 7:1–8

GOD-MADE WEAKNESS

Gideon's messengers gather a fighting force of some 32,000 men. That may seem like a lot, but the Midianites have more than 135,000. Nevertheless, the Lord wants to make clear that He alone is delivering Israel, and He alone is to receive the glory.

Gideon first reduces the troops to 10,000. This is in line with God's commands in Deuteronomy 20:8. Holy war cannot be fought except by men of faith, who have confidence in the Lord and no fear. Incredibly, though, God further reduces the number. The second reduction comes through choosing men who drink water in a unique way. This leaves Gideon with the 300 men God wants. The ratio is now 450:1. God's providence has made His people recognize their utter dependence on Him for their salvation.

📄 7:9–15

GOD'S ENCOURAGEMENT IN WEAKNESS

When Gideon accepts God's offer of assurance, God kindly strengthens his faith. God's message of encouragement comes through a Midianite private, who correctly interprets his friend's dream. Note that Gideon's reputation is known among his enemies. This soldier recognizes that the barley loaf—the bread of the poor—flattening the Midianite tent means doom. Overhearing this, Gideon bows in worship before the Lord.

📄 7:16–22

GOD'S GLORY THROUGH WEAKNESS

Gideon has received special instructions from the Lord for the battle plan. It would be missing the point to simply say it was psychological warfare. The dew-drenched, Spirit-anointed men and their deliverer are now images of the coming of God's glory cloud, complete with fire, a trumpet, and a voice.

📄 7:23–25

IRONIC JUDGMENT

Two commanders of the Midianite army are captured and killed by Ephraim. The places where they are killed become landmarks of God's ironic and holy humor. The Israelites used to hide in rocks (6:2), but now Oreb is killed, possibly trying to hide in a rock himself. Gideon once hid in a winepress (6:11), but now Zeeb is killed at a winepress. Their heads being cut off remind us of the theology of the crushing of Satan's head.

📄 8:1–3

JUDGMENT IN A SOFT ANSWER

Ephraim's concern is for personal glory. But Gideon decides to turn away their anger with a soft answer (Proverbs 15:1). Ephraim can be commended for what they have done right, even if it is wrapped in seeking personal gain (see Philippians 1:15–18). Gideon does mildly rebuke them, noting that God delivered these princes into their hands.

📄 8:4–17

JUDGMENT FOR UNFAITHFULNESS

Succoth refuses to risk their immediate safety by openly trusting God's promise of deliverance in the light of risky circumstances. They will not side with the Lord in His blessing, and so they come to know the Lord in His discipline (8:16). Even worse is the city of Penuel. They are not afraid of the enemy, but their trust is not in the Lord. Their trust is in their big tower. Gideon's judgment upon them is not only to destroy their tower, but to kill the men of the city as well. God is a jealous God, and He will not share His glory with any other.

Take It Home

God is not in the business of making life more secure or more comfortable. That is not His goal. His goal is His glory—revealing Himself to humanity. Sometimes, in order to share this glory, He makes us weak—so that in our weakness we are able to see Him more clearly.

JUDGES 8:18–32

SHADOWS ON GIDEON

Setting Up the Section

Gideon is a man of faith. He is listed in the "hall of faith" in Hebrews 11. He has the kind of faith we are to imitate, the kind of faith that perseveres to the end. But there are other lessons to learn from Gideon. God does not give us stories like fairy tales, where the good prince goes off and lives happily ever after. In fact, one of the greatest lessons to learn from the end of Gideon's life is that we must never rest on our laurels or think that we are no longer susceptible to temptation. We must learn the importance of finishing well and the incredible covenantal connection between us and future generations.

📖 8:18–21

SHADOWS OF SLIPPING IN GIDEON

Gideon, as Jerubbaal, the servant of the Lord for the people of Israel, has the right and obligation to put to death these princes of Midian. But in this short discourse, we see the beginnings of something dark taking place. Gideon does not correct Zebah and Zalmunna when they imply he is a king (8:18). Perhaps misusing his power for vengeance, he seeks to disgrace them by having his young son slay them (and, like his father was earlier, Jether is afraid).

📖 8:22–23

SHADOWS OF SLIPPING IN ISRAEL

The people now seek to establish a dynasty in Gideon. But he only judges as one appointed by God, and it was the Lord who delivered them. The people's trust is moving away from the Lord again, toward an earthly throne. Unfortunately, the story doesn't end after Gideon's faithful answer.

📖 8:24–27

COMPROMISED WORSHIP, COMPROMISED GOVERNMENT

What happens next, though, is a small picture of the real problem. When we are faithful in our worship of God, then the Lord truly is the King, and human kings are no threat to God's glory or to the liberty of the people. But in 8:24–27, Gideon starts changing the rules for worship and starts acting like one of the pagan kings.

8:28–32

GIDEON'S DEATH AND POSTERITY

Verses 28–29 and 32 emphasize the fact that Gideon's life was blessed by God, and that overall, his service to the Lord was faithful. Nevertheless, notice the name change from *Jerubbaal* to *Gideon* between verses 29 and 32. This suggests that Gideon does not end up acting as a Baal-fighter, but a pagan king, influenced by Baal-like gods.

Abimelech, Gideon's son of a concubine, is named "my father is king." Most of us know the struggle of making our practice as holy as our theology. Gideon has denied the throne, but in his dreams, and in some of his actions, he has been letting this temptation simmer, slowly and quietly permeating the aroma of his life.

Demystifying Judges

Gideon probably justifies making a new ephod out of the Midianite plunder because God had instructed him to sacrifice and had spoken to him specifically. The original ephod, in the distant tabernacle, was a golden tunic worn by the priests. It bore the Urim and Thummim, used by the high priest to determine the word and will of God. With this new object, located in Gideon's hometown of Ophrah, the Israelites begin to follow Gideon as a pseudo-king and priest.

JUDGES 8:33–9:57

GIDEON'S EVIL SON

Setting Up the Section

Following Gideon's forty years of peace, the consequences of sin and compromise weave a web of great judgment upon the next generation. The story of Abimelech is a warning.

8:33–35

FAITHLESSNESS, AGAIN

Gideon's time as a judge is a mixed bag, but he must have restrained the worship of Baal effectively, because it isn't until after his death that the Israelites begin engaging in Baalism again. *Baal-Berith* is literally "lord of the covenant." Much like "God bless America," this title could appeal to God-fearing Israelites and Baal-worshiping Canaanites alike. But this mushy theology leads to a terrible curse and judgment from the true Lord of the covenant.

📖 9:1–6

THE CONSPIRACY OF ABIMELECH AND SHECHEM

Gideon's half-Canaanite son Abimelech ("my father is king") confronts Shechem's leaders, his uncles on his mother's side. He calls for loyalty to Baal-Berith and not to the Baalfighter and his God. Implied is Abimelech's argument that for Shechem to make a clean break, all of Jerubbaal's sons must be killed, for surely their intent is to rule over them.

Shechem's citizens agree and give Abimelech seventy shekels (perhaps one for each son) out of Baal's treasure. The thugs Abimelech hires with it capture all seventy sons (minus one who escapes), and one by one they are executed upon a stone, like sacrificial animals. Abimelech is then crowned king at the very place Joshua had set up a memorial stone for the people of Israel (Joshua 24:1, 24, 26), most likely employing a bit of historical revisionism to a people who have forgotten God.

📖 9:7–21

THE CURSE UPON ABIMELECH AND SHECHEM

Gideon's youngest son, Jotham, proclaims a parable from the mount of blessing, Gerizim. It is a curse and a call to repentance. The people have obviously been seduced to believe that what they have done is right and just, and that they have acted in truth and sincerity. Jotham warns them that if they do not turn from their loyalty to Abimelech, they will be burned by this same tyrant. Once again, rebellious sin becomes the very instrument of judgment upon a people.

📖 9:22–29

THE JUDGMENT UPON ABIMELECH AND SHECHEM

Evil is self-destructive; evil people will be at one another's throats soon enough. But in His graciousness to His own people, God sends an evil spirit to speed things along. The people of Shechem turn against Abimelech, who has ruled them for three years, and begin to rob travelers passing by.

Gaal, in the midst of a great harvest festival (remember, Baal is a god of the harvest), calls for pure devotion to the god and people of Shechem. In the drunkenness of the feast, he calls on Abimelech to come out and fight.

📖 9:30–41

FIRE OF THE BRAMBLE UPON GAAL

Zebul, a city leader, hears about Gaal and warns Abimelech, who then plans a preemptive strike. Gaal spots movement, but Zebul convinces him he sees shadows until it's too late. In 9:38, we see that Zebul gets the last laugh before the battle. Gaal and his Canaanite followers are chased from town. But like a brush fire, Abimelech's wrath has just begun.

9:42–45

FIRE OF THE BRAMBLE UPON SHECHEM

The people of Shechem figure that the crisis is over and head back out to the harvest. But Abimelech, fresh from one victory, comes down upon the field and the city, destroys, kills, and curses the land with salt (see Deuteronomy 29:23). We begin to see the hand of the Lord bringing His judgment on the land using the instrument of Abimelech, who is himself an enemy of the Lord.

9:46–49

FIRE OF THE BRAMBLE UPON BAAL

The leaders of the tower flee to the inner chamber of El-berith ("God of the covenant"). Just as Gideon had burned the altar of Baal, so Abimelech now brings bramble-fire judgment upon Baal's house.

9:50–57

FIRE OF THE BRAMBLE UPON ABIMELECH

Abimelech's lust for power presses him further, to what appears to be an easier target: Thebez. God's irony is everywhere. Another tower, another woman, another stone—but this time, his own head (perhaps representing the serpent) is crushed.

Although we clearly see the chastisement of God upon Gideon's family, still these verses declare that God is at work avenging the family of Gideon, the Baal-fighter.

Critical Observation

In Jotham's parable of the trees and the bramble (9:7–15), the trees represent Israel; they are seeking for a king to rule over them. The three fruitful trees (olive, fruit, and grapevine) are associated with Israel throughout scripture. There is a strong contrast made between the fruitfulness and blessing of these trees working according to their calling and the bramble's worthlessness; he is a fire hazard. The bramble is an emblem of the curse that came upon humanity because of sin (Genesis 3:18). Part of the practical consequences of this curse is the tyrannical reigns of evil men over others. Of course, in this case, this is God's description of Abimelech.

JUDGES 10:1–18
RETURN TO APOSTASY

Setting Up the Section

Following the accounts of Gideon and Abimelech, passages like 10:1–5 (and 12:8–15, at the end of this section) seem to be filled with minor details, but that is not always the case. Consider their placement in light of the greater passages and the whole book to make sense of what they offer.

📖 10:1–5

TOLA AND JAIR

Verses 1–5 provide a quick description of two judges of Israel. Tola served as judge for twenty-three years, yet no children are listed. Jair's description includes thirty sons.

Critical Observation

What we can see in this opening description, as with the account of Gideon, is the struggle to establish a dynasty. Keep in mind that there was not a prohibition against having many wives in the Old Testament, and having many children was a sign of blessing. This is why the count of children is significant here.

The Lord grants rest after the work of the first judges (3:11, 30; 5:31; 8:28). With these regimes following Abimelech, though, there is no mention of rest for the people. Life goes on, but it is as if the people are constantly falling away from their faith. Instead of rest, there is only more human activity.

In the opening description, you also see an emphasis on burials, which actually began in the account of Gideon. Gideon was buried in Ophrah; Tola in Shamir; Jair in Kamon; Jephthah in Gilead; Ibzan in Bethlehem; Elon in Aijalon; and Abdon in Pirathon. With the judges listed here in verses 1–5, we know nothing of their battles. They are described as judges, but we hear nothing of the people crying out or of the Lord sending these men as deliverers or saviors. Their graves are reminders of the temporary nature of their reigns.

The fact that God keeps raising up judges to rescue and protect and lead His people is a sign of His grace. Judges 10:6 and 13:1 both point to the fact that after these judges rule, Israel falls back into idolatry. This seems to tell us that, during their administrations, they kept the people from idolatry.

📖 10:6–9

FORSAKING THE LORD AGAIN

Verses 6–9 reveal yet another forsaking of faith. It seems every time a judge dies, the people fall back into idolatry, but the situation described here is to the fullest extent. Seven gods are named, yet this may imply more gods than this since it seems to include the gods associated with these deities. The issue at hand is that the Israelites have forsaken God.

Critical Observation

While our modern view of sin often boils down to breaking a set of laws or rules, here we see that sin is also the offending of a personal and jealous God. The object of God's wrath was not simply at Israel's sins, but upon Israel herself (10:7). His anger was evidenced in the life of the nation; from that year on they were shattered and crushed as the land was invaded (10:8–9). This oppression lasted for eighteen long years and came from both the northeast (Ammonites) and the southwest (Philistines).

📖 10:10–14

SORROW UNTO DEATH

Apparently, Israel's cry of repentance is received by the Lord as just another song and dance (10:10–14). The Lord reminds Israel that seven times (a number denoting completeness) He delivered them, yet each time they fell away and served other gods. God sees no change in their hearts and responds with the chilling words of verses 13–14. God has given fair warning that He will respond in kind (Deuteronomy 32:37–38). These frightening words, however, are used by God as a means to give Israel true repentance (Judges 10:15–16). They once again put away their false gods and serve the Lord.

📖 10:15–18

A GODLY SORROW

Notice that in verse 16 it does not say God is impressed or moved by the repentance of the people. In fact, it says that God's soul cannot endure their misery. This is a reminder that hope in the mercy of God does not rest in the sincerity of a person's repentance but in the intensity of God's compassion. Repentance, like faith, is never the ground of our salvation or pardon. Instead, that ground is the mercy of God.

Critical Observation

We get a glimpse in verse 16 of the personality of God. The God who decrees everything that comes to pass is also the living God of scripture. It is possible for Him to be sovereign over the earth and the people in it yet respond authentically to the events at hand.

JUDGES 11:1–12:15

JEPHTHAH

Setting Up the Section

The beginning of the story of Jephthah is full of comparisons and contrasts. First, notice that Jephthah looks a lot like Abimelech. Both are sons of a mix representing faithfulness and unfaithfulness. Both are surrounded by worthless men. But Jephthah is listed as a believer, a man of great faith (Hebrews 11:32), a mighty man of valor (Judges 11:1), one who speaks with and worships the Lord (11:11). In addition, this part of the story (Gilead and Jephthah) closely parallels the exact situation of Israel and the Lord.

📖 11:1–11

AS GOD WAS REJECTED

In verses 1–3 Jephthah is rejected, much as God is rejected in chapter 10 (10:6). Then Gilead comes to Jephthah (11:4–6), much as Israel made an attempt to return to the Lord (10:10).

Considering that parallel, in the same way that God rejected Israel's cry for help after they fell away from faith (10:11–14), Jephthah at first rejects the cry of his family who calls out to him because they need his help (11:7). And in the same vein of comparison, when Gilead appeals, Jephthah does return to his family (11:8–11)—in some fashion like the second cries of Israel and the answer of the Lord (10:15–16). The parallel here is more flawed, for Jephthah is imperfect in his motives.

📖 11:12–28

JEPHTHAH'S MESSAGE OF PEACE

In sending messengers to Ammon, Jephthah is revealed to be a man of peace (11:12). The Ammonites claim that Israel has taken their land, and they want it back (11:13). Jephthah responds with a series of diplomatic arguments.

First Argument (11:14–18): As Israel passed through the eastern side of the Jordan, she always attempted to remain at peace with the nations of Edom, Moab, and Ammon, respecting their borders.

Second Argument (11:19–22): The disputed land that Israel took was the territory of the Amorites under King Sihon, not the Ammonites.

Third Argument (11:23): The Lord gave this land to Israel.

Fourth Argument (11:24): Jephthah charges them to live with what their god, Chemosh, has given them. One God is greater than another, and Jephthah makes that case clear.

Fifth Argument (11:25): Jephthah also attempts to avoid war with threats. Balak couldn't contend with Israel, so what makes Ammon think they will?

Sixth Argument (11:26): Israel has occupied the land for three hundred years.

Seventh Argument (11:27): Jephthah's true faith is seen here. His final appeal is to the Lord, who is the true judge of Israel.

Even faced with these arguments, however, Jephthah's diplomacy is rejected (11:28). When Ammon rejects the proposal for peace, the nation brings judgment upon itself. In this case, rejecting Jephthah's words is, in effect, rejecting the Word of God Himself, because Ammon refuses to surrender to God's will as defined by the Israelite judge.

📖 11:29–33

JEPHTHAH'S VOW AND CONQUEST

Jephthah is given a great victory over Ammon, but we are given very little information on the battle. Rather, the focus of the story is on the vow that Jephthah makes and the results of that vow. He has declared his faith in the Lord. Now, the Spirit of the Lord comes upon him.

The commitment Jephthah makes in verse 31 is similar to a tithe-offering. In essence, it is a kind of firstfruit. In most cases this term refers to the first of a harvest, but in this case it reflects the first product of this newly established peace. By offering this firstfruit, Jephthah is dedicating the peace, the result of his conquest, to God. (Jacob made a similar vow in Genesis 28:20.)

📖 11:34–40

JEPHTHAH'S DYNASTY

Verses 34–40 constitute one of the most debated passages in the Old Testament. Did Jephthah actually take his daughter to the tabernacle, where the Levites would kill, skin, and section her, offering her up as a burnt offering? Some would argue that this is the only interpretation this scripture allows. Others disagree.

Another perspective is that the word translated *burnt offering* is not a Hebrew word that necessarily implies the *burning* of the offering (other offerings not referred to as burnt offerings were indeed burnt). Instead, an offering that is burnt up can carry with it the idea that the entire offering ascends to God. No portion is reserved back, even for the priests.

Another insight that seems relevant is that Leviticus 27:1–7 describes the redemption contract for those who have been consecrated by a vow to the Lord. There are those who are irrevocably devoted to God and cannot be redeemed, however, as in this case (11:28). In a holy war ban, also, those who had been irrevocably devoted to God would be killed (11:29). (These deaths were not considered human sacrifices.)

However one interprets Jephthah's vow, it is a vow of dedication to the Lord for victory, and it includes the promise to devote the firstfruits of peace coming from his home to the Lord. Jephthah promised to give him or her entirely away to the Lord. Consequently, however, Jephthah is shocked when God appoints his only daughter to be the one. This would seem to stand in the way of Jephthah establishing any kind of dynasty in Gilead.

Both father and daughter, in faith, submit to the vow and, as she is Jephthah's only child, sacrifice the hopes of the continuing reign of the family line. The young woman bewails her virginity with friends who would have been in her wedding party. Then Jephthah fulfills his vow. Some believe that this means his daughter then went to serve at the tabernacle as other women did (Exodus 38:8; 1 Samuel 2:22). Many others believe it means she was killed as a sacrifice.

The chapter closes with the resulting annual Israelite custom in commemoration of the great sacrifice made by this judge and his only daughter.

📄 12:1–7

THE REBELLION OF EPHRAIM

This is the second time in the book of Judges that Ephraim claims they have been left out of the action and the resulting glory (8:1–3). Here, in verse 1, they actually threaten Jephthah, God's appointed judge, something the law condemns (Deuteronomy 17:12).

Judges 12:5–6 reveals a kind of humorous irony on God's part. Jephthah's men capture the fords of the Jordan where the Ephraimites had to cross to return to their home (after they had made an offensive attack on Gilead). The irony of this event is that this is the same tactic Ephraim had used against Midian (6:3). Because of the ingenuity of Jephthah's men, 42,000 Ephraimites fall under God's judgment.

Jephthah's reign was a mere six years (12:7). Perhaps the six years of judging (contrasted with the idea of seven, which is often associated with completeness in the Bible) represents the shortcoming of man's rule to bring about God's kingdom and rest.

📄 12:8–15

MINOR JUDGES

As with the opening of chapter 10, chapter 12 closes with a brief history of three judges: Ibzan, Elon, and Abdon. The last in this list of minor judges, Abdon, has seventy sons (or grandsons), yet Elon has no children listed. Ibzan, like Jair in the opening of chapter 10, has thirty sons listed.

Also, as with the list at the opening of chapter 10, these short histories give facts regarding not only the number of children, but also the places of burial. While these judges rule for a time, theirs is not an ongoing dynasty.

JUDGES 13:1–25

SAMSON'S PARENTS

Setting Up the Section

Over a thousand years before the birth of Jesus, an angel appeared to a woman. He told her that she would conceive in a miraculous way and give birth to a son. He said that her son would be set apart for the Lord from his birth on and that he would start to save his people from their enemies. We have learned from our study in Judges that these are not simply coincidences. The background of the birth of Samson reveals that this unintentional deliverer is a gift from God.

📖 13:1

THE HAND OF THE PHILISTINES

The oppression of the Philistines is mentioned in Judges 10:7, but it is in the story of Samson (along with Samuel, and later, David) that we hear of the conflict. Samson is born and raised during these years of oppression.

The Danites lived in great compromise (1:34–36; also chapters 17–18). This time, there is no narrative of the people crying out for deliverance. Instead, they are a people seemingly so used to bondage that they do not even call out for relief (15:11). But here is a picture of the grace of God. He doesn't wait for us to make the first move. His grace is greater than all of our senseless sin. He takes the initiative, even if it requires a miracle.

📖 13:2–7

THE NAZIRITE AND THE PROMISE

In these verses, and also in Numbers 6:1–8, we learn that *nazar* generally means "to be separated, consecrated," and can be used as a crown of sorts, signifying the one set apart for something special. Nazirites are like priests, set apart for a particular service for the Lord, either for a particular time, or as we see in some cases, for their entire lives.

Demystifying Judges

The Nazirite abstained from any product made from vine fruit—wine, juice, or even the grapes themselves. This act of abstinence signified the idea that he was set apart for special service. This text regarding Samson is not a biblical argument for everyone abstaining from drinking wine, but rather a description of a specific scenario (Judges 9:13; Psalm 104:15). In this case, Samson is representing Israel and is not in a time of rest until he has finished his vow (Numbers 6:20).

Manoah's wife is to keep the Nazirite vow herself, until the child is born, for her son has been consecrated to the Lord from the womb. Here is more proof from the scriptures that an unborn child is a living person, a person who can even be in relationship with his mother and with God.

By his life and by his death, Samson will begin a process of deliverance. But it will take Samuel and, finally, David before the Philistines will be completely crushed.

The Nazirite's holiness is connected to long hair (Numbers 6:5). A man or a woman who takes a Nazirite vow represents the whole nation to God as a bride, one set apart and devoted to her husband. The long hair is a crown, and at the end of the time of the vow, the Nazirite cuts his long hair and offers it up as a sacrifice to God, much as we will take our crowns and cast them before the Lord in heaven (Revelation 4:10).

In addition, the Nazirite is to ceremonially separate himself from death (Numbers 6:6–8), a sign of uncleanness.

13:8–14

MANOAH AND HIS WIFE

The Lord continues to show His distance with Manoah, even while answering his prayer. This savior will not come in a natural way. In one sense, Manoah has nothing to do with it (although his wife will conceive by Manoah).

Manoah wants to know about this boy, what they will do for him, and what his work will be. The angel of the Lord returns and answers, coming first to the woman and answering Manoah's questions about the boy by speaking about the requirements for his mother (13:12–13). God is not going to give Manoah any more details for now.

13:15–16

GETTING YOUR OFFERINGS STRAIGHT

There is a clear contrast in this scene to Gideon in Judges 6. Gideon's offering (a peace offering of sorts) was accepted. But God refuses Manoah's (and thus, Israel's) offer of a meal.

Communion, the peace-meal with God, could not occur because in Manoah's day, the people had not cried out to the Lord; there was no peace with God and mankind (13:1). First, an *olah*—a whole burnt offering, an ascension offering—must be made. The writer parenthetically tells us that Manoah is not confused regarding the order of offerings (as we might be). Rather, it is only because he does not yet know that this is the angel of the Lord that he wrongly offers to sit and eat in peace with this man.

📄 13:17–23

THE NAME OF GOD

Manoah has another question: *What is your name?* The God whose name is *Wonderful* (Isaiah 9:6) did wondrous things in the sight of Manoah and his wife. The angel of the Lord (who is the Lord Himself) ascends in the flame of the offering. Then Manoah knows that he has seen the Lord (13:22).

Critical Observation

We do not realize all that we are asking when we—like Manoah in chapter 13—ask God for His name, for we do not think of names in the same ways that the ancients did. When a person was named, his or her character was revealed and, in a way, dominion was claimed over that person in that they were defined by that name. Parents take some kind of dominion over their children by naming them—the act of naming is a part of the parents laying claim to their little ones. In the account of creation, Adam expressed the dominion God gave him in part by naming the animals. It is telling, then, that the angel of the Lord says that God's name is wonderful (or secret). It is beyond our ability to fully comprehend and certainly beyond our ability to have any kind of dominion.

When God reveals who He is and what He is doing, the result is never simply an ascent to truth. Dull religion (in your heart) betrays your presumptive spirit. Those who realize they have seen God fall on their faces.

📄 13:24–25

ONE MORE SIMILARITY IN GOD'S STORYTELLING

While so much attention is given to the events surrounding the birth of Samson, after his birth we learn very little about him until his adult ministry is initiated. We are told that from this point, God's Spirit began to move in him. God's wonders will be displayed not only on behalf of this deliverer, but actually through him.

JUDGES 14:1–20

SAMSON

Setting Up the Section

The account of Samson is one of the strangest stories in the book of Judges. He is surprising in his actions and in his strength. At first it doesn't seem that Samson is acting as a judge but rather just doing his own thing. But we are told that the Lord raised up Samson to begin to deliver Israel (13:5) and that the Spirit of the Lord had begun to move upon him (13:25). To understand the stories of Samson, we should keep in mind three things: first, Samson's association with Philistine women; second, Samson's Nazirite vow; and third, Samson's ministry of stirring up a sleeping Israel and his work of beginning a deliverance from the Philistines.

📖 14:1–4

SAMSON'S DESIRES

Instead of getting ready for war, Samson is in the mood for a wedding. Against his parent's desires, he finds a woman among the Philistines. We find ourselves easily siding with the parents on this one. But that would be siding against the Lord, who is intending to do something about the dominion of the Philistines over Israel even with as unwitting an accomplice as Samson seems to be.

📖 14:5–9

SAMSON'S SURPRISING MIGHT

The Nazirite finds himself in the vineyards of Timnah, where the fruit of the vine is to be enjoyed in this glorious land given to Israel by the Lord. But it has been taken from them. A lion (an unclean beast) attacks Samson, but the Spirit of the Lord comes mightily upon him, and he tears the lion apart with his bare hands. Later, Samson comes back and finds honey in the carcass, scrapes some out and eats it, and then gives some to his parents. But he keeps these strange events to himself.

As a Nazirite, Samson is not supposed to touch the unclean carcass. Yet he enjoys and shares a token of what is promised by his deliverance in that the land would again be a land of milk and honey for God's people.

📖 14:10–18

SAMSON'S RIDDLE

Samson's father provides a wedding for his son, and a seven-day feast ensues. During this time, the occasion comes to move against the Philistines, but with a riddle. Samson really wins because the Philistines have to coerce his wife through fear to squeeze the information out of Samson. The point is not Samson's weakness, but his wife's unfaithfulness. The bride is supposed to forget her own people (Psalm 45:10), come out, and be made one with her husband. How often does Christ's bride, the church, forget or betray her husband?

📖 14:19–20

SAMSON'S VENGEANCE

Like the lion, the Philistines have attacked Samson in the contest of the riddle, and the Spirit of the Lord comes mightily upon Samson again. This isn't a fit of rage—this is the Lord's administration of justice upon the Philistines. Afterward, Samson's anger is roused (toward his wife) and he leaves her, going back up to his father's house.

JUDGES 15:1–20

SAMSON'S BATTLES

Setting Up the Section

Holy violence sounds like an oxymoron and brings to some an image of religious fanaticism. The story of Samson is neither for the squeamish pacifist nor the Victorian prude. But the story is for the people of God, that they might fear a mighty and holy God and rest alone in the life, provision, and vengeance of the Savior.

📖 15:1–5

JUDGMENT FIRE

We are not told why Samson returns to his father's home without his wife. The story picks up as Samson returns to have relations with her. It is important to note this because it bears upon the eye-for-an-eye justice he will bring. The problem lies with the Philistines of Timnah. They have robbed him of his wife and fertility, and so he responds by attacking their fertility. The choice of foxes (wild animals—possibly jackals), three hundred of them, sent in pairs, all lead to questions that are hard to answer. It is clear that this is not a fit of rage on Samson's part when we hear his words in verse 3.

A HEAP OF VENGEANCE

Samson's wife has been afraid of being burned by her own people, and so she betrays her husband (14:15). She ends up receiving the very judgment she sought to escape. But she is Samson's wife, and so he brings vengeance with a great slaughter. Those who do not turn in repentance after receiving a slighter judgment will find that God has been patient in withholding His full wrath.

JUDAH'S BETRAYAL

Like Samson's wife, the men of Judah fear the Philistines more than God. In fact, they are quite bothered for the ruckus that Samson has raised. They may have been enslaved by the Philistine culture, but at least they are at peace. Judah is the tribe that originally had faithfully gone into battle (1:1–20); they have now become cowards. But something else is being pictured here. God's own people are betraying their messiah, and this messiah is going along with it, with a greater plan of judgment and deliverance.

JAWBONE HILL

Once again, the Spirit of the Lord comes upon Samson, frees him, and sets him on a holy war. Picking up the fresh jawbone of a donkey (another unclean animal), Samson kills a thousand Philistines, one by one. Then the Nazirite throws the jawbone away, separating himself from that which is unclean.

"I'M THIRSTY"

If we do not have water, we die in a matter of days. God, in a clear reference to the forty-year wilderness wanderings, humbles this deliverer to show him that God alone must provide for all his needs. Just as the rock was Christ in the desert, so this rock is Christ, the water of life. This is more than physical refreshment. As Samson represents Israel, we are reminded that we are always in need of God for the water of life. As Samson represents Christ, remember we sing in Psalm 110 of our Messiah drinking from a brook and lifting up His head.

Critical Observation

Over and over, Judah and Israel turn their back on the deliverers God sends to them. Even in the first century, Jesus' rejection and His trial and execution are an extension of this same pattern (John 11:49–52).

JUDGES 16:1-31

SAMSON AND DELILAH

Setting Up the Section

There are many literary parallels between Judges 14–15 and Judges 16. In both, a woman is approached by Samson, she obtains and betrays a secret, Samson is bound, and there is a great slaughter of Philistines. But there is a significant contrast. Three times in Judges 14–15 the Spirit of the Lord comes upon Samson. In Judges 16, amidst Samson's sin, the Spirit is not mentioned and then later is mentioned as having departed.

📖 **16:1-3**

SAMSON LOOKS FOR A BRIDE

In chapter 14, Samson has pure motives as he looks for a woman to be his bride (14:1). But this time he approaches a woman with eyes of lust. And Samson is representing Israel again. Judges 15 concludes as each story of deliverance in the book of Judges concludes: with judgment on Israel for many years. The first verse of Judges 16 begins with the same pattern established back in 2:16–17. Samson is being led by his lusts just as Israel has been led by hers.

Samson goes deep into Philistine territory where he sleeps with a harlot. When he finds out that he is going to be attacked, he thwarts the attackers' plans with a preemptive strike. He picks up the gates of the city and puts them where Hebron can see that Gaza is ripe for the picking. And then he leaves, and sleepy Israel does nothing. While Samson remains strong, there is no mention of the Spirit. Samson may think he escaped this mess, but he is clearly on the wrong trajectory.

📖 **16:4-5**

DELILAH THE BETRAYER

Samson continues to forsake his calling and his vows. Delilah will be the one who betrays him this time. She turns him over for silver.

Samson is probably not all that big and muscular, because Delilah and Samson begin to play guessing games with what kind of magic has brought this amazing power upon him. But the Philistines are not playing a game.

PLAYING GAMES WITH SIN

Samson has fun ridiculing the Philistines' belief in magic. But we also see Samson playing around with his vow. He mentions the number seven and later mentions his hair. Samson does not need to fear magic, but he does need to fear compromise, and Delilah playfully pouts and seduces her way to the truth.

BLINDED WITH LUST

Samson's focus is primarily upon his lusts, and he has lulled himself into thinking he is invincible. Giving in to Delilah's vexing, Samson tells her that if his hair is shaved, his strength will leave him. Delilah lulls him to sleep upon her knees (a veiled allusion to his sexual immorality), and like the harlot in Proverbs, her "feet go down to death" (Proverbs 5:5 NIV). Like Israel, Samson has been raised up out of a barren womb, set apart to be holy, received grace after grace, and deliverance after deliverance. Like Israel, Samson chases after other lovers, taking God's grace as license for any sin that pleases him. And like Israel, Samson is sent into exile.

PROVOKING THE LORD

Verse 23 mentions that Samson's hair is growing back. This is a sign of the stupidity of the Philistines, but also a sign of Samson's strength returning

The Philistines call for a great party, and their victory is their theme. But Dagon has nothing to do with their victory; it is not Dagon's power, but the Lord's absence. They bring out Israel's great deliverer and publicly mock him (16:25), and we should see the foreshadowing of another Deliverer, betrayed for silver, blinded and mocked by the Roman guards (Luke 22:64).

VENGEANCE IS MINE

The servant of the Lord will be avenged, for the Lord's name will be avenged. The Lord answers the prayer of His suffering servant—Samson's death does not picture a suicide, but a victorious self-sacrifice. Once again we are told of the burial of a judge, a memorial of sorts, until the day that the greater Samson will come, die, and leave His grave empty in complete victory over His enemies.

🏠

Take It Home

Samson's life was not a life typified by humility. His life can serve as a reminder to us where our strength and our accomplishments find their source. It is not a difficult thing to lose sight of that reality and begin to view our accomplishments as our own. Whether individuals or nations—those who trust in their own strength are setting themselves up for a fall.

JUDGES 17:1–13

FALSE PRIESTS

A False Tabernacle   17:1–6

A False Priesthood   17:7–13

Setting Up the Section

The book of Judges begins with two introductory passages and concludes with two appendices. The accounts in chapters 17–21 most likely took place before the first judges came upon the scene. Moses' grandson is mentioned in Judges 18:30 and Aaron's grandson in Judges 20:27–28. Their placement here at the end of the book is to emphasize what went wrong in Israel and why she fell into idolatry so often. The first appendix is contained in chapters 17–18.

Some see Judges 17 and 18 as a parody of the story of Moses. Moses delivered the people of Israel, and through him God established a house of worship, a priesthood, and the promise of conquest of a land. Judges 17 perverts this history of an established worship and priesthood, and Judges 18 will pervert the story of the conquest. This parody displays for us why Israel falls into such apostasy time and time again throughout the following generations (described in the first 16 chapters of Judges) and is told through the life of the priest who is the grandson of the same Moses.

📖 17:1–6

A FALSE TABERNACLE

In Judges 16, Samson has been betrayed with 1,100 pieces of silver (16:1–4), and in the opening of Judges 17, we see 1,100 pieces of silver again surrounding a betrayal. Micah steals the silver from his mother but returns it because he fears her curses. While Micah returns what he has taken, he makes no restitution as required by laws, such as those in Leviticus 6:1–7, nor is any trespass offering made.

Micah's mother, unnamed in this passage, dedicates the silver to the Lord, but then uses it to make a carved image and a molded image, openly breaking the second commandment. According to verse 5, Micah has a shrine (a false tabernacle), an ephod (a false garment for fortune-telling), and household idols. These idols are *teraphim*—little messengers to gods—as opposed to the seraphim who serve God. Micah also sets up his son as the priest of his own worship house.

Verse 6 reveals Israel's lack of a king. Had there been a king who loved and kept God's laws, actions like Micah's would have been stopped. Deuteronomy 13 and 17 confirm that idolatry (including idolatry that is combined with true religion) is not only a sin, but a crime against society. Rather than adhere to the laws of their religion, the people of Israel do whatever they think is right in their own eyes.

A FALSE PRIESTHOOD

From Micah's perspective, things seem to get better. A Levite from Bethlehem (which means "the house of bread") comes looking for work. This maverick priest is hired to serve in Micah's false tabernacle before false idols in false worship. This priest will even get a suit of clothes (contrasted with the first high priest's garments of glory and beauty).

Critical Observation

Part of the role of the Levites in Israel's history was as a substitution for the firstborn of Israel. By the laws of God given to these ancients, the firstborn always belonged to God, as well as the firstfruits of a crop. (This practice carries over today in the practice of offering a tithe or offering to God first from our income.)

In this substitutionary role, the Levites gave up certain freedoms. They lived in appointed cities because they had no land, and they also served in the towns of Israel, more or less like pastors of synagogues. The Levites were to reveal God's truth and lead true worship. Unfortunately, in the first 16 chapters of Judges, the Levites are conspicuously absent.

As presented in the Old Testament, priests are also to be like fathers, leading and protecting and teaching their flock. But Micah's priest becomes like a son, manipulated by Micah rather than rebuking him (Malachi 2:7–9). Micah manipulates the gods he owns rather than submitting to the true Lord. Once he determines that he has this perverted form of religion under control, he believes that the Lord will bless him for sure.

Take It Home

The tabernacle at Shiloh and, later, the temple in Jerusalem are simply shadows of the true temple of God. In actuality, we are the reality: The temple of God is the body of Christ. More than that, we are the priesthood, under our High Priest, Jesus.

We still can be tempted to worship God however we see fit, without regard for His commands. We still can be tempted to attempt to manipulate God with our accomplishments or outward rituals of worship. These externals are not where God observes us, though. God sees right into the temple of our hearts (Matthew 15:8–9).

JUDGES 18:1–31

DAN'S DECEIT

Setting Up the Section

In the days of Moses and the Exodus, the Lord led His people out of Egypt, established His priesthood, sent His spies, and conquered the land, burning the first city, Jericho. This section is similar to that story but is more of a distorted parody. This account reveals how the people of Israel, during the times of the judges, continue to miss the mark, fall into the sin of idolatry, and find themselves under God's wrath. Their story is a reminder of the importance of walking in faithfulness.

The account here gives the details of the Danites' compromise, something that has already been mentioned in Judges 1:34 and even in the account of Joshua, the first Israelite leader in the land of Canaan (Joshua 19:47).

📄 18:1–2

THE DANITES IN THE HOUSE OF MICAH

In the days when there was no king in Israel, and long before the mighty Samson, the Danites were unable to conquer the portion of the land that had been given to them when the Israelites returned to the land. When they didn't establish their promised inheritance, they made an attempt to establish their own, sending spies in to explore possible sites.

📄 18:3–6

THE DANITES WITH THE PRIEST OF MICAH

Verses 3–6 describe these spies' interaction with Micah's personal priest. Even though the priest readily admits that he is Micah's priest (rather than God's), the spies ask him to predict their future. Rather than go to Shiloh, the place where the Israelites worshiped, these men go to this priest, who tell them just what they want to hear.

RECRUITING THE PEOPLE TO TAKE THE LAND

The spies return with news that the land is good and an attack could be successful. In contrast to the first spies during the Exodus, who were afraid to trust the Lord and go into the land, these spies are not afraid. Unfortunately, what looks like trusting the Lord is really a justification to disobey. This becomes obvious when they arrive at Micah's house.

RECRUITING THE PEOPLE TO TAKE THE GODS

The spies recruit Micah's Levite. The law requires that they burn Micah and his shrine to the ground. But what do they do? Their perspective seems to be that since they are going to take a land, they will need a priest and an altar. In some twisted way, they can construe this Levite as God's provision. There is even a great promotion for their good friend, the priest. Verse 20 says the priest was happy in his place among the Danites (contrast this with Numbers 2:17).

MANHANDLING MICAH

Micah was a thief and an idolater. In the end, he could not stop his gods from being stolen. The thief is robbed, and the idolater's gods are in the control of men.

MANHANDLING LAISH

Just like Jericho, the Danites come in and burn the first city of their conquest to the ground. The Lord calls for holy war, and in certain cases, whole cities are to be utterly destroyed. The people are to represent the Lord's holy fire of judgment.

FINAL TRIBUTE TO DAN

Verses 30–31 describe a final tribute to Dan that includes an element of irony given the mention of the house of God in Shiloh along with the idols Micah had made. The carved images that the Danites set up are idols clearly prohibited by the Law of Moses. Yet the people remained successful even though they openly worshiped these idols. This is a good example of the fact that the consequences of breaking God's law are not always immediate. Eventually, at the hand of the Philistines, the Danites' "luck" ran out.

Take It Home

The account of the spies holds a lesson for all of us. Whose voices do we listen to? These spies were not only attracted to the priest's voice, but to his worldview. Like these spies, we, too, can convince ourselves that we are serving God, but we are listening to the voices that say what we want to hear.

JUDGES 19:1–30

THE LEVITE'S CONCUBINE

Setting Up the Section

This section includes one of the most shocking stories in the Bible, a horror story of sorts. But God has a purpose in it for us. One structure that has been applied to these appendices is this:

1) Chapters 17–18 show us that the Levites fail to protect the people from idolatry.

2) Chapters 19–21 show us that the Levites fail to protect the people from immorality.

In the Bible, idolatry leads to immorality. If we don't love God exclusively, we will not love others.

📖 19:1–3

UNFAITHFUL WIFE

Verses 1–3 give the account of a concubine. In this era and culture, in places where polygamy was practiced, a concubine was like a second-class citizen, a second wife. The male head of the household was still considered her husband, but she wasn't always referred to as his wife.

In this case, the Levite's concubine is unfaithful and finally deserts her husband to return to her father's household. After he waits for her return for four months, he seeks to win her back to himself by traveling to the father's house.

Critical Observation

The story of the Levite following his second wife to bring her back is seen by some as reminiscent of God's wooing of Israel, though the nation was spiritually unfaithful over and over again. Israel played the part of an unfaithful bride throughout Judges, rejecting her Lord as husband and returning to the gods of her ancient forefathers (Joshua 24:2, 14).

DELAYING THE RETURN

According to verses 4–9, the Levite's father-in-law repeatedly delays the departure. There is nothing wrong with this display of hospitality in itself. But the way the story is told, we sense the Levite's anxiousness to be on his way, and so the repeated delay seems awkward. The Levite needs to return, but we do not know why.

Jerusalem is referred to as Jebus in verse 10. This is the name of the city before the Israelites settled there. The traveling family should have been able to stay in Jebus, but the fact that it had not yet become an Israelite city is troublesome for the Levite.

SODOM IN ISRAEL, NOT GIBEAH OF THE BENJAMITES

They travel on to Gibeah, an Israelite city, but find it empty, dark, and ominous (19:14–15). Their choice to wait in the city square is not unusual in this day. Hospitality, even to strangers, was expected. They would have expected to be invited to someone's home for the night. When they finally do receive a single offer, it is not from a citizen of Gibeah but from an old man transplanted from Ephraim (19:16–21).

Critical Observation

From this point on in the story of the Levite, the storyline becomes somewhat reminiscent of the angelic visitors of Genesis 19, who call on Lot to warn him of the coming destruction of Sodom and Gomorrah. In both accounts, the response of the townsmen to the newcomers is a chilling example of wickedness.

In the Genesis account of Lot in Sodom, the wicked men who attack the household are struck blind, and the attack ends. Here in Judges, there is no such rescue. The woman is victimized and killed.

Once the Levite and those traveling with him settle into the old man's home, wicked Gibeanites pound the doors requesting the Levite have sex with them. The response from within is awful. First, the old man offers his daughter and the Levite's wife. Then the Levite forces his wife out to be victimized by the men (19:22–24). The fate of the virgin daughter and especially of the concubine is so horrible that it is remembered throughout Israel (Hosea 9:9; 10:9).

Demystifying Judges

It's important to understand the account of the Levite in a broader context. When the Israelites entered Canaan to claim it as their inheritance from the Lord, each tribe was assigned a territory. It was that tribe's responsibility to conquer the territory and drive out all those who would threaten the faithful worship of the Israelites. The Benjamites had failed to trust God and follow Him to battle against the Canaanites. They never conquered the land or claimed it for their religion. By this point in their history, they have come to live like Canaanites rather than forcing the Canaanites to adopt the Israelite way of life.

📖 **19:25–30**

THE CRUELTY OF THE LEVITE, THE WICKEDNESS OF MEN

In Judges 17–18 we see the consequences of a Levite living for himself. Here in verses 25–28 we see the consequences of a Levite failing to protect his wife, even if she is a concubine. And in 29–30, he makes the corpse of his bride some kind of message to Israel. What is the point of the Levite's actions here? He creates a kind of picture of Israel. She is dead, torn apart, in her sin and treachery. Idolatry has given birth to immorality, and that has resulted in captivity and death.

Take It Home

What application can we make for our own lives out of this horrific story? While the events are grotesque, the hearts that allowed those actions are not unfamiliar.

When we fall away from worship, our lives change. As idolatry leads to immorality, we are numbed to the ways in which we start looking out for our own interests, sometimes to the deficit of others. While we may stay within acceptable moral standards for our culture, the heart issue is the same. First we fall away from the Lord, and in doing so, we fall away from one another.

JUDGES 20:1-48

RESPONDING TO THE CRIME

Setting Up the Section

At the close of chapter 19, a Levite responds to the brutal death of his concubine, or second wife, by cutting her corpse into twelve pieces and sending each piece to a tribe of Israel. Judges 20 records the response of the tribes of Israel against the tribe of Benjamin on behalf of the crime committed against the Levite and his concubine.

Some consider the Levite's decision to act in this way to be a picture of Israel that is torn apart by sin and unfaithfulness.

20:1–11

A QUICK REVIEW

At the opening of Judges 20, the tribes gather to hear the Levite's story and to decide how to respond. All of Israel, from the northernmost city, Dan-Laish, to the southernmost, Beersheba, gather as one (20:1, 8, 11) in full fighting force to respond to the evil the Levite and his concubine endured.

20:12–17

ALL EXCEPT ONE

While all the rest of Israel has gathered together in Mizpah, a city in Benjamin, the tribe of Benjamin remains absent. An offer of peace is made to them if they will turn over the men who are guilty of raping and killing the woman, following the laws of war in Deuteronomy 20:10–11. But Benjamin refuses and instead prepares for battle. This reveals the hearts of the people of Benjamin, that they would fight for those who had victimized the powerless.

20:18–25

FIRST AND SECOND BATTLES

The campaign against Benjamin begins just as the battles against the Canaanites began in Judges 1. Judah is selected to go first. Two battles and two terrible losses later, we are reminded of the battle of Ai in Joshua. The problem is not that they shouldn't be fighting the battle, but that Israel is sinful and does not have God's blessing.

📖 20:26–28

THE LORD PURIFIES HIS PEOPLE

In verses 26–28, the Lord purifies His people. This time there is weeping and fasting. Also, this time there is an ascension offering and a peace offering. The fasting portrays their need for God over anything else. Their ascension offering is the atonement granted by a substitute, wholly offered to God. Their peace offering is the communion meal when fellowship is restored. The Lord purifies and nourishes His people. The covenant with Yahweh is renewed. Now they are ready for battle.

Critical Observation

Sometimes in reading a biblical account, the details provided in one book reveal context for the information in another book. Verse 28 is such a case, where the mention of Phinehas, son of Eleazar, helps to put this event in a historical context. Phinehas is mentioned in Numbers 25:10–13.

Demystifying Judges

The ark of the covenant, mentioned in verses 27–28, was Israel's most holy shrine, a box made to God's specifications that held artifacts like the first high priest's rod and a sampling of the manna that provided food for the Israelites in the desert. The ark was usually kept in the national place of worship and was naturally where the people would go to seek God's will. It was considered God's presence, and there were even times when the armies would carry the ark into battle with them in the hopes that it would imbue them with God's power (1 Samuel 4:2–3).

📖 20:29–36

THE BATTLE OF BENJAMIN

The battle of Benjamin described here is reminiscent of a previous battle at Ai, at least in terms of strategy (Joshua 8:1–26). This battle, however, is not only a battle against the Benjamites, but a victory for Israel over the spirit of the Canaanites. Verse 35 offers a theological summary of the battle when it states that it is God who won the battle. The strategy of the battle is an ambush (Judges 20:36–48).

📖 20:37–48

IMPORTANT DETAILS

Drawing the Benjamites out of the city, Gibeah is burned to the ground (20:40).

There is a relentless pursuit of the fleeing Benjamites. The word translated *struck down* in verse 45 is the same word that is used with regard to the abuse leveled at the concubine in Judges 19:25. In both situations, the idea of a brutal, awful, and complete harvest is in mind. Her life was cut down, and Gibeah is cut down. A small remnant finds refuge in the battle at the rock of Rimmon and stays there four months. Besides them, the destruction is total—men, women, beasts, and cities fall under the wrath of the Lord.

Take It Home

Gibeah (similar to Sodom) faced God's wrath and was destroyed with fire. There are several lessons we can learn from their fate:

1) Every individual and every people group will face God's judgment for the way they have lived their lives. Either they will face it through faith in the work of Jesus, or they will face it by themselves.

2) The people were judged because they became like the Canaanites. In other words, rather than spreading God's way of living to the people around them, they took on the lifestyle of those people. We face the same temptation today to become like the evil we are exposed to rather than transforming and influencing change in the culture around us.

3) The tribe of Benjamin was judged, but Israel was saved. Even in this unfortunate incident, God's grace was evident in the stand that the eleven tribes took against Benjamin. God disciplines His people and calls them back to righteousness.

JUDGES 21:1–25

THE REBELLION OF BENJAMIN

The Failure of Benjamin	21:1–4
Another Vow	21:5–9
Utter Destruction	21:10–14
Extending Peace	21:15–25

Setting Up the Section

As we end this story of the rebellion of Benjamin, we see the grace of God in this final chapter. The Levites have been unable to protect the people from idolatry and immorality, and thus the judgment of the Lord falls hard upon the house of the Lord in chapter 20. The tribe of Benjamin is dead. And God, in His extraordinary and unpredictable ways, resurrects the tribe.

📄 **21:1–4**

THE FAILURE OF BENJAMIN

In verses 1–3, there are six hundred men of Benjamin left at the rock of Rimmon (20:47), but they have no wives. Why? Israel had sworn an oath, a curse upon herself if she gave any daughters to Benjamin (21:1, 18). In light of the wicked heart of Benjamin, this was an honorable vow (Deuteronomy 7:3–4). But the excommunication of the tribe of Benjamin brings no joy to Israel (Judges 21:3); it is not a moment of triumph. Instead, it is heartbreaking for even one tribe to fail. Their question—*Why?*—is in essence a prayer for restoration.

Take It Home

Israel had already offered sacrifices for their sins, but in verse 4 they do so again for all of Israel, including Benjamin, as they cry out to the Lord for Benjamin's restoration. While the motivation had some national interest unique to this situation, it still stands as an example of the kind of covenant connection that would serve the church well when a member has fallen away from the faith (1 Corinthians 5:6; Ephesians 4:4–6).

📖 **21:5–9**

ANOTHER VOW

The sacrifices described in verses 2–4 provide a basis for the tribe of Benjamin's forgiveness and restoration, but they don't provide one practical need—wives so that the remnant of the tribe can repopulate. Therefore, Israel is still mourning (21:6). But the nation had taken another vow as well (21:5). Jabesh Gilead became the loophole that could solve the puzzle. This tribe had refused to come to Israel's assistance when every other city had sent men to battle the Benjamites. In this way, Jabesh Gilead had stood against the efforts of Israel—and thus the perceived efforts of the Lord—by doing nothing.

Critical Observation

Was the vow to shun the tribe of Benjamin a typical response in this situation? When Deborah judged Israel, the city of Meroz was cursed but not utterly destroyed (5:23). Both of these scenarios are an example of internal conflict and thus an internal judgment call. Deuteronomy 17:7 certainly seems to support the action taken against the Benjamites as an effort to rid Israel of the evil that had risen up from within the nation.

📖 **21:10–14**

UTTER DESTRUCTION

In verses 10–14, another Hormah is carried out (1:17). In the days of Phinehas, twelve thousand men are gathered together and all are killed, leaving only the virgin women. This is a repeat of yet another slaughter against the Midianites described in Numbers 31. After the destruction, there were four hundred women to give as wives to the six hundred Benjamites.

EXTENDING PEACE

A peace offering has already been made (21:4), and peace has been extended to the remnant of Benjamin (21:13). In verses 16–24, the Benjamites are brought to Shiloh, the place of rest (peace), to receive the first four hundred wives and to provide them with this third episode of peace and reconciliation with God and with His people.

Verses 16–18 reveal that the remainder of Israel wants to see the full restoration of Benjamin in spite of the curse placed upon these men.

This dance of virgins described in verses 18–24, the festival in Shiloh, must have declared the desire of these women to be married or their father's declaration to give them in marriage, maybe in a way similar to when we see a group of women scrambling to catch the bouquet at a wedding (21:19–24). The fathers had declared that they would never give their daughters to Benjamin, but the fact that the men took the women during the festival provided an end run around that declaration. In an unexpected way, the tribe of Benjamin is reborn.

Take It Home

On the one hand, the book of Judges is a history of dark days for the people of Israel. We see their constant rebellion, the Levites' failure to protect and lead the people out of idolatry and immorality, and the recurring consequences of oppression by God's enemies. On the other hand, the cycle of God's deliverance reveals His overriding grace for those He had promised to protect.

The broad context of this book is the rule of Israel without a king (21:25). If Samuel, or someone in Samuel's day, is writing, he is contrasting the lack of a godly king to the eventual rule of David as king of Israel. While David was a righteous king, he was still a man. David's own family will lead the people back into sin. The history of Israel is evidence of the fact that humanity needs more than itself to be righteous. This is why God sent Jesus, to do the work in the hearts of His people that neither they nor their leaders could do for themselves.

Consider the modern church. She experiences God's grace, yet struggles with temptations. God brings reformation. She grows. She falters again and again. God continues to raise up modern leaders to call the church back to true faith, but the struggle continues. On an individual level, we face the same dilemma—the struggle with falling away from the grace and faith we've been given. But God continues to bring voices into our lives to call us back. And ultimately, Christ's sacrifice stands in for our failings. God will not leave you, just as He did not leave Israel. And after all of your struggle with sin and failure and falling, He will give you salvation for all eternity.

LIST OF BIBLICAL JUDGES

Judge	Biblical Reference	The Enemy They Fought
Othniel	Judges 3:9–11	Mesopotamia
Ehud	Judges 3:15–30	Moabites
Shamgar	Judges 3:31	Philistines
Deborah and Barak	Judges 4:4–5:31	Canaanites
Gideon	Judges 6:7–8:35	Midianites
Tola	Judges 10:1–2	None listed
Jair	Judges 10:3–5	None listed
Jephthah	Judges 10:6–12:7	Ammonites
Ibzan	Judges 12:8–10	None listed
Elon	Judges 12:11–12	None listed
Abdon	Judges 12:13–15	None listed
Samson	Judges 13:2–16:31	Philistines
Eli	1 Samuel 1–4	None listed
Samuel	1 Samuel 7–9	Philistines

RUTH

INTRODUCTION TO RUTH

Ruth is a small book, only four chapters, that reveals God's work of providence in the details of people's lives.

AUTHOR

Even though there has been speculation about possible authors, no one knows who wrote the book of Ruth. We do believe, however, that the book was written during the time of King David. This seems reasonable because of the genealogy included at the end of the book, a genealogy that includes David's ancestors.

PURPOSE

One option for the purpose of this book is to reveal how a Moabite—a non-Jew—can become a faithful follower of Yahweh, Israel's God. Another option is that it is meant to be a contribution to the genealogy of David, an ancestor to Jesus. Just as likely, however, the primary purpose of the book of Ruth is to illustrate how simple, obedient people can be saved by God's providence and become part of His larger plan.

OCCASION

It's unclear when the book of Ruth was written, though it likely was written during King David's reign, thus the genealogy at the end of the book. In the English Old Testament, it comes right after the book of Judges. This placement may allow Ruth to provide a stark contrast to the greed and disobedience displayed by God's people during the time of the judges. In the Hebrew Old Testament, this book follows Proverbs, displaying Ruth as an example of the virtuous woman described in Proverbs 31.

THEMES

The book of Ruth focuses on divine providence. Through obedience and lovingkindness, God's people continue in His plan even in the face of obstacles and mistakes.

HISTORICAL CONTEXT

Throughout Christian history, the book of Ruth has been considered part of the historical record of God's people. In addition to a story about love and obedience, Ruth reveals the workings of religious laws related to widowhood, as well as a part of the genealogy of Christ—even through a Moabite woman.

RUTH 1:1–22

THE JOURNEY

Setting Up the Section

This chapter has a poignant lesson: God's providence is certain and He makes no mistakes. As He unfolds the intricacies of His divine purpose in our lives, He does so with a goal in mind. We also see how the saving purposes of God often begin in the sometimes dark periods in someone's life.

📖 1:1–5

FROM BETHLEHEM TO MOAB

At the opening of chapter 1, Bethlehem faces a lack of food, but there is also a famine in spirituality, faith, and morals. The book of Ruth describes an era in Israel's history before the monarch was established. The people were ruled by judges or national champions. It was described as a time when, rather than following the laws of God, every person did what was right in his or her own eyes. Within that context, this famine could be seen as a judgment on Israel for wandering from the faith.

Elimelech's family leaves Judah, the only land to which God has given specific promises of blessing, for the neighboring country of Moab. Soon Elimelech dies, leaving Naomi with her two sons, Mahlon and Kilion, and their Moabite wives, Orpah and Ruth (1:3–4). After about ten years, Naomi's sons die, leaving her alone with her daughters-in-law. Naomi is away from the land of her God, her immediate family, and any extended family. Naturally she would long for her home and for the company of people with similar faith.

📖 1:6–18

RUTH'S CHOICE

Naomi hears that the Lord has returned blessing to Bethlehem but sees a problem with her daughters-in-law returning there. They cannot be guaranteed marriage partners. According to Jewish customs, the women would be married to their nearest relative in order to continue the family inheritance of their deceased husbands. But as Naomi points out, she has no other sons and is too old to have more (1:6–7). As widows, all three would be poverty-stricken beggars, eking out an existence. As foreign Moabites, the daughters-in-law would struggle even more than Naomi herself (1:8–9).

At first, both daughters-in-law refuse to leave Naomi despite her recommendation that they stay in Moab (1:10), but Naomi explains that their best chance for remarriage is to stay. Naomi, even in difficult circumstances, believes in the faithfulness of God's providence (1:9–13).

While Orpah decides to stay in her Moabite culture (1:15), Ruth's choice to return to Bethlehem with Naomi (1:14) reveals her depth of family commitment. Commentators believe Ruth learned some of the principles of God's people by watching Naomi persevere in her beliefs despite great odds (1:16–18) and that her decision reflects Naomi's impact in her life. Ruth is prepared to forsake her past and future and put her trust in Naomi's God and people (1:15–17).

📄 1:19–22

GOD'S HUMBLING POWER

As Naomi returns home, her look has changed (1:19); pain and sorrow have etched their way into her very visage. She had gone away full, but she has come back empty, even requesting she be called by the name *Mara*, which means "bitter," rather than *Naomi*, which means "pleasant" (1:20–21).

Critical Observation

The last sentence of this chapter gives a hint of promise by mentioning the barley harvest (1:22). Troubling things have happened in the lives of the main characters so far, but a harvest is coming. This harvest may not be accomplished without hard work, but the narrator is hinting that a time of blessing and abundance is near.

RUTH 2:1–23

THE COUPLE

Ruth Gleans in Boaz's Field	2:1–3
Boaz Provides for Ruth	2:4–17
Ruth's Harvest	2:18–23

Setting Up the Section

In discovering how Naomi and Ruth are to survive, we are introduced to Old Testament laws of gleaning, which were meant to provide for the poor and for the widow.

📄 2:1–3

RUTH GLEANS IN BOAZ'S FIELD

The opening information about Naomi's relationship to the family of Elimelech implies Naomi has a plan (2:1). When Ruth offers to go glean in Boaz's field, a man related to Elimelech, Naomi encourages her (2:2–3).

Demystifying Ruth

The national religious laws of Israel state that after harvesting a field, a certain amount must be left on the side of the field and in the corners of the field for the poor and for those who cannot provide for themselves (Leviticus 19:9–10; Deuteronomy 24:19–22). Often women and widows used this provision to find sufficient grain to make food for one, two, or even three days, but no more than that. To survive only from the grain gleaned from a harvested field was a menial and difficult existence.

📄 **2:4–17**

BOAZ PROVIDES FOR RUTH

Boaz is a businessman, yet his first words to his workers are of God. The writer presents Boaz as a man of character (2:4). His inquiry about Ruth alludes to an attraction toward her (2:5). His workers explain that she has asked to be allowed to glean and is currently resting (2:6–7).

Boaz finds Ruth and advises her to stay in this particular field and to follow his maids (2:8). He tells her he has ordered his servants not to touch her, an indication that such fields can be dangerous, but he is providing for her safety. He also allows her to drink from his servants' water jars (2:9). Boaz is providing for Ruth beyond what is required by Levitical law.

When Ruth inquires about Boaz's kindness toward her, he explains that he has heard of her widowhood and her devotion to her mother-in-law, particularly in her leaving her homeland to join Naomi's people (2:10). This story has all the elements of romance and an awakening of interest as Boaz sees in Ruth a character that is attractive to him (2:11).

Boaz asks God's blessing on Ruth's work, noting that Ruth has come to Israel to seek God's shelter. He uses the metaphor of being under God's wings, a protective gesture that mother hens provide for their baby chicks. And as the narrative unfolds, similar language is used about Boaz's relationship to Ruth; Boaz takes a surrogate role of protector and responsibility for Ruth. He takes her under his wing, just as he prays God will do for her (2:12).

Ruth acknowledges that Boaz is treating her like one of his own maidservants, even though she is a stranger (2:13). When Boaz invites Ruth to eat dinner with the reapers, Ruth not only gets full, but has leftovers. What a gift for a woman who is usually dependent upon the leftovers of others for her daily sustenance.

When it is time for Ruth to go back to gleaning, Boaz commands his servants to expand the areas where she is allowed to glean, and specifically orders them not to harass her, but to leave extra (2:15–16). Again, Boaz is going well beyond the requirements of the law. Because of his generosity, Ruth is able to work in the field all day, with access to water and a full meal, and leave the field that evening with about thirty pounds of barley (2:17).

RUTH'S HARVEST

The text tells us that Ruth takes her thirty pounds of barley back to Naomi and shares it with her (2:18). Naomi must have known that the volume of the harvest is more than expected, because she asks God's blessing on the generous person. When Ruth tells her it is Boaz's field, Naomi repeats her blessing and explains that he is one of their closest relatives (2:20).

Demystifying Ruth

In addition to the law of gleaning, the Hebrew people also operated under the law of the kinsman redeemer: If a woman was left as a widow and childless, the nearest relative would take her as his wife, yet any children that she bore would be considered the heirs of her previous husband (Deuteronomy 25:5–6). In this way, the kinsman redeemer was helping continue that family line rather than his own. Naomi may have been already hoping that this kinsman's kind treatment of Ruth would lead to a marriage.

When Ruth tells Naomi that Boaz instructed her to work with his servants until the end of the harvest (2:21), Naomi supports this instruction. Several times in the book of Ruth, the narrator hints that the harvest fields can be a dangerous place for women. Harvest time could also be a time of drinking and celebration, intensifying the risk for vulnerable workers. Thus, Naomi agrees that staying near Boaz's servants would decrease the risk of someone attacking or mistreating Ruth (2:22–23).

Take It Home

Ruth does her duty to her mother-in-law by moving to Israel with her and gleaning in the fields. By doing so, God's plan to connect her to Boaz will be fulfilled. Sometimes it's not in the extraordinary things that we find the guidance of God, but in the small business of going about our ordinary, day-to-day work.

RUTH 3:1–18

THE AGREEMENT

Setting Up the Section

The narrative of the book of Ruth is clearly leading to Ruth and Boaz's marriage, which will fulfill God's plan for the line of David, leading to the birth of Jesus. Also of note is the setting of daytime and nighttime. Chapter 3 begins in daytime, then moves to night, and ends in daytime again. In the middle of the night, the greatest risk occurs.

📖 3:1–5

NAOMI'S PLAN

Naomi presents a plan to Ruth that would ensure Ruth's future (3:1). As a widow and a nonnative of Israel, the future most likely consists of gleaning for survival. Naomi reminds Ruth of the kinsman relationship to Boaz and the promising relationship between Ruth and his maids (3:2). On a night when Naomi knows that Boaz will be at the threshing floor, she instructs Ruth to wash, anoint herself, put on her best clothes, and go to him. Knowing the dangers of harvest time, her suggestion that Ruth go to the threshing floor both after dark and after the men have been eating and drinking carries some risk (3:3).

The risk in this plan isn't solely for Ruth. In addition to placing Ruth in a vulnerable position, following Naomi's instructions to lie down at Boaz's feet could put Boaz in a compromising position as well. The events of the evening described here will require faith on the part of all three people (3:4–6).

📖 3:6–18

BOAZ'S RESPONSE

According to the Hebrew, there is a shudder in the middle of the night, and Boaz awakens to find Ruth at his feet. It is astonishing that Boaz, after food and drink, reacts to this situation with such composure (3:7–8).

In response to Boaz's question about her identity, Ruth's answer is pointed. She identifies herself as one of his maids and uses a phrase that asks him to take her under his wing, a word picture he has already used with her. In this case, Ruth's request is a pledge of marriage. She even uses the language that will remind him that he is a close relative with a right and possibly a responsibility in this situation (3:9).

Boaz asks God's blessing on Ruth and suggests that her gesture of interest in him, even though he is not a young man, impresses him (3:10). He continues, telling her not to fear, referring to her reputation as an honorable woman (3:11). Could Boaz be assuring Ruth that she doesn't have to fear the rumors of what can happen to vulnerable women on the threshing floor?

Boaz's response to Ruth's presence indicates his intention to treat her with honor. However, he explains that while he is, indeed, a close relative, there is someone even more closely related to Ruth who, according to the law of kinship, has first claim to her. Boaz will defer to this relative (3:12–13). In other words, while Boaz's heart has been won over by Ruth, he will do what is right according to God's law.

Demystifying Ruth

Naomi and Ruth's closest kinsman is under obligation to make sure that Naomi's lineage (the lineage of her deceased son) is maintained (Deuteronomy 25:5–6). In this case, the redeemer also bought the land belonging to Elimelech's sons. This would have provided financially for Naomi as well as provide for her son's inheritance.

When morning arrives, Boaz makes sure no one knows he came to the threshing floor (3:14). The message here is that Boaz wants Ruth's reputation to remain unblemished. Boaz, however, also wants his commitment to Ruth and Naomi to be clear. He sends Ruth home with another significant load of barley (3:15–17). Hearing Ruth's summary of the night, and seeing this message from Boaz, Naomi assures Ruth that Boaz will move to marry her (3:18).

Take It Home

It's only through the grace of God that this chapter ends with the reputations of all the major players intact. Ruth's obedience to her superiors and Boaz's obedience to the law ensured both emerged safely from temptation.

RUTH 4:1–22

THE LEGACY

Setting Up the Section

In chapter 4, the fulfillment of God's plan is evident for not only Naomi and Ruth, but also for the beginning of the line of David. Boaz has fallen in love, but he's not the nearest kinsman.

4:1–15

RUTH AND BOAZ MARRY

Boaz waits at the town gate, the place of business in the ancient world, and finds the man who is related to Naomi's deceased husband, Elimelech—her closest relative (4:1). Boaz also finds ten men to witness the transaction (4:2–3).

Demystifying Ruth

In ancient times, the city gate was the place where justice was administered. If you had a case that needed to be resolved in some way, you would go to the city gate and call upon the elders to make a judgment.

Boaz explains his interest in Naomi's land, but defers this option to the nearest kinsman, who agrees to purchase it from Naomi, until he realizes that the land comes with the widow, Ruth (4:4). Because this man would jeopardize his own family's future by taking on another, he hands over the right of redemption to Boaz. In this culture, the passing on of this responsibility is symbolized by handing over a sandal (4:6–7). For the record, Boaz announces to all the witnesses the result of the transaction: He has acquired everything that belongs to Naomi, and Ruth will be his wife in order to continue Elimelech's line (4:9–10).

When the people ask that the Lord make Ruth like Rachel and Leah (wives of Jacob), they are stating their hopes for a large family (4:11). Rachel and Leah bore Jacob twelve sons. The reference to Perez here is because he is the ancestor of Boaz, revealing the family connection (4:12). This section reveals the answer to Naomi's prayer in Ruth 1:8 for her daughter-in-law.

Boaz and Ruth marry and have a son. The narrator's phrasing emphasizes the belief that children are a gift from God (4:13). The women of Bethlehem respond to Naomi, and it is significantly more hopeful than when she returned from Moab. They ask God's blessing on Naomi's grandson, and call Ruth the Moabitess, describing her as someone who is better to Naomi than seven sons, a powerful indication of Ruth's standing in the eyes of the community (4:14–15). Naomi becomes the nurse to her grandson, Obed, whose name means "servant," and who will become grandfather to King David (4:16–17).

Take It Home

God will stop at nothing for those whom He has determined to bless, even when we seem at times to get in the way through our choices. The story of Ruth is also the story of Naomi. God's blessing came to them both through a variety of twists and turns, some of which could have drawn them further from God's plan rather than closer.

📖 4:16–22

THE LINE OF DAVID BEGINS

The genealogy here traces the line of Judah from Perez, son of Tamar, through Boaz to David (4:16–22). These names hold significance; they show that God's plan of sending the Messiah through the house of David will be fulfilled and that God can work through all kinds of circumstances to ensure His plan of salvation.

CONTRIBUTING EDITORS:

David Hatcher has been in the ministry for over 20 years and has been the pastor of Trinity Church in Kirkland, WA, for the last 10 years. David and his wife, Kim, have six covenant children from the ages of 20 to 8. David completed his pastoral studies at Greyfriars' Hall in Moscow, Idaho.

The late **J. Hampton Keathley III, Th.M** was a 1966 graduate of Dallas Theological Seminary and a former pastor of 28 years. Hampton wrote many articles and on occasion taught New Testament Greek at Moody Bible Institute, Northwest Extension for External Studies in Spokane, Washington. In August 2002 he succumbed to lung cancer and went home to be with the Lord.

Dr. Stephen Leston is pastor of Kishwaukee Bible Church in DeKalb , IL. He is passionate about training people for ministry and has served as a pastor at Grace Church of DuPage (Warrenville, IL) and Petersburg Bible Church (Petersburg, Alaska).

Dr. Robert Rayburn holds a Master of Divinity degree from Covenant Theological Seminary and a doctorate in New Testament from the University of Aberdeen, Scotland. His commentary on Hebrews was published in the Evangelical Commentary of the Bible.

Dr. Derek W. H. Thomas is professor of practical and systematic theology at Reformed Theological Seminary. After pastoring for 17 years in Belfast, Northern Ireland, Dr. Thomas returned to the US in 1996 where, in addition to his work at the seminary, he serves as the *Minister of Teaching* at First Presbyterian Church in Jackson, Mississippi. He has been married to his wife, Rosemary, for almost 30 years. They have two adult children.

CONSULTING EDITOR:

Dr. Tremper Longman is the Robert H. Gundry Professor of Biblical Studies at Westmont University. He has taught at Westmont since 1998 and taught before that for 18 years at the Westminster Theological Seminary in Philadelphia. Dr. Longman has degrees from Ohio Wesleyan University (B.A.), Westminster Theological Seminary (M.Div.), and Yale University (M.Phil.; Ph.D.). He has also been active in the area of Bible translation, in particular he serves on the central committee that produced and now monitors the New Living Translation.

WITH SPECIAL THANKS TO BIBLE.ORG

Bible.org is a non-profit (501c3) Christian ministry headquartered in Dallas, Texas. In the last decade, bible.org has grown to serve millions of individuals around the world and provides thousands of trustworthy resources for Bible study including the new NET BIBLE® translation.

Bible.org offers thousands of free resources for:
- Spiritual formation and discipleship
- Men's ministry
- Women's ministry
- Pastoral helps
- Small group curriculum and much more. . .

Bible.org can be accessed through www.bible.org.